ROCK CLIMBING

ROCKY MOUNTAIN NATIONAL PARK

THE
CRAG AREAS

ROCK CLIMBING
ROCKY MOUNTAIN NATIONAL PARK
PARK

THE CRAG AREA.

Richard Rossiter

Chockstone Press
Evergreen, Colorado
1996

CK CLIMBING ROCKY MOUNTAIN NATIONAL PARK: THE CRAG AREAS

'er photo: Richard Rossiter and Greg Carelli on *Xenomorph,*
Ville 3 Pinnacle. Photo by Bonnie Von Grebe.

k photo: Joyce Rossiter on *Dags in Beanland.* Photo by Richard
:siter.

uncredited photos by Richard Rossiter.

N: 0-934641-34-X

ARY OF CONGRESS CATALOGING-IN-PUBLICATION DATA
siter, Richard, 1945-
Rock Climbing Rocky Mountain National Park.   The Crag areas /
:ichard Rossiter.
      p.   cm.
Includes index.
ISBN 0-934641-34-X (alk. paper)
1. Rock climbing--Colorado--Rocky Mountain National Park-
Guidebooks. 2. Rocky Mountain National Park (Colo.)--Guidebooks.
   Title.
:V199.42.C62R628   1996   96-5537
17.88'69--dc20   CIP

.ISHED AND DISTRIBUTED BY:
·ckstone Press, Inc.
t Office Box 3505
rgreen, Colorado 80437-3505

Guaranteed Binding
This book binding is sewn with nylon thread to withstand
the rough treatment of the active climber. OUR GUARANTEE:
If the binding of this book falls apart send us the book and
we will replace it with a good copy of the same edition.

WARNING: CLIMBING IS A SPORT WHERE YOU MAY BE SERIOU INJURED OR DIE. READ THIS BEFORE YOU USE THIS BOOK.

This guidebook is a compilation of unverified information gathered from many different climbe The author cannot assure the accuracy of any of the information in this book, including the top and route descriptions, the difficulty ratings, and the protection ratings. These may be incorrec misleading and it is impossible for any one author to climb all the routes to confirm the inform about each route. Also, ratings of climbing difficulty and danger are always subjective and depe on the physical characteristics (for example, height), experience, technical ability, confidence an physical fitness of the climber who supplied the rating. Additionally, climbers who achieve first ascents sometimes underrate the difficulty or danger of the climbing route out of fear of being ridiculed if a climb is later down-rated by subsequent ascents. Therefore, be warned that you m exercise your own judgment on where a climbing route goes, its difficulty and your ability to sa protect yourself from the risks of rock climbing. Examples of some of these risks are: falling du technical difficulty or due to natural hazards such as holds breaking, falling rock, climbing equ ment dropped by other climbers, hazards of weather and lightning, your own equipment failure failure or absence of fixed protection.

You should not depend on any information gleaned from this book for your personal safety; your safety depends on your own good judgment, based on experience and a istic assessment of your climbing ability. If you have any doubt as to your ability to s ly climb a route described in this book, do not attempt it.

The following are some ways to make your use of this book safer:

1. Consultation: You should consult with other climbers about the difficulty and danger of a ticular climb prior to attempting it. Most local climbers are glad to give advice on routes in their area and we suggest that you contact locals to confirm ratings and safety of particula routes and to obtain first-hand information about a route chosen from this book.

2. Instruction: Most climbing areas have local climbing instructors and guides available. We re mend that you engage an instructor or guide to learn safety techniques and to become fam with the routes and hazards of the areas described in this book. Even after you are profici climbing safely, occasional use of a guide is a safe way to raise your climbing standard an learn advanced techniques.

3. Fixed Protection: Many of the routes in this book use bolts and pitons which are permanen placed in the rock. Because of variances in the manner of placement, weathering, metal fat the quality of the metal used, and many other factors, these fixed protection pieces shoul always be considered suspect and should always be backed up by equipment that you plac yourself. Never depend for your safety on a single piece of fixed protection because you n can tell whether it will hold weight, and in some cases, fixed protection may have been removed or is now absent.

Be aware of the following specific potential hazards which could arise in using this b

1. Misdescriptions of Routes: If you climb a route and you have a doubt as to where the route go, you should not go on unless you are sure that you can go that way safely. Route descri tions and topos in this book may be inaccurate or misleading.

2. Incorrect Difficulty Rating: A route may, in fact, be more difficult than the rating indicates. not be lulled into a false sense of security by the difficulty rating.

3. Incorrect Protection Rating: If you climb a route and you are unable to arrange adequate p tion from the risk of falling through the use of fixed pitons or bolts and by placing your o protection devices, do not assume that there is adequate protection available higher just because the route protection rating indicates the route is not an "X" or an "R" rating. Every is potentially an "X" (a fall may be deadly), due to the inherent hazards of climbing – including, example, failure or absence of fixed protection, your own equipment's failure, or improper use climbing equipment.

THERE ARE NO WARRANTIES, WHETHER EXPRESS OR IMPLIED, THAT THIS GUIL BOOK IS ACCURATE OR THAT THE INFORMATION CONTAINED IN IT IS RELIABL THERE ARE NO WARRANTIES OF FITNESS FOR A PARTICULAR PURPOSE OR THA THIS GUIDE IS MERCHANTABLE. YOUR USE OF THIS BOOK INDICATES YOUR ASS TION OF THE RISK THAT IT MAY CONTAIN ERRORS AND IS AN ACKNOWLEDGM OF YOUR OWN SOLE RESPONSIBILITY FOR YOUR CLIMBING SAFETY.

ce Rossiter on Ellipse, Lens Rock.

TABLE OF CONTENTS

reface

ecided to write a guide book to Rocky Mountain National Park during the
nmer of 1984. It is embarrassing to admit that I have been working on it
more than a decade, but I can partly excuse myself by having written five
er guide books during the same period and established a successful train-
business. Still, this project may qualify me for lifetime membership in
Dull Men's Club. Toward the end, I wouldn't do anything with anyone if it
n't have something to do with this book. It always seemed that the book
uld be ready by the following spring, but it never was. Then I thought I
uld just write a "Selected Climbs" guide and save myself an enormous
ount of work, but there was still no "Complete" book from which it might
drawn. Further, no one (other than Walter Fricke) had put much effort into
turing the historical aspect of the sport. My fate was sealed. The only way
was through. I lost my wife, I lost my friends, I lost my identity, my
ley developed an oil leak, and my computer broke down. The last chapter
s written in blood. But I pressed on to the end.

Acknowledgments

Many of the names and dates of first ascents before 1980 are borrowed fr
A Climber's Guide to the Rocky Mountain National Park Area by Walter Fric
Jr., *The High Peaks* by Richard DuMais, and *Lumpy Ridge, Estes Park Rock
Climbs* by Scott Kimball. First ascent information for newer routes is from
personal research and from the many climbers who submitted informatio
and addenda to the interim version of this book.

I wish to thank the following people for contributing route information,
topos, photos, and/or first ascent data: Roger Briggs, Jeff Lowe, Greg Dav
Ed Webster, Joe Burke, Charlie Fowler, Dan Hare, John Marrs, Larry Coats,
Randy Joseph, Bob Bradley, Malcolm Daly, Alec Sharp, Gary Neptune, Kyle
Copeland, Gene Ellis, Jon Estabrook, Mike Caldwell, Peter Hubbel, Doug
Redosh, Todd Swain, Dr. Roger Clark, Paul Kunasz, Doug Allcock, Craig
Luebben, Jim Detterline, Clay Jackson, Bernard Gillett, Bruce Hildenbrand
Ron Olson, Dan Bradford, Lawrence Steumke, Greg Sievers, Kris Walker an
the late, great Derek Hersey.

Many of these climbers worked with me in person, pouring over photos a
topos of routes they knew well or of which they had made first ascents. N
effort was spared in the name of accuracy. Chances are good I have misse
few people who sent me information, and I sincerely apologize if your na
does not appear in this list.

Roy McClenahan volunteered his time and a steady hand with production
aspects of the book. A special thank-you to Bonnie Von Grebe, who devot
many hours (and weekends) to the final production.

IN PRAISE OF TEA

The first cup moistens my lips and throat.

The second cup breaks my loneliness.

The third cup searches my barren mind

To find therein some five thousand volumes of words.

The fourth cup raises a slight perspiration,

All the wrong of life passes through my pores

At the fifth cup I am purified.

The sixth cup calls me to a realm of immortals.

The seventh cup, ah..., but I could take no more!

—*Lotung, eighth-century Chinese poet*

INTRODUCTION

Equipment

Appropriate climbing hardware can vary drastically from one route to ano[cut] er, and what a climber chooses to carry is a matter of style and experience[cut] There is, however, at least in terms of crack width, a general array of devi[cut] that most parties would want to carry. Thus, a "standard rack" (SR) might [cut] consist of the following gear.

    A set of RPs
    Wired stoppers up to one inch
    Two or three slung stoppers, Hexes, or Tri-cams
    Various camming devices up to three inches
    Six or seven quickdraws (QDs)
    Three to five runners long enough to wear over the shoulder
    One double-length runner
    Six to eight unoccupied carabiners (usually with the runners)

On some routes this rack would be overkill; on others, it might be weak i[cut] certain areas. Snow and ice climbs such as the *Notch Couloir* typically wil[cut] require crampons, ice ax(es), snow pickets or flukes, and ice screws as we[cut] as some part of the rock climbing gear listed above and perhaps a few pitons. Equipment suggestions are given with some route descriptions; ot[cut] erwise, the gear listed above is recommended.

Ratings

The system used for rating difficulty in this book is simply a streamlined version of the so-called Yosemite Decimal System. Which is to say that th[cut] class five designation is assumed and that 5.0 through 5.14 is written as [cut] through 14 without the 5. prefix. The Welzenbach classes 2 through 4 hav[cut] been retained and appear in route descriptions as (cl3), (cl4), and are writ[cut] out in route names as Class 3 or Class 4. The Roman numeral grades I through VI for overall difficulty are also retained but are not applied to c[cut] routes. The water ice rating system WI1 through WI6 is used for winter ic[cut] climbs. Alpine snow and ice routes are described verbally. Mixed ice and [cut] is rated M1 through M6.

The potential for a long leader fall is indicated by an **s** (serious) or **vs** (ve[cut] serious) after the rating of difficulty. A climb rated **s** will have at least on[cut] notable run-out and the potential for a scary fall. A climb rated **vs** typical[cut] will have poor protection for hard moves and the potential for a fatal or near-fatal fall. The absence of these letters indicates a relatively safe clim[cut] providing that it is within the leader's ability.

The rating of a climb represents an informal consensus of opinion from some of the climbers who have completed a route. Some of the routes in [cut]

Introduction

ok may never have been repeated which makes the ratings extremely sub-
ctive. But even the ratings of long established climbs are still debated,
nich indicates that numerical ratings are merely approximate and must be
ken with "a grain of salt." In the end, it is your skill and judgment that will
ep you alive on the rocks.

eather and Snow Conditions

mbing in the high peaks is done primarily from June through September.
ring this period one can expect comfortable to hot daytime temperatures,
nny mornings, and afternoon thundershowers. Until July, many peak
mbs involve snow travel; thus, an ice ax and mountain boots may be use-
for some part of the approach, climb, or descent. From mid July through
gust, the weather is usually hot during the day and many climbs can be
ne without snow travel. There is sometimes an auspicious period of two or
ee weeks in midsummer distinguished by a lack of afternoon thunder-
rms but there is no telling if or when this will happen. Temperatures cool
September but it is still reasonable to climb on warm days, even on the
amond. By October the first serious snows come and windows of opportu-
y for rock climbing are rare, however, the alpine ice gullies are at their
t. In November, it gets cold and the winter ice climbs begin to form up.
ter ascents of the Diamond and other major features are not uncommon,
it's a whole different ball game than during summer. Spring is avalanche
e in the Rockies. Check with the rangers for conditions.

k climbing at Lumpy Ridge and the lower crags has a much longer sea-
: the most congenial weather is from April to October; however, it is
netimes warm enough to climb even during winter on south-facing fea-
s.

vironmental Considerations

ky Mountain National Park, which includes Lumpy Ridge, is one of the
nest and best maintained parks in the country. To preserve the natural
uty and ecological integrity of our climbing environment, a few sugges-
s are offered: Use rest rooms or outdoor toilets where possible.
erwise, deposit solid human waste far from the cliffs and away from
s of approach and descent. Do not cover with a rock but leave exposed
he elements where it will deteriorate more quickly. Carry used toilet
er out in a plastic bag or use a stick or Douglas fir cone. Do not leave
-made riffraff lying about: if you pack it in, pack it out. Take care to pre-
e trees and other plants on approaches and climbs. Scree gullies and
s fields usually have sections that are more stable; thrashing up and
n loose scree causes erosion and destroys plant life. Always use trails
foot paths where they have been developed and demonstrate human
ution by removing obstructions, stacking loose rocks along trail sides,
picking up trash. When hiking across tundra, follow foot paths or step
ocks to avoid crushing the fragile plant life.

Introduction

Fixed Protection

Fixed protection has become a major point of contention with park manage[r]
and powerful wilderness lobbies such as the Audubon Society. The very co[n]
cept of "climbing management" and resultant closures and restrictions has
developed around climbers' use of bolts and other forms of fixed anchors,
especially in high profile areas. If we are to have access to public lands an[d]
preserve the freedom that we have enjoyed in the past, it is critical that we
promote a sensible and responsible public image. Climber organizations
such as The Access Fund do much to help this cause but our actions in the
field are even more important.

Bolts, pitons, and slings that can be seen from the ground (or through bin[oc]
ulars) are easy targets for complaint. Dangling slings are highly visible and
should be kept to an absolute minimum. Bolt hangers should be camou-
flaged. For those in the first ascent business, it is wiser to place bolts in th[e]
most useful possible position for someone leading the route. Bolts that are
hard to reach or those that precede long, unprotected cruxes usually have
slings hanging on them — let's get them it the right spot for leading the
climb. Bolt anchors are best fitted with lap links or cold shuts because the[y]
are permanent and much less visible than slings.

Knowing that every bolt and piton we place will be counted and document[ed]
by some regulatory agency or wildlife organization, it is obvious that som[e]
restraint on our part is necessary. As for new free climbs requiring bolts:
ONLY THE VERY BEST LINES SHOULD BE DEVELOPED. Contrived and medioc[re]
routes should be left undone. When the decision is made to place bolts on [a]
new route, only the best gear should be used so that it is reliable and perr[ma]
nent. Whether bolts are placed on rappel or on the lead is irrelevant. The
emphasis should not fall on the first ascent but on the resultant route.
Regarding that a good route will be climbed thousands of times and that
holes drilled in the rock will last for millennia, it is obvious that THE QUA[LI]
TY AND POSITIONING OF FIXED GEAR MUST TAKE PRECEDENCE OVER OTHE[R]
CONSIDERATIONS. Note: The use of power drills is currently banned inside
Rocky Mountain National Park, presumably with the hope of limiting the
application of bolts. Climbers are still permitted the use of hand drills.

Areas Covered in this Book

Estes Valley, a name of convenience, is formed by the confluence of Fall
River, Big Thompson River, Fish Creek and Black Canyon Creek, all of whic[h]
comprise the head of the Big Thompson River Valley. Scattered about this
area, in a manner defying logical description, are many crags of interest t[o]
climbers. These crags are listed in this book by area, beginning with Prosp[ect]
Mountain, then from left to right in a clockwise arc as they would appear i[n]
panorama from the summit of Prospect Mountain: Twin Sisters Mountain, [ ]
Mountain, East Portal, Fern Canyon, Fall River Canyon, Lumpy Ridge, Cow
Creek Canyon, Dry Gulch and Big Thompson Canyon. Some of these areas
within the boundaries of Rocky Mountain National Park and some are loca[ted]
in the Roosevelt National Forest. All crags and routes are listed from left t[o]
right.

Introduction

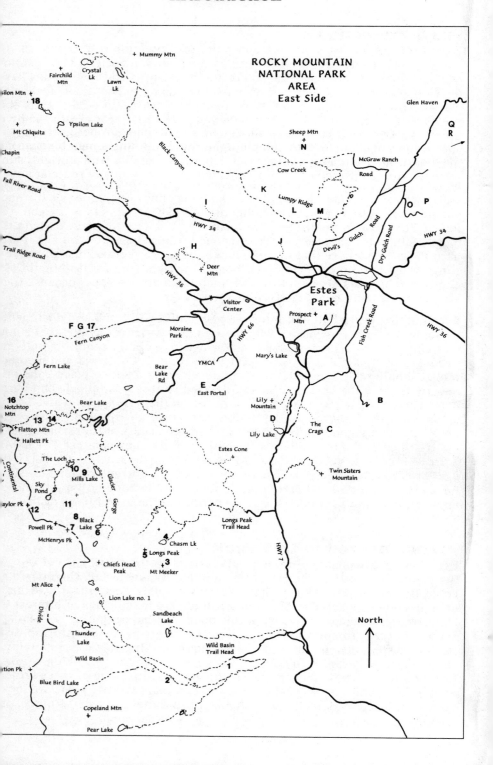

Introduction

Limitations of this Book

This book is intended for the experienced climber; it is not a manual of instruction, but a guide to the routes. It assumes that the reader is already proficient in the placement of climbing hardware, the use of a rope, and ha climbed before in the mountains. Climbing schools are available for those who seek instruction or the service of a guide. Whereas this book contains much useful information, it cannot take the place of skill and good judgment. Take care in planning an ascent. Be sure to have proper gear and clot ing. Allow adequate time to complete the route – an unplanned bivouac can be disastrous. Mountain weather can deteriorate rapidly, and a bright, sunn day can turn into a violent storm. Rockfall can occur on any route at any time. Regardless of experience, if the situation in which you find yourself does not look good, consider retreat. You can always return another day.

ROCKY MOUNTAIN NATIONAL PARK AREA
(East Side)

CRAG LOCATOR	ICE CLIMB LOCATOR ★
A. Thumb and Needle	1. Hidden Falls
B. DeVille Rocks	2. Ouzel Falls
C. The Crags	3. Dream Weaver
D. The Fin	4. Columbine Falls
E. Cottontail Crag	5 Notch Couloir
F. The Lost World	6. Black Lake Ice
G. Rock of Ages	7. Big Mac Couloir
H. Deer Mountain Buttress	8. Hourglass Couloir
I McGregor Slab	9. All Mixed Up
J. Window Rock	10. Necrophilia
K. Sundance Buttress	11. Thatchtop-Powel Ice
L. The Book	12. Taylor Glacier
M. Twin Owls	13. Dragon Tail Couloir
N. Sheep Mountain Rock	14. Emerald Lake Ice
O. Eagle Rock	15. Ptarmigan Glacier
P. Crosier Dome	16. Grace Falls
Q. Combat Rock	17. Jaws
R. Seam Rock	18. Y Couloir

★ For more detail on the ice climbs listed here, see the second boo in this series, *The High Peaks of Rocky Mountain National Park.*

Prospect Mountain

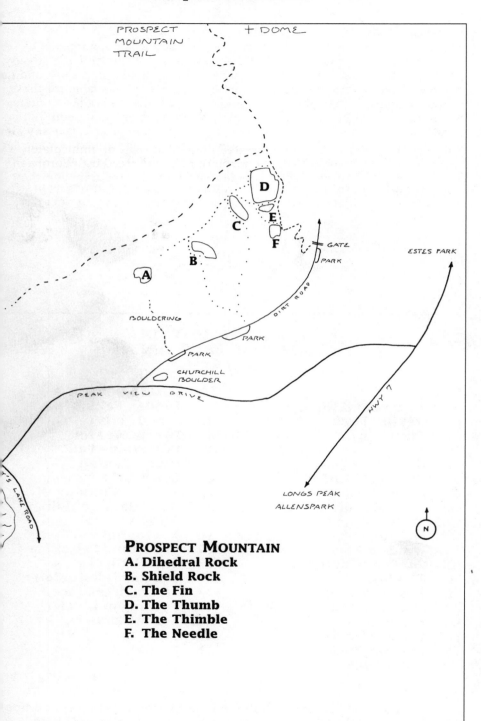

PROSPECT MOUNTAIN
A. Dihedral Rock
B. Shield Rock
C. The Fin
D. The Thumb
E. The Thimble
F. The Needle

PROSPECT MOUNTAIN

Prospect Mountain is the large, forested dome that rises up immediately south of downtown Estes Park. Its northern flank is graced by a European-style telepherique (tram) that is popular with tourists. The tram and the observation deck near the top of the mountain likely will be of little interes to climbers but the unique cluster of crags around on the east side is anoth story. To reach The Thumb and Needle and other nearby features, take Highway 7 from Estes Park and turn right on Peak View Drive. After a mile so, turn right on a dirt road and park as shown in the map. DO NOT BLOCK THE GATE; the road is used by the tram operators. The formations are liste from left to right as one faces the mountain from the east. Dihedral Rock, t southernmost feature has a name, but I have no information on its routes.

SHIELD ROCK
Shield Rock is located about 100 yards southwest from The Fin. Approach from the south as shown in the map or follow a game trail across from The Thumb.

1. **The Shield   12c** ★
   FA: Lawrence Stuemke, 1991.
   This route climbs the very steep left wall of the huge dihedral in sout east face and takes the roof above. Four bolts, three pins, and a fixed nut.

Prospect Mountain

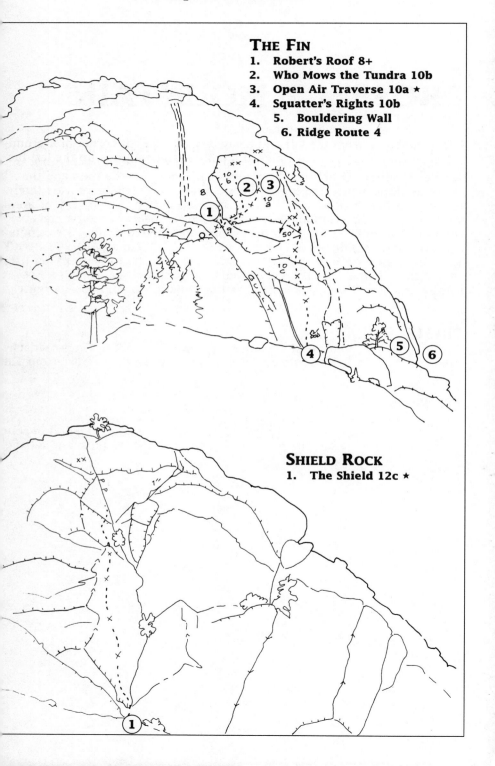

THE FIN
1. Robert's Roof 8+
2. Who Mows the Tundra 10b
3. Open Air Traverse 10a ★
4. Squatter's Rights 10b
5. Bouldering Wall
6. Ridge Route 4

SHIELD ROCK
1. The Shield 12c ★

THE FIN

The Fin is the dome-like buttress to the south and below The Thumb. Approach from The Thumb or from the south as shown in the map on page 6. Do not confuse this feature with The Fin on Lily Mountain a few miles to the south.

1. **Robert's Roof   9**
   FA: Bernard and Robert Gillet, 1987.
   Scramble in from the left and belay beneath the left corner of a prominent roof. Climb over a bulge at a bolt (9) and continue up the left-facing dihedral above (8).

2. **Who Mows the Tundra   10b**
   FA: Lawrence Stuemke and Jim Hurst, 1991.
   Begin as for *Robert's Roof,* but after the first bolt, move right out of the corner and climb straight up past three more bolts (missing) to a bolt anchor.

3. **Open Air Traverse   10a ★**
   FA: Stuemke and Hurst, 1991.
   Also known as *When Do the Deer Turn into Elk.* Begin as for *Tundra,* but traverse up and right above the roof past three bolts, then climb a blunt arête to a bolt anchor.

4. **Squatter's Rights   10b**
   FA: Stuemke and Judy Lovedokken, 1991.
   Begin down to the right from the roof described above and to the left of an orange lichen streak. Follow three bolts up to a bolt anchor.

5. **Bouldering Wall**
   Find several long boulder problems to the right of the orange lichen streak.

6. **Ridge Route   4**
   Begin at the right (southeast) side of the buttress and follow the ridge to the top.

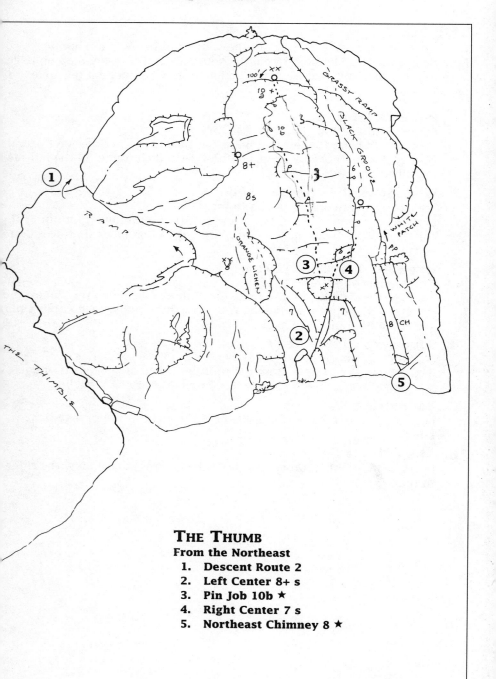

THE THUMB
From the Northeast
1. **Descent Route 2**
2. **Left Center 8+ s**
3. **Pin Job 10b ★**
4. **Right Center 7 s**
5. **Northeast Chimney 8 ★**

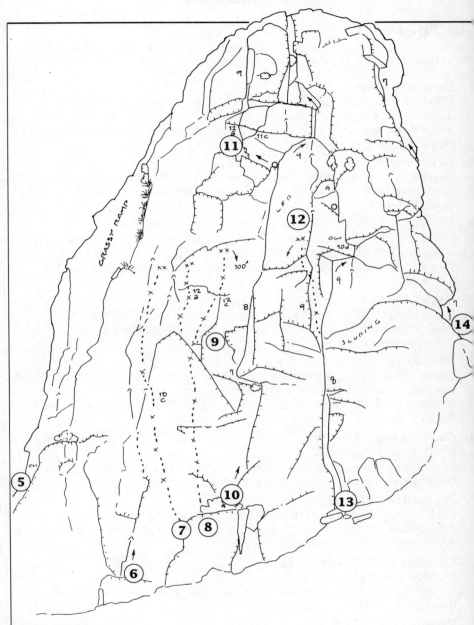

THE THUMB
From the North

5. Northeast Chimney 8 e
6. Grey Arête 10 s/vs
7. Zig Arête 10d ★
8. Confines of Power 12a ★
9. Vapor Trail 12d

10. North Overhang 9 ★
11. Mind over Matter 12a ★
12. Pigeon Perch 9 s
13. North Roof 10c
14. Uphill Cracks 7

HE THUMB

e Thumb is the largest crag of the group and features several interesting utes. It is located a short way up the slope to the west of The Needle.

1. Descent Route 2
Begin on the south side, in the cleft between The Thimble and The Thumb. Climb any of several ways to reach a broad ledge that wraps around the south side of the tower. Follow the ledge to its west end and climb a groove to the summit.

2. Left Center 8+ s
Begin beside a ten-foot pillar at the bottom of the east face and beneath an orange lichen streak. Climb straight up the face, then work left into an exit groove.

3. Pin Job 10b ★ — beware loose rock @ bottom
Begin just right of a ten-foot pillar at the bottom of the east face. Climb a short dihedral to a large block with a rappel anchor, then work straight up the fine face past some fixed gear to a bolt belay and a ledge.

4. Right Center 7 s
Begin about 20 feet right of the pillar of *Left Center.* Work up and right past some fixed pins and belay on a ledge. Climb straight up a large black groove to the summit.

5. Northeast Chimney 8 ★
Begin about 40 feet around to the right from the preceding route. Climb a steep chimney to a bench with some old pitons, then continue up a crack to the belay beneath the black groove. Climb the groove as for **Right Center**.

6. Grey Arête 10 s/vs
FA: Duncan Ferguson.
Ascend the steep, gray, lichenous arête down and left from the North Overhangs (the big roofs at the top of the north face).

7. Zig Arête 10d ★
FA: Lawrence Stuemke and Jim Hurst, 1992.
Also known as *Jane's Arête,* this is the bolt line just right of the *Grey Arête.* Five bolts to a two-bolt anchor.

8. Confines of Power 12a ★
FA: Stuemke and Hurst, 1992.
A topic the US. government should consider. Follow seven bolts to a fixed anchor just right of *Jane's.*

9. Vapor Trail 12d
Begin with *Confines of Power* but branch right at the fourth bolt. Three bolts up an overhanging wall to a fixed anchor.

10. North Overhang 9 ★
Climb the steep left-facing dihedral in the middle of the north face and skirt the upper roof on the right.

11. Mind over Matter   12a ★
FA: Mike Caldwell and Dan Ludlam, 1986.
This route originally began to the right of the *North Overhang,* turned
roof via a wide crack (10d), then made an awkward traverse left to tak
on the upper roof (see *North Roof*). It is more reasonable, however, to
do the upper roof by starting with *North Overhang.* This version takes
the left branch in the crack through the upper roof.

11A. Never Mind, It Doesn't Matter   11c
This is the right branch in the crack through the upper roof.

12. Pigeon Perch   9 s
FA: Stuemke and Hurst, 1991.
Climb the dihedral as for *North Roof.* Branch left at the sloping shelf
and climb past a single bolt to a bolt anchor.

13. North Roof   10c
Begin with a left-facing dihedral to the right of the *North Overhang.*
Climb the dihedral (8) to a large sloping ledge, then jam a wide crack
through a roof (crux) and belay in a niche. Follow a crack up and left t
join the *North Overhang* where it passes the upper roofs (9).

14. Uphill Cracks   7
Begin around to the west from the preceding routes. Climb an overhar
and move right to a crack. From the crack, go left over an awkward
bulge.

15. A Reason to Bolt   9+ s
Begin toward the right side of the west face below some orange lichen
streaks. Make committing moves over steep rock to get started, then
work up the face past three bolts and two pins, the last of which is ju
right of a short roof.

16. West Face   6 s
This is a somewhat indistinct line that joins the descent route about
halfway up. Begin about 25 feet right of *Reason.*

THE THIMBLE
This is the large detached block at the south side of The Thumb. The route
are usually toproped.

Toprope Wall. At least three 40-foot lines in the 8 and 9 range exist on the
wall that faces The Thumb.

School Slab. A few very easy lines may be toproped on the east side of The
Thimble.

THE NEEDLE
From the North

1. Angels Overhang 11 (TR)
2. Suburban Hangover 11a ★
3. Momentary Lapse of Ethics 11a or 12a ★
4. Temple of the Dog 13a (?)
5. And the Damage Done 11b ★
6. North Lieback 10a
7. Bustin' Move 12b ★
8. Uphill Slab 8 s
9. Descent Route 4

THE NEEDLE

The Needle is the rock nearest to the gate. Park on the right just before the gate and follow a good path up to the northeast corner of the rock – a five-minute walk. The routes are numbered counterclockwise around the pinnacl beginning with the farthest left route on the north side.

1. **Angels Overhang   11 (TR)**
   FA: John Gill, 1960s.
   Climb overhanging rock and pass a nose-like bulge just left of the mor obvious *Suburban Hangover* (that must be climbed first to set the toprope).

2. **Suburban Hangover   11a ★**
   FA: Lawrence Stuemke and Jim Hurst, 1991.
   Where the approach trail first reaches The Needle, this excellent short route appears on the arête at left. Stick-clip the first bolt, then climb u and around the nose past three more bolts to a bolt anchor.

3. **Momentary Lapse of Ethics   11a or 12a ★**
   FA: Stuemke and Hurst, 1991.
   Begin a short way right of *Suburban Hangover* beneath a bulging wall. Five bolts with the crux between the last two.

4. **Temple of the Dog   13a (?)**
   Begin a few feet right of Route 7 beneath a left-facing corner that leads to a roof (medium Friends). Five bolts with the crux above the roof — a time of writing, only two hangers appear on the route. Lower off from the anchor atop Route 7, 60 feet.

5. **And the Damage Done   11b ★**
   FA: Stuemke and Hurst, 1991.
   This route takes the roof to the right of *Temple of the Dog* and stays right of an arête. Four bolts with some radical moves passing the roof.

6. **North Lieback   10a**
   Climb in from the right and lieback to the top of a flake. Exit left acros a ramp.

7. **Bustin' Move   12b ★**
   FA: Stuemke and Hurst, 1991.
   Begin a short way right from the left-facing dihedral of *North Lieback*. Climb up through a series of left-angling roofs to a bolt anchor on the flat northwest face. Five bolts with a lunge after the third.

8. **Uphill Slab   8 s**
   Climb the steep face past two bolts, both of which need hangers. This route is easily toproped from a bolt anchor at the top.

9. **Descent Route   4**
   As an ascent, begin with a shallow, crescent-shaped, right-facing dihedral or the face to the right and continue up the easy slab above.

0. Hanging Over New Years   9+
Start at the left side of the south face in a chimney at the left side of a pillar. Work up and left over steep rock to a sloping ramp. Climb up to a bulge that is passed via a thin crack.

1. South Face   7
Climb the right side of a pillar to a ledge with a two-bolt anchor (one hanger is missing). One also may climb easy rock up the outside of the pillar. Work up a steep, left-facing dihedral past another bolt and continue on steep rock to the top.

2. About Face   7
Climb the face to the right of the *South Face* chimney. Take right or left options of equal difficulty from a ledge about 30 feet up.

3 History Lesson   8+
Two pins and two bolts to an anchor. The lower part of the route was previously climbed as *Southwest Corner.*

4. Southeast Corner   10c
Begin at the right side of the south face and climb the blank wall to the right of the large detached flake. Work up and right past a small roof via three bolts. Lower off or rappel 75 feet from a bolt anchor.

e author on Xenomorph, DeVille 3 Pinnacle. Photo: Greg Carelli

TWIN SISTERS MOUNTAIN

Twin Sisters Mountain is located on the east side of Highway 7, five miles south of Prospect Mountain and 5.6 miles east-northeast of Longs Peak. Though a popular trail leads to the double summit, if it is of no use in reaching DeVille Rocks or The Crags – two excellent rock-climbing areas on the north shoulder of the mountain. Reach Twin Sisters Mountain via Highway 7 either from Estes Park or from Lyons and the South Saint Vrain Canyon.

DEVILLE ROCKS

DeVille Rocks is a group of isolated buttresses above a deep ravine on the north shoulder of Twin Sisters Mountain. The first known route on these rocks was established by Layton Kor, who had a way of coming up with weird names for his climbs, such as *Ruper* and *Kloeberdanz.* He named this first route *DeVille 3,* which is no less strange, and somehow became the name associated with the whole area.

There are four distinct features: The highest and farthest north is the UFO Dome, a rounded buttress that reaches 9400 feet in elevation. Below and to the west, the DeVille 3 buttress protrudes from the north side of the ravine. Near the west end of the buttress, a vertical fault has opened and formed a separate pinnacle, which has upon its west face the route *DeVille 3.* A large recess or amphitheater drops back to the south of the DeVille 3 Buttress. To the right of the recess, the South Buttress rises in steps to a summit. Farther south and nearer to the stream is a free-standing tower called Petit or Little DeVille, which has a short easy route on its southeast side (4) and a difficult toprope problem on its north face (11c).

Below DeVille Rocks, at the mouth of the ravine, is Cheley Camp, a Christian summer youth camp. Though these crags lie within Roosevelt National Forest, the only reasonable approach is via the road that leads into the camp which is private property. Cheley Camp will allow climbers to park within or just outside their property and walk through to the DeVille Rocks. They ask that climbers call (970) 586-4244 before they come and get parking instructions since certain events may require parking just outside the gate to the camp. *It is very important that we be polite and reasonably quiet while passing through so that we do not disrupt camp activities.* During the winter, the gate may or may not be open. If it is open, you may park in front of the office, but the gate may be locked after 6 p.m. Don't get locked inside.

Approach. Drive Highway 7 to a hairpin turn about a half mile south of Mary's Lake. Turn south on Fish Creek Road and stay right at the first junction. One also may reach this junction by turning onto the north end of Fish

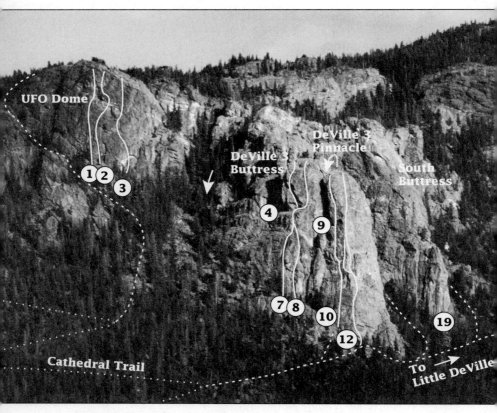

DeVille 3
From the Northwest
UFO Dome
  1. Yellow Peril 9
  2. Alien 7 ★
  3. Grey Matter 7
DeVille 3 Buttress
  4. Sky Lab 9
  7. Lightning Crack 8 ★
  8. Kornerstone Edge 7 ★
  9. Moonlight Lady 8 ★

DeVille 3 Pinnacle
  10. No Respite 9 ★
  12. Xenomorph 9 ★
South Buttress
  19. Easy Slabs 4 ★

Creek Road from Highway 36, just east of Lake Estes. From the junction, continue south, then turn left and follow the road into Cheley Camp. Park at the office, the first significant building on the right.

Cathedral Trail. Walk past the office and veer left on a dirt road. After about 300 feet, turn right and follow this road south (uphill) to the Cathedral Trailhead, which is on the left. The trail makes several switchbacks up the forested hillside below and northwest of DeVille Rocks, then swings around to the northeast side of the ridge, where a spur leads back to the top of the highest dome. All features are accessed from the Cathedral Trail before it crosses to the northeast side of the crest.

UFO DOME

Above and northeast of DeVille 3 is this prominent dome, the northwest side of which is quite steep. To reach the UFO Dome, hike up the Cathedral Trail to the highest switchback, then hike straight up the forest slope to the bottom of the northwest face. To descend from the top, hike northeast, then follow an easy gully back down to the bottom of the face.

1. **Yellow Peril   9**
   FA: Bob Culp and Layton Kor, c. 1962.
   Begin from a sloping ramp beneath the middle of the northwest face.
   1. Climb excellent rock to the left of a dihedral with yellow lichen and belay on a ledge beneath some overhangs (6, 120 feet).
   2. Pass the overhang "at its worst place" and continue to the top of the dome (9, 80 feet).

2. **Alien 7** ★
   FA: R. Rossiter, solo, 1995.
   Some of us are not from this planet. Begin as for *Yellow Peril,* at the bottom of a left-facing dihedral streaked with yellow lichen.
   1. Climb straight up the rib that forms the right side of the yellow dihedral (excellent rock with good holds) and continue to the white roofs high on the wall. Turn the right side of the roofs, then belay up and left on a ledge (7, 150 feet).
   2. Work up and left and climb the headwall (6, 60 feet).

3. **Grey Matter   7**
   FA: Kimball and Wroblewski, 1981.
   Begin about 70 feet down and right from the ramp at the bottom of the previous routes.
   1. Climb knobby rock right of an obtuse white dihedral, pass a bulge and follow a vague ramp up and left to a tiny alcove.
   2. Climb a crack through the top of the alcove and continue up easier rock to a final headwall that is passed via a finger crack.

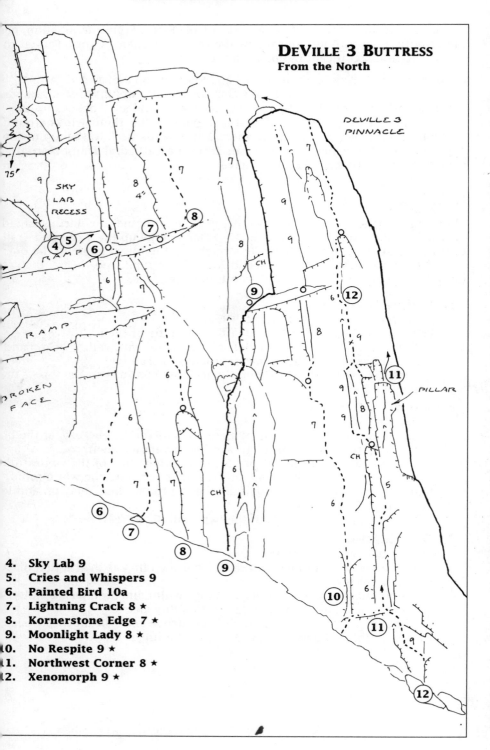

4. **Sky Lab 9**
5. **Cries and Whispers 9**
6. **Painted Bird 10a**
7. **Lightning Crack 8 ★**
8. **Kornerstone Edge 7 ★**
9. **Moonlight Lady 8 ★**
10. **No Respite 9 ★**
11. **Northwest Corner 8 ★**
12. **Xenomorph 9 ★**

DEVILLE 3 BUTTRESS

DeVille 3 is the most prominent feature of the group and strikes an impressive profile from Highway 7. The huge detached tower that forms the west end of the buttress is called the DeVille 3 Pinnacle and offers steep climbing on excellent rock. Routes have been established on the north, west, and south sides of the buttress.

Approach. Follow the Cathedral Trail for about a quarter mile to where it emerges at a rocky overlook, and continue to the seventh switchback above the overlook. This point may be identified by a retainer log along the right side of the trail and a small cairn. Leave the trail and make an ascending traverse southward to the desired point along the buttress.

Descent. To escape from the ridge crest above the north face, scramble up the crest until it is possible to descend a wooded gully to the northwest. It also possible to rappel from trees. For routes that finish on the summit of the detached pinnacle, step across the fault to the east, then scramble down a ramp to the south and gain a gully that leads down to the west.

4. **Sky Lab   9**
   FA: Kimball and Harrison, 1979.
   In the middle of the north face, beneath two pinnacles, is a square-cut recess. Gain the recess by climbing the first pitch of *Lightning Crack* or traverse in from the left. Climb the steep crack at the left inside corner of the recess.

5. **Cries and Whispers   9**
   FA: Neri and Kimball, 1976.
   Undercling and lieback an orange flake on the right wall of the recess.

6. **Painted Bird   10a**
   FA: Kimball and Salaun, 1979.
   1. Climb the steep wall just left of the blunt rib of *Lightning Crack* and continue to the highest ledge (which is continuous with the bottom of the Sky Lab recess, but out to the right).
   2. Climb an overhanging left-facing dihedral just right of the recess (crux

7. **Lightning Crack   8 ★**
   FA: Joe Hladick and Kevin Hanolin, 1976.
   Begin at a blunt rib about 40 feet left from the big fault that splits the buttress.
   1. Step off a block and climb the rib, followed by a left-facing corner, and gain the ledge that runs out right from the *Sky Lab* recess.
   2. Climb the prominent, left-leaning crack/dihedral in the upper wall (8

8. **Kornerstone Edge   7 ★**
   FA: Layton Kor and Bob Culp, c. 1962.
   Begin about 30 feet left of the big fault, beneath an inset formed by two dihedrals that face each other.
   1. Climb the right side of the slot, pass a tricky bulge, and belay on a pillar.
   2. Continue up the face and gain the ledge that runs out right from the *Sky Lab* recess.
   2. Traverse out right and climb the middle of the upper wall.

9. Moonlight Lady   8 ★
FA: Duncan Ferguson and Carol Peterson, 1978.
This route is on the upper east (left) wall of the big fault.
1. Climb the buttress just right of the fault and belay on a scree ledge inside of the fault. One also may rappel to this ledge from the top of the buttress.
2. Climb the long crack that requires pro up to 2.5 inches (8, 150 feet).

eVille 3 Pinnacle. *The following routes ascend the impressive, 400-foot-high* *nnacle that forms the west end of the DeVille 3 Buttress.*

0. No Respite   9 ★
FA: Larry Dalke and Bob Culp, 1967.
This route takes the middle of the narrow north face of the DeVille 3 Pinnacle, to the right of the big fault.
1. Take discontinuous cracks up the nebulous wall to a stance (6, 130 feet).
2. A right-facing dihedral leads to a big ledge (8, 80 feet).
3. Follow an overhanging hand crack to the top of the pinnacle (9, 80 feet).

1. Northwest Corner   8 ★
Begin beneath the middle of the north side of the pinnacle as for *No Respite.*
1. Climb up onto a sloping ledge and traverse right until very near the arête. Follow a shallow corner system for about 75 feet, then move around to the right side of the arête and continue past a big ledge to the top of a prominent pillar (6, 160 feet).
2. Work up and right across a steep black wall (crux), then follow an easy corner system straight up to a ledge high on the face (8, 140 feet).
3. Climb a thin crack up the exposed headwall and gain the top of the DeVille 3 Pinnacle (7, 70 feet). The last pitch can be avoided by climbing the upper northwest arête, but it is too easy to be fun.

2. Xenomorph   9 ★×
FA: Richard Rossiter, Greg Carelli and Gail Effron, 1995.
Begin at the bottom of the west face, about 15 feet right of the northwest corner of the DeVille 3 Pinnacle.
1. Climb a small left-facing dihedral, then work up and left over steep rock past the left end of a roof and gain the northwest corner of the tower. Climb just left of the arête for about 75 feet, then move around right and continue to a big ledge left of a prominent pillar (9, 150 feet).
2a. Step around to the north side of the arête and climb a vertical crack for about 50 feet (9). Pull around right and continue up the spectacular arête past a bolt to a ledge formed by a blunt flake (9, 130 feet).
2b. Climb a yellow, overhanging left-facing dihedral just left of the pillar (8), then continue straight up the arête as for 2a.
3. Move up and right and follow a thin crack to the top of the pinnacle (7, 90 ft.).

A. Parallel Universe   11c ★
FA: Rossiter, Effron and Carelli, 1995.
From a belay on top of the pillar, climb straight up the middle of the wall utilizing an obvious thin crack that fades after about 25 feet. Very difficult face climbing continues past several bolts to the top of the blunt flake (11c, 100 feet).

13. Polycontrast   10c ★
FA: Billy Westbay, Carl Harrison, Scott Kimball, 1981.
Begin at the bottom of the west face as for *Xenomorph*.
1. Work straight up the steep face past an overlap and turn a roof (crux), then climb a small left-facing dihedral with a second roof and continue straight up to a big ledge below the left side of a prominent pillar (10c, 150 feet).
2 and 3. Finish as for *Xenomorph*.

14. DeVille 3   8 ★
FA: Layton Kor and partner, c. 1962.
Begin at the bottom of the west face, about 25 feet right of the northwest corner (just right of a dead tree).
1. Surmount a bulge, then work up and right along obvious features to the right end of the roof. Climb straight up past a small tree and belay on a ledge (7, 120 feet).
2. Climb past a tricky bulge to a big ledge at mid face, then climb a chimney on the left and belay atop a prominent pillar (7, 75 feet).
3. Work up and right across a steep black wall (crux), then follow an easy corner system to a ledge high on the face (8, 140 feet).
4. Climb a thin crack up the exposed headwall and gain the top of the DeVille 3 Pinnacle (7, 70 feet).

15. Wind Song   8 ★
FA: Bob and Jane Culp and Huntley Ingalls, 1963.
1. Climb *DeVille 3* to the small tree, then work up and right to the big ledge at mid face (7, 160 feet).
2. Follow a prominent crack system that angles up and right to a niche near the right edge of the face (8, 100 feet).
3. Step left and climb a right-facing dihedral system, then jam a finger crack to the top of the wall (7, 120 feet).

16. Ghost Dance   9 s
FA: Bill Wylie and Scott Kimball, 1980.
This route ascends the southwest corner of the pinnacle.
1. Climb directly up the southwest corner to a belay stance (9, 120 feet).
2. Climb up and then left into a right-facing corner and gain the belay niche on *Wind Song* (8, 100 feet).
3. Start up a right-leaning, right-facing dihedral (9), then crank around onto the west face. Thin moves lead to easier ground and the top of the pinnacle (9, 100 feet).

17. Plastic Ono Climb   10
FA: Kimball, East, and Harrison, 1980.
This route begins on the right wall of the deep cleft, around to the right from the southwest arête of the DeVille 3 Pinnacle.
1. Climb a vertical wall and right-facing dihedral to the left of a reddish streak. Undercling right beneath a roof and continue up difficult rock a belay (10).
2. Climb past the right end of another roof and follow an easier dihedral to the walk-off ledge (9).

DeVille 3 Pinnacle – West Face

11. Northwest Corner 8 ★
12. Xenomorph 9 ★
13. Polycontrast 10c ★
14. DeVille 3 8 ★
15. Wind Song 8 ★

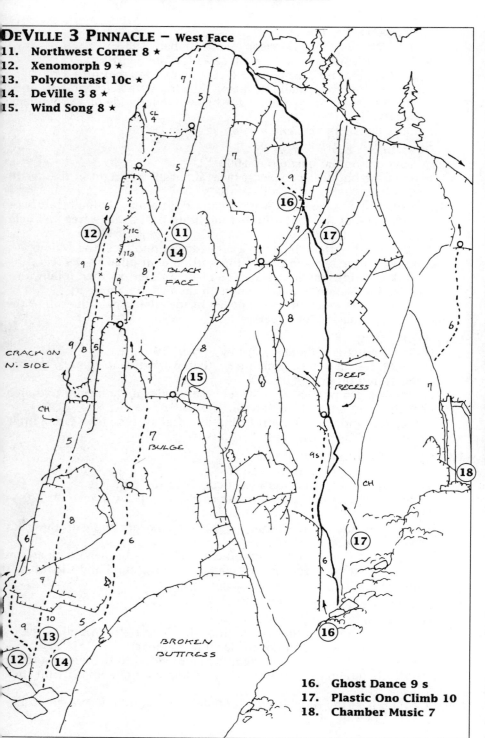

16. Ghost Dance 9 s
17. Plastic Ono Climb 10
18. Chamber Music 7

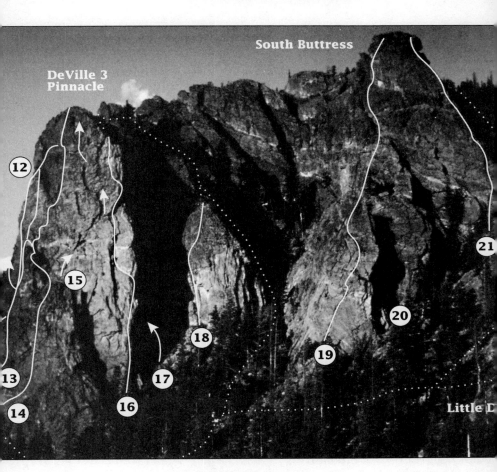

DeVille Rocks
From the Southwest
DeVille 3 Pinnacle
12. Xenomorph 9 ★
13. Polycontrast 10c ★
14. DeVille 3 8 ★
15. Wind Song 8 ★
16. Ghost Dance 9 s
17. Plastic Ono Climb 10
18. Chamber Music 7
South Buttress
19. Easy Slabs 4 ★
20. Chainhand's Lament 8
21. Planet of the Bovinoids 8

8. Chamber Music   7

This route follows cracks up the west face of a smaller buttress that sits between the DeVille 3 Pinnacle and the descent gully. Begin just right of a large flake. Climb a brushy slot that tapers to a crack, pass a black bulge, then break right and climb to the top of the buttress. Scramble up to the walk-off ramp.

»uth Buttress. The following three routes ascend the large stepped buttress *the right (south) of the descent gully. Escape from the summit by hiking* *ɔwn the forested gully on the south side of the buttress.*

9. Easy Slabs   4 ★

FA: Bob and Jane Culp, c. 1963.
Follow cracks and slabs up the west face of the South Buttress. Three pitches.

0. Chainhand's Lament   8

FA: Kimball, Hladick, and Knowles, 1979.
Begin this climb at the bottom of a narrow face around to the right from *Easy Slabs.*
1. Follow a seam and flake system to a small ledge.
2. Work right and follow a black groove to a large ledge.
3. Climb a blank face left of center and gain the top of a large flake.
4. Climb a short steep pitch.
5. A long easy pitch leads to the top of the buttress.

1. Planet of the Bovinoids   8

FA: R. Rossiter, solo, 1995.
This route is dedicated to mass consciousness — perhaps the best oxymoron of all time...on this planet anyway.

ıe upper part of the South Buttress forms a large pyramid with a sort of *'uashed summit. Climb a long pitch up the steep south edge of the west face,* *ıen continue more easily to the top.*

THE CRAGS

The Crags are a seldom visited group of towers, ribs, and buttresses on the northwest shoulder of Twin Sisters Mountain. The area hosts many interesting routes and is among the most spectacularly scenic climbing spots in Colorado. The average belay is graced with sweeping views of the Continental Divide from the Meeker-Longs massif to the Mummy Range, wit an unparalleled surveillance of the Estes Park Valley and Lumpy Ridge. The rock is generally solid, consisting mostly of gneiss and schist that has erod ed to produce numerous irregularities and rugosities. Thus, many routes, even those having good cracks, are primarily face climbs.

That few climbers visit the area is likely due to the primitive approach, and to the fact that there are no great classic lines such as *Mainliner, The Nose, Pear Buttress;* nor are there enough bolt-protected face climbs (one so far) t attract the clip and run aficionados. Yet, The Crags have a definite appeal: a high and lonely air, an arcane beauty, and some very unusual routes and rocks.

Approach A. Turn off Highway 7 at the Lily Lake Visitor Center, then turn left (north) and follow a dirt road to a parking area just beyond the Bald Pa Inn. Hike north along the dirt road (administered by Larimer County Parks) for a half mile, then head up the forest slope on the right (east) and continu to the talus field beneath Rib Rock. This is more difficult than it sounds because, once in the trees, it is impossible to see where you are going. If th correct line is found, it takes about 30 minutes to reach Rib Rock from the parking area. This is the more pleasant of the two approach options and ca be used to reach any of the features.

Approach B. Park at the Lily Lake Visitor Center on the east side of Highwa 7, across from Lily Lake. Start up a dirt road that runs south behind the vis tor center. Just before reaching a gate, turn east and hike up the hillside through an area of lodge pole pine that, for some reason, has been thinned with the cuttings left in large piles. Continue east through dense forest, windfall, and brush veering ever so slightly north. With luck, the bottom of long talus field will be found that leads to the southeast corner of the Lowe Great Face. The entire walk is barely a mile long, but it takes about 45 min utes to get out of the trees, even if you do everything right. Use this approach to reach the Lower Great Face, Crosswinds, Castaway Crag, and th Upper Great Face.

THE RIBS

The Ribs consist of three parallel fins or narrow buttresses at the lower left aspect of The Crags. The northern rib is broken and uninspiring but the other two, Mid Rib and Rib Rock, are precipitous and relatively well formed A narrow fin called Treasure Islands resides at the top of the gully between Mid Rib and Rib Rock. The Ribs are very near to each other, separated by deep mossy talus gullies so that most routes are shady and cool. However, these narrow channels create a clandestine atmosphere and provide surrea views of the Mummy Range to the west. Routes are described counterclock wise around each feature beginning at the top of the north face.

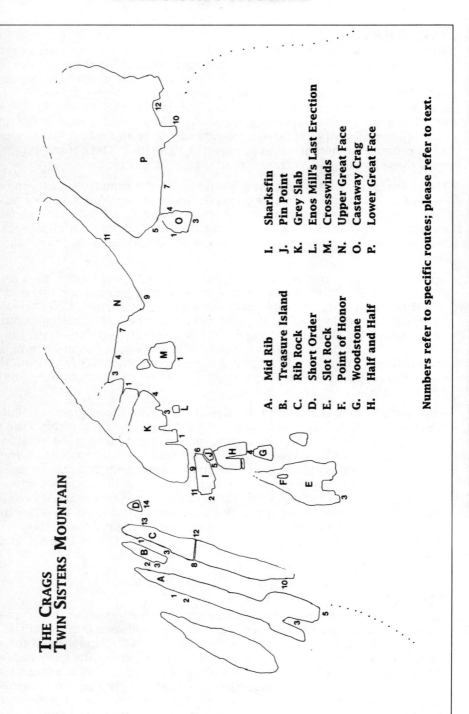

THE CRAGS
TWIN SISTERS MOUNTAIN

A.   Mid Rib
B.   Treasure Island
C.   Rib Rock
D.   Short Order
E.   Slot Rock
F.   Point of Honor
G.   Woodstone
H.   Half and Half

I.   Sharksfin
J.   Pin Point
K.   Grey Slab
L.   Enos Mill's Last Erection
M.   Crosswinds
N.   Upper Great Face
O.   Castaway Crag
P.   Lower Great Face

Numbers refer to specific routes; please refer to text.

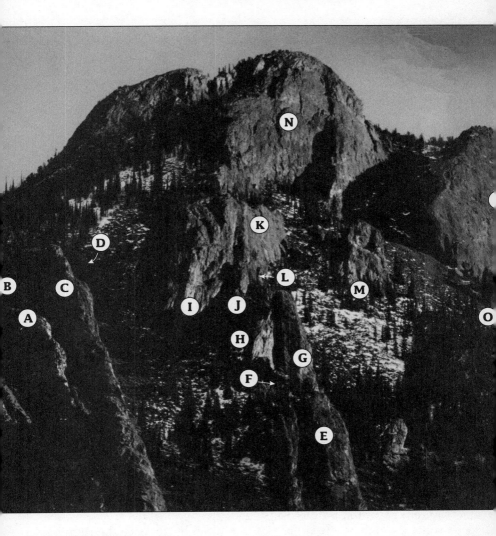

THE CRAGS
TWIN SISTERS MOUNTAIN

A. Mid Rib	I. Sharksfin
B. Treasure Island	J. Pin Point
C. Rib Rock	K. Grey Slab
D. Short Order	L. Enos Mills' Last Erection
E. Slot Rock	M. Crosswinds
F. Point of Honor	N. Upper Great Face
G. Woodstone	O. Castaway Crag
H. Half and Half	P. Lower Great Face

MID RIB

This is the middle of the three long buttresses. The lower west buttress of Mid Rib is offset to the south and has its own summit separated from the main ridge by a notch. Escape from the ridge crest by scrambling east until the rib merges with the main slope. It also is easy to downclimb the south side just below the level of *Treasure Island* (cl4).

1. Under the Rainbow   9 ★
FA: Scott Kimball and Eric Ming, 1981.
This route ascends a left-facing dihedral in the steep red wall near the upper end of the north face. It begins in a thicket of trees and is marked with a small cairn. Climb the dihedral to where it fades and continue with a shallow chimney. One pitch.

2. Better Rocks and Gardens   8
FA: Scott Kimball and Annegret Wroblewski, 1981.
This route lies just right of the thicket of trees near the top of the gully. Begin at a tiny pillar about 20 feet right of the first fir tree. Gain a shallow left-leaning right-facing dihedral, climb to its top, and belay beneath a red roof. Pass the roof on the right and continue to the ridge crest.

3. Trouble with Rubble   9+
FA: Kimball, Kennedy, and Snively, 1982.
A short way up the along the north side of the initial buttress is an out-leaning banded wall. Climb the intimidating crack in the middle of the wall, pass a right-facing corner, then move up and left to belay. Step left into another crack and continue past a roof to the top of the wall.

4. Horizontal Element   7
FA: Layton Kor and Larry Dalke, 1962.
Climb a dihedral at the left side of the west face and belay on the crest. Traverse left across the upper north face and gain the notch in the crest of the ridge. Scramble up the ridge crest to where it merges with the talus.

5. Mid Rib   7
FA: Layton Kor and Bob Culp, c. 1962.
This route ascends the west face of the initial buttress to the right of the preceding route. Face climb up the lower west face and gain a crack after about 75 feet that is followed to a belay. Continue over a minor summit, switch left to the main rib, and stay on the crest all the way.

TREASURE ISLAND

This is a small but engaging fin of rock at the top of the gully between Mid Rib and Rib Rock. Escape from the summit by scrambling off to the east.

1. Czechoslovakian Crystal Collector   8 s
FA: Kimball and Hladick, 1983.
Climb a precarious flake twenty feet left of *Ironsides*.

2. Ironsides 9 ★
FA: Kimball and Randy Joseph, 1981.
Jam a prominent hand and finger crack in dark red rock just left of an arête. A bolt anchor with chains has been installed near the top of the face a short way right of this crack; its purpose is not known, however one could use it to toprope *Ironsides* or the face and arête to the right.

3. Pirates Cove 7 ★
FA: Joseph, Wroblewski, and Kimball, 1981.
Climb the prominent right-facing dihedral at the lower right side of the north face.

4. Treasure Island 9
FA: Kimball and Johnson, 1979.
This route ascends the narrow west face. Climb through an undercut and avoid the loose central roof via face holds to the right.

5. Junk Pile 9
FA: Kent Lugbill and Kimball, 1982.
Climb the loose and precarious crack at the lower left side of the sout face.

RIB ROCK

Rib Rock is the rightmost and higher of the three ribs. It has several fine routes on its north face. Note that the north face is divided by three distinc chimneys that aid in locating the routes, most of which are within a rope-length of the middle chimney (*Flesh Flagellation*). The lowest chimney cuts all the way through the rib to the south face. The large, overhanging wall o the lower north face has no routes. Escape the ridge crest by scrambling of to the east.

1. Green Street 7
FA: Snively and Kimball, 1981.
At the upper east side of the north face is a large right-facing dihedra which contains the higher of the three chimneys. Climb a handcrack u the gray left wall of the dihedral.

2. Dark Canyon 7 or 9 s
FA: Kimball and Harrison, 1978.
Begin about 25 feet up and left from the middle chimney.
1. Follow a seam for about 40 feet, then work left to a recess in the fa and belay at bottom of a right-facing dihedral (9 s). Or begin another feet to the left and climb more easily to the same fate (7).
2. Move up and right into a finger crack and continue to the ridge cre (7).

3. Flesh Flagellation 9
FA: Kimball and Lugbill, 1982.
This route ascends the central chimney. Climb over the chockstones and gain a classic hand and finger crack in a shallow left-facing dihe-dral (9). Move right at its top and follow a right-facing corner to the ridge crest.

4. Personal Space Hammer   9+ ★
FA: Bernard Gillett and Jerry Hill, 1992.
1. Jam an overhanging hand crack immediately right of the central
chimney and belay on a good ledge as for the following route (9+).
2. Climb a squeeze chimney and continue straight up to the ridge crest
(8), or climb an offset left-facing dihedral just to the right (9).

5. Consumption of the Ages   10b ★
FA: Ming, Kimball, and Kennedy, 1981.
This route ascends the overhanging crack around to the right of the
central chimney.
1. Hand traverse up and right to gain the crack and jam to a good ledge
(10b).
2. Climb the squeeze chimney and continue to the ridge crest (8).

6. Face Lift   10a ★
FA: Snively and Kimball, 1981.
This route ascends the middle of the wall between the central and lower
chimneys. Begin about 35 feet up and left from the lower chimney
(*Anatomy Asylum*).
1. Lieback in from the left (10a) and jam a left-leaning crack to a ledge.
2. Start with a thin crack, then face climb up and over a roof and angle
right to the ridge crest (8).

7. Kaleidoscope   10b ★
FA: Kimball and Matt Rembaum, 1984.
This route ascends the steep wall just left of *Anatomy Asylum*.
1. Climb poorly protected rock up and slightly left to some better nut
placements, then break left (10a) and gain a crack that is followed to a
stance beneath a left-leaning left-facing dihedral.
2. Climb the bulging dihedral, then work around to the right on easier
rock and gain the ridge crest.

8. Anatomy Asylum   7
FA: Kimball, 1984.
This route ascends the right (lower) chimney. Climb up past some
chockstones, then worm up through the interior of Rib Rock and gain
the crest of the ridge.

9. Marriage on the Rocks   8
FA: Kimball and Wroblewski, 1981.
This route ascends the wall just right of *Anatomy Asylum*.
1. Start up the chimney but break right and climb a right-leaning, left-
facing dihedral. Pass a small roof, then work up and right to a long
ledge (8).
2. Gain a short hand crack that is followed to the crest of the ridge (7).

0. Higher Rib   5
FA: Layton Kor and Larry Dalke, c. 1965.
This route ascends the entire rib from bottom to top. Begin with a large
left-facing dihedral (viewed from the west) and continue up the crest to
where it merges with the slope of the mountain.

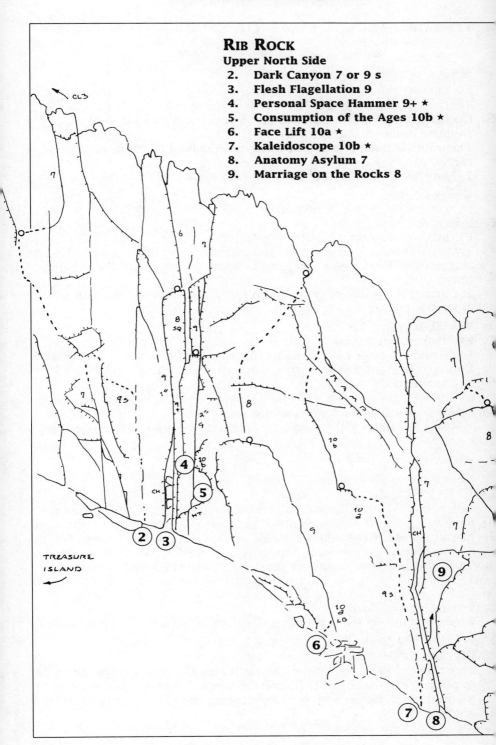

RIB ROCK
Upper North Side
2. **Dark Canyon 7 or 9 s**
3. **Flesh Flagellation 9**
4. **Personal Space Hammer 9+ ★**
5. **Consumption of the Ages 10b ★**
6. **Face Lift 10a ★**
7. **Kaleidoscope 10b ★**
8. **Anatomy Asylum 7**
9. **Marriage on the Rocks 8**

CL3

7

6

7

8 SQ

9

9

1"

7

9 5

9

9+

2"

9

10 b

CH

HT

2

3

4

5

8

10 b

10 2

7

7

CH

7

7

8

9

9 5

TREASURE ISLAND

10 2 LD

6

10 2 LD

7

8

9

outh Face. *The following routes ascend the south face of Rib Rock across a road gully from the Sharksfin.*

1. A Day at the Crags   8
FA: Kimball, Syphax, and Anderson, 1976.
This route climbs the face left a major chimney/fault near the middle of the face (*Ginger Snap*). Begin about 15 feet down and left from the chimney beside a 35 foot fir tree.
1. Stem up a steep left-facing corner to a good belay stance (7, 100 feet).
2. Traverse out left and follow a groove through a ceiling (8).

2. Ginger Snap   9
FA: Kimball, Harrison, and Westbay, 1981.
Across from the Sharksfin, locate a chimney/fault that goes through to the other side of the rib (*Anatomy Asylum*).
1. Stem out of an indentation at the bottom of the chimney and climb a blank brown face, pass a roof, and belay at an opening in the chimney (9).
2. Climb through the opening at the top of the chimney and gain the crest of the ridge (2).

3. Rockhounds   10
FA: Hladick and Kimball, 1979.
Begin under a large roof at the top of the south face. Jam a handcrack through the eight-foot roof, then work up the face and tackle a smaller and easier roof.

ort Order. *This is a small pinnacle just south from the top of Rib Rock. It s a single route up its flat west face. Climb a thin crack up the left side of e face.*

LOT ROCK
ot Rock is the large square buttress across the gully to the south from the ottom of Mid Rib. It is easily identified by a huge square-cut slot in its west ce. Routes are described counterclockwise beginning with the north face. cape all routes by hiking around the west and north sides of the summit ock to the talus on the northwest shoulder. It also is possible to scramble over the top.

1. Sword in the Stone   9
Begin near the center of the north face and climb a reddish left-facing dihedral that is capped by a roof.

2. Pigeon Arête   8
Begin toward the right side of the north face and gain a ledge the leads to a wide crack on the right. Climb the crack to its end, then work up the face to the ridge crest and belay. Follow the easy ridge to the summit area.

3. Slot Machine 8
FA: Larry Dalke and George O'Brien, 1970.
This route ascends the buttress that forms the left side of the slot.
1. Begin from the low-point of the buttress and climb to the first ledge
2. Identify a wide crack in tan colored rock on the right. Move right of
the crack, around a prow (8), and gain a stance at the bottom of a right
facing dihedral.
3. Follow the dihedral to the top of the buttress (7).

4. Could Be Wales 7 ★
This route ascends the right margin of the buttress forming the left si
of the slot. Begin around the corner left from the bottom of the slot.
1. Climb a short easy wall and belay on a big ledge.
2. Work up and right to the outside edge of the slot, then climb a fractured slab past a fixed pin and continue up a 40-foot flake.
3. Climb a vertical blocky wall on the left.

5. Slot Left 7
Climb two leads up the left inside corner of the slot.

6. Slot Direct 9 ★
FA: Larry Dalke and Bob Culp, 1969.
This route ascends a wide crack up the middle of the wall in the back
the slot.
1. Climb in from the left and belay at a stance in the central crack.
2. Jam up the steep crack, which widens to four inches.

7. Slot Right 7
Climb the right inside corner of the slot for two pitches of gardening.

8. Lichen It or Not 9+
FA: Kimball and Hladick, 1983.
So punny. Climb the corner of *Slot Right*, but halfway up the second
pitch, jam the crack in the vertical right wall and finish on the expose
arête.

9. Roofs Ridiculous 9
FA: Bob Culp and Bob Beal, 1970.
This route ascends the west face of the buttress to the right of the slc
1. Begin from the northwest corner of the buttress and climb to a ledg
2. Climb a red and orange left-leaning flake through the out-leaning
middle of the buttress.
3. An easy pitch leads to the top.

10. Lakeview 7
Sounds like a suburb of Seattle ... instead, locate a cave at the bottom
of the south face. Begin with a line that proceeds from the left edge o
the cave and climb moderate rock to the top.

Point of Honor is a narrow 40-foot tower on the shoulder just east from th
top of Slot Rock. It features a very nice steep route on its north face (6).
Downclimb the route or fashion a rappel from the tiny summit.

WOODSTONE

Woodstone is the prominent square spire a short way southeast from Point of Honor. Escape the summit by a 75-foot rappel into the notch on the east side.

1. Chimney Stone 7
Climb the chockstone chimney at the upper left side of the north face.

2. Hardwood 8
Climb an obvious chimney followed by a hand crack along the right side of the north face.

3. Woodstone 7 ★
This route ascends the highly textured west face. Turn a roof 20 feet off the deck and belay on a big ledge. Climb a right-facing dihedral and continue to the summit.

HALF AND HALF

Directly east of Woodstone is a squared-off tower, split in half by a deep chimney. Rappel from the north buttress via questionable anchors; walk off from the south buttress. A gully (cl3) allows north-south passage just east of Half and Half.

1. Transformation of Waste 8
Left from the central chimney, is a flake that is detached from the main buttress. Climb the north edge of the flake for 70 feet past a roof and a thin crack. Move right and climb the west face of the main buttress or jam a crack/flake to finish (9).

2. Chimney Route 5
Climb a recess up the east side of the fin/flake of the preceding route.

3. Interiors 9
FA: Kimball and Harrison, 1981.
Begin in the chimney that divides the crag into halves. Climb a left-leaning hand crack in the right wall finishing with a bombay slot.

4. Disarmament 9 ★
FA: Al Czecholinski, c. 1970.
This route ascends excellent rock up the left side of the west face to a belay in a thin red crack beneath the upper roof. Step right and crank over the roof.

5. Letting Go 7
FA: Mike Neri and Kimball, 1976.
This route ascends the right side of the west face in one long pitch. Climb face holds right of center, turn a roof at mid-height, then continue more easily to the top.

SHARKSFIN

The free-standing tower of the Sharksfin is perhaps the best single formatic at The Crags and has one of the very best routes on its narrow north face. I is steep on all sides but the southwest, which allows a reasonable down-climb. An uncircumcised-looking pinnacle called Pin Point thrusts up across a narrow notch from the southwest corner of the main tower. Routes are described counterclockwise beginning from the left side of the north face.

Descent. Reverse the *Sharksfin* route or rappel 75 feet east from an anchor near the south end of the summit ridge.

Shark Alley. A deep talus gully descends to the north between the Grey Slab and the east face of the Sharksfin. This gully allows reasonable passage between the northern and southern features of The Crags. On the south side instead of climbing down around the bottom Enos Mills' Last Erection, traver a narrow ledge south from the notch on its east side. There also is a passabl gully (cl3) between Pin Point and Half and Half.

1. **North Face Left 8 ★**
   FA: Ray Northcutt and George Lamb, 1955.
   This is the left to a parallel route on the right side of the north face. Spartan pro.
   1. Climb a line of discontinuous cracks up the left side of the narrow face to a ledge (8, 100 feet).
   2. Continue up the left side of the face to the summit (6).

2. **North Face Right 8 ★**
   FA: Northcutt and Lamb, 1955.
   Classic.
   1. Follow a discontinuous crack system up the right side of the north face and belay on a ledge (8, 100 feet).
   2. Climb the middle of the upper face to the summit (6).

3. **Cracks and Terrace 9**
   Begin about 30 feet on the northwest corner.
   1. Climb a handcrack through a bulge and belay on a grassy ledge (9).
   2. Work up and right and follow cracks to a chockstone notch on the summit ridge (8).

4. **West Face 6**
   1. Begin left of the middle of the west face and follow a fissure to a grassy ledge.
   2. Angle up and left and gain the chockstone notch near the summit.

5. **Sharksfin 2**
   FA: Bill Eubank and Brad VanDiver, c. 1950.
   This is the easiest way to reach the summit and was the line of the fir ascent of the tower. Scramble up a gully to ledges on the south side o the west face (near Pin Point), work up and left across the upper west face to the chockstone notch on the summit ridge.

N POINT AND SHARKSFIN From the Southeast

. **Loan Shark 8 ★**
. **Religious Zealot 9 ★**
. **Big Tears 10a ★**

11. **Sharkstone 8 ★**
13. **Buns Up 9**
14. **Shark Bite 8 ★**

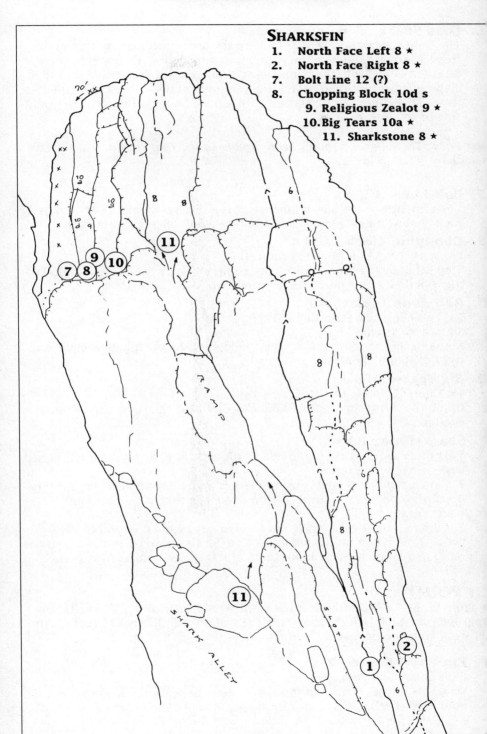

SHARKSFIN

1. North Face Left 8 ★
2. North Face Right 8 ★
7. Bolt Line 12 (?)
8. Chopping Block 10d s
   9. Religious Zealot 9 ★
   10. Big Tears 10a ★
   11. Sharkstone 8 ★

6. Loan Shark 8 ★

This route ascends excellent rock up the steep and narrow south buttress. Begin at the low point of the buttress, below the gap that separates Pin Point from the main tower. Climb a right-facing dihedral to a sloping ledge (optional belay), then follow a crack to the top of the buttress. This climb can be started with a right-facing dihedral at the right side of the buttress.

East Face. The following routes begin up on a shelf that runs across the east face above Shark Alley.

7. Bolt Line 12(?)

The east side of the south buttress forms a narrow column of dark red rock. Follow a line a six bolts up to a two-bolt anchor with chains.

8. Chopping Block 10d s

FA: Mark Termini and Randy Nance.
Step off a jagged block and follow a thin crack up the shallow right-facing dihedral just right of the previous route.

9. Religious Zealot 9 ★

FA: Eric Ming and Scott Kirby, 1979.
SR to a #4 Friend.
Jam a hand and fist crack up the shallow left-facing dihedral eight feet right of *Chopping Block.*

10. Big Tears 10a ★

FA: Kimball, Wylie, and Harrison, 1981.
Climb the left-facing, left-leaning dihedral near the right end of the shelf.

11. Sharkstone 8 ★

This route ascends the right side of the east face. Begin from the northeast corner of the tower.
1. Gain a ramp that angles up to the left and climb to near its top, then break right in a crack and belay on a ledge with a large clump of *heuchera* (6).
2. Climb straight up a crack and a steep left-facing dihedral to the chockstone notch on the summit ridge (8). Or continue to the top of the ramp and climb a crack about ten feet left of the regular finish (8).

PIN POINT

Pin Point is the fat little tower at the southwest corner of the Sharksfin, the upper half of which is separated from the main tower. Rappel 75 feet northeast from slings to escape the summit.

12. Pin Point Route 7

FA: Kimball and Neri, 1976.
Scramble up the *Sharksfin* route to a ledge beneath the north side of Pin Point and climb a wide crack up the right side of the north face.

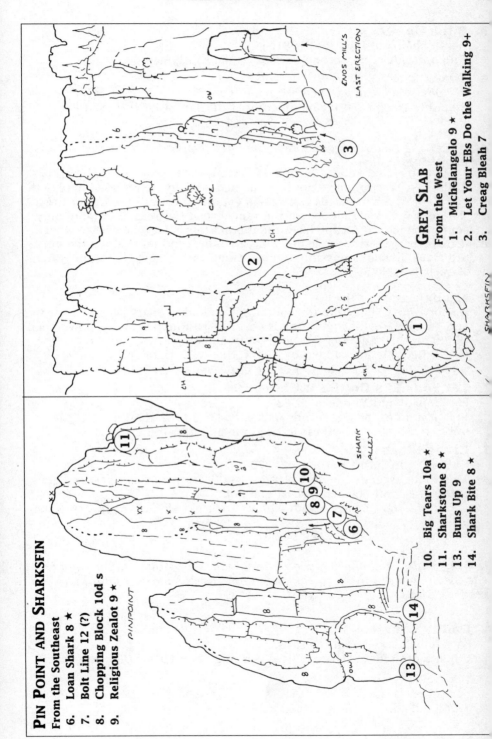

Grey Slab
From the West

1. Michelangelo 9 ★
2. Let Your EBs Do the Walking 9+
3. Creag Bleah 7

Pin Point and Sharksfin
From the Southeast

6. Loan Shark 8 ★
7. Bolt Line 12 (?)
8. Chopping Block 10d s
9. Religious Zealot 9 ★

10. Big Tears 10a ★
11. Sharkstone 8 ★
13. Buns Up 9
14. Shark Bite 8 ★

3. Buns Up   9
FA: Kimball and Harrison, 1981.
Climb a wide crack through a roof on the south face.

4. Shark Bite   8 ★
FA: Dave Mondeau and Scott Kimball, 1983.
Stem the steep right-facing dihedral at the southeast corner of Pin Point.

REY SLAB

ne steep orange and yellow buttresses directly east of the Sharksfin and
nos Mills' Last Erection have not been named, and so are grouped here with
e Grey Slab, which proceeds from them southeast toward the Upper Great
ce. These features are all part of the same broad buttress, separated only
/ facet or crevice. To escape from the top of any route, hike east to where
e buttress merges with the main slope, then descend talus along the north
south sides. It also is possible to downclimb the narrow gullies on either
de of Michelangelo.

1. Michelangelo   9 ★
A short way uphill from the south (upper) end of Shark Alley is a steep
and narrow, west-facing buttress covered with orange and yellow lichen.
Climb up the middle of the buttress in one long pitch. Aim for a small
left-facing dihedral capped by a roof, then veer right and jam a "sculp-
tured" hand crack to the top of the buttress.

2. Let Your EBs Do the Walking   9+
FA: Kimball and Mondeau, 1983.
Just around to the right from *Michelangelo,* on the south face of the
buttress, climb the farthest left right-facing dihedral.

3. Creag Bleah   7
FA: Bob Culp and Tom Haig, c. 1970.
This route ascends the next buttress south from *Michelangelo* and about
100 feet east of Enos Mills' Last Erection.
1. Climb a right-facing dihedral along the right side of the buttress and
belay at its top.
2. Finish with a broad open book.

*ne Grey Slab. The following two routes are located around to the right from
eag Bleah on a southwest-facing gray slab, directly across a talus gully
om Crosswinds.*

4. Daddy Longlegs   9
FA: Kimball and Mondeau, 1983.
Climb a prominent right-facing dihedral 25 feet left of *Diamond Dust.*

5. Diamond Dust   9
FA: Kimball and Haze Johnson, 1983.
Near the middle of the slab, identify a left-leaning dogleg crack. Start below the crack and face climb up to a big ledge, stem up a slot, then work the face along the dogleg.

ENOS MILLS' LAST ERECTION
This abrupt little tower shows its best profile from the east and gives new meaning to the term Die Hard. It is located about 300 feet southeast of the Sharksfin and just below the dihedral of *Creag Bleah*. Use a long sling to rappel from the summit or downclimb *Penis Mills*.

1. North Crack   6
Also known as *Penis Mills* – climb the 35-foot crack on the north side.

2. Split Ends   9
Climb the wide crack on the south side of the tower.

ENOS MILLS'
LAST ERECTION

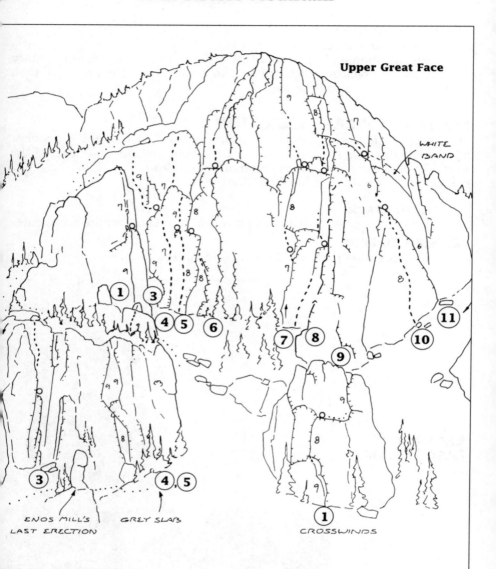

UPPER GREAT FACE
From the West

1. **Over Thirty Club 9** ★
3. **High Clutch 9 s** ★
4. **A Few Moments' Pleasure 7** ★
5. **Sky King 9 s**
6. **Tom's Travesty 8** ★

7. **Kor-Northcutt 9** ★
8. **Erac's Crack 6**
9. **Right Buttress 8** ★
10. **Southwest Face 8 (?)**
11. **Indian Peaks Arête 7**

CROSSWINDS

Crosswinds is a free-standing tower several hundred feet beneath the Upper Great Face and a short way south of the Grey Slab. Escape from the summit via the *Normal Way.*

1. Crosswinds 10

Begin at the bottom center of the west face.

1. Jam a difficult handcrack (10), or climb cracks and flakes on the righ (9), then follow a reddish right-facing dihedral to a sloping ledge.
2. Move right and stem an overhanging, left-facing dihedral above the right end of the ledge (9).

2. Normal Way 2

Climb the chimney at the southeast corner of the tower.

UPPER GREAT FACE

High on the northwest ridge of Twin Sisters Mountain and towering above al the other formations is the 500-foot-high buttress of the Upper Great Face. The main wall faces west and is bound on the right by a large buttress (the Right Rib) beyond which the wall bends around to face southwest.

Descent. For routes that finish along the left side of the west face, scrambl down the northwest ridge to a chimney with a chockstone. Sling the chockstone and rappel 75 feet to the talus. For routes that finish near the summit hike south, then descend the talus gully between the Upper Great Face and the Lower Great Face.

1. Over Thirty Club 9 ★

This route is located on a narrow buttress down and left from the main west face. Identify a vertical hand crack above a dark gray slab.

1. Begin with the slab and climb to the top of the crack (9).
2. Follow easier cracks to the top of the buttress.

To descend, scramble north, then down to the west.

2. Old and Forgotten 7(?)

Begin behind a tall fir tree at the far left side of the west face and follow a right-facing-dihedral to the crest of the ridge.

3. High Clutch 9 s ★

FA: Kimball and Czecholinski, 1976.

Begin with an arch at the lower left side of the west face.

1. Climb through the top of the arch, then follow a crack and corner system to a ledge beneath a rectangular recess (9).
2. Make a committing traverse left to a right-facing dihedral system an follow it to the ridge crest (9 s).

4. A Few Moments' Pleasure 7 ★

This is a worthy route up the middle of the left wall. Begin a short way right the aforementioned arch at a faint right-facing corner.

1. Climb the corner to a ledge, then follow edges and incipient cracks a ledge beneath a rectangular recess (7).
2. Climb a crack out the right side of the recess, and continue more ea ily to the ridge crest.

5. Sky King   9 s
FA: Kimball and Snively, 1981.
This route ascends the face left of the huge right-racing dihedral of *Tom's Travesty.*
1. Do a long lead up the poorly protected face and belay at a large flake (8).
2. Climb the unprotected face above the flake, then continue more easily to the top (9 s).

6. Tom's Travesty   8 ★
FA: Bob Culp and Tom Haig, c. 1960.
This route ascends the main dihedral system up the right margin of the left wall. Begin at a bent tree, about 40 feet right of a big right-facing dihedral system.
1. Jam a left-arching wide crack and veer left into the main corner system (8).
2. Follow the corner to where it arches right and belay on a ledge at right (7).
3. Climb a crack and turn a roof 30 feet right of the main dihedral and continue up the ridge to the summit.

7. Kor-Northcutt   9 ★
FA: Layton Kor and Ray Northcutt, 1959.
This route climbs the center of the main face to its top. Begin a short way left of the Right Rib (the large buttress that marks the right side of the main face).
1. Climb an easy chimney/corner and belay in a niche.
2. Climb up past the left end of a small roof, then jam a wide crack to a ledge and belay beside a large block (8).
3. From the top of the block, move a bit left and follow a shallow right-facing dihedral system to the top of the face (9).

8. Erac's Crack   6
FA: Ken Brin and Larry Beardsley, 1962.
This route ascends the huge left-facing chimney/dihedral formed by Right Rib. Finish in the steep upper dihedral or climb the clean face to the left.

9. Right Buttress   8 ★
Climb directly up the Right Rib, then finish with a right-facing dihedral or the face just to its left.

10. Southwest Face   8(?)
Old pitons suggest that the southwest face of the Right Rib has been climbed.

11. Indian Peaks Arête   7
Begin about halfway up the gully that runs along the bottom of the southwest face and follow a broken crest for two pitches. The final pitch ascends light-colored rock up the right edge of the Right Rib.

The author on What's My Line, Castaway Crag. Photo: Bonnie Von Greb

ASTAWAY CRAG

astaway Crag is a small buttress just below the northwest corner of the ower Great Face. To escape from the summit, downclimb a chimney on the outheast side (see *Old Way*).

1. Air Conditioning   7 ★

Begin with a left-facing corner on the northwest side, then jam a hand-crack that arcs up and left and finish on knobby rock.

2. Flying Wallenda   10c

FA: Kimball and Harrison, 1979.

Lieback up a right-facing, right-arching corner and finish with difficult twin cracks.

3. What's My Line   10b ★

FA: Kimball and Joseph, 1981.

Follow thin cracks up the right side of the west face, then finish with the duel cracks of the preceding route or work around to the right.

4. Old Way   0

This is a chimney on the southeast side used for descent.

OWER GREAT FACE

he Lower Great Face is the farthest south of the features normally climbed The Crags. It is located near the top and a short way north of the talus eld described in the approach to The Crags. The broad, west-facing wall is out 600 feet high and is divided by three large buttresses: one at either d of the wall and one in the middle. the Lower Great Face is separated om the Upper Great Face by a broad talus gully. To descend from the top of e wall, scramble east over the crest, then hike northwest down the broad lly between the two Great Faces.

5. DuMais Route   8

FA: Dick DuMais and party, c. 1978.

This route ascends the blunt northeast buttress. Scramble up to the highest ledges and set the belay. Climb the right side of the conspicuous slab that forms the lower buttress and belay near its top (8, 160 feet). Follow easier rock for several hundred feet to the top of the crag.

6. Beside the Seaside   8

FA: Harrison and Dennis Laird, 1979.

About 150 feet right of the *DuMais Route,* identify a right-facing flake/dihedral that leads to a ledge with a fallen tree.

1. Climb the corner and belay atop a large flake (7).

2. Continue up the flakes weaving past two roofs and a short dihedral (8).

3. Face climb to the top.

7. Northcutt-Kor 9 ★
FA: Ray Northcutt and Layton Kor, 1966.
Classic. Begin with a right-facing flake in the far right of the flake/dihe-drals toward the left side of the face. A smooth gray wall extends to the right of this system.
1. Climb a flake/crack and belay beneath the roof that is formed as the corner arches right.
2. Climb through the roof (9) and belay at a stance.
3. Continue up the right-facing corner, which gets easier higher up (8).

8. Crossword Puzzle 9
This route ascends a faint dihedral up the gray slab to the right of *Northcutt-Kor.*
1. Climb easy slabs and belay just right of a rectangular recess with some shrubs.
2. Climb straight up a dihedral to where it begins to fade. Traverse right past a fixed stopper into the next corner/crack system (9).
3. Work up and then left through a roof, then run-out the rope to the top of the climb.

9. Righthand Fault 7 A1
This old aid line ascends a large left-facing dihedral just left of the *Central Buttress.* Mossy and wet.

10. Central Buttress 7 or 10b ★
This route ascends the prominent buttress in the middle of the face. Previous guide books describe this route as ascending a "left-facing dihedral system" up the "front" of the buttress. The route and variation described below were climbed by R. Rossiter and Bonnie Von Grebe during 1994: the relationship to previous ascents is unknown.
Begin a short way up along the south side of the buttress beneath a clean right-facing flake with a tiny tree about eight feet up.
1. Climb the flake/dihedral past a steep spot and belay on a big ledge (7, 100 feet).
2a. Climb a large right-facing dihedral for about 100 feet, then veer left in a smaller dihedral and belay on a small ledge at the top of the buttress (6, 165 feet).
2b. Start up the big dihedral, but after about 15 feet, hand traverse left into a small right-facing dihedral. The small dihedral also may be reached by climbing straight up the prow of the buttress. Climb the dihedral, then work up and left over beautiful steep rock to a ledge (optional belay). Climb a left-facing dihedral to where it curves left and branches. Start up the left branch, then crank right into a very steep and clean left-facing dihedral (crux) that is followed to the ledge at the top of the buttress (10b, 160 feet).
Move the belay along a level section of the crest to the bottom of a steep wall.
3. Climb the wall to where the angle eases off (6, 160 feet).
4. Continue to the top of the wall and belay at a tree (4, 150 feet).
Scramble another 60 feet to the crest.

Twin Sisters Mountain

CASTAWAY CRAG AND LOWER GREAT FACE

From the West

1. Air Conditioning 7 ★
2. Flying Wallenda 10c
3. What's My Line 10b e
4. Old Way 0
5. DuMais Route 8
6. Beside the Seaside 8
7. Northcut-Kor 9 ★
8. Crossword Puzzle 9
9. Righthand Fault 7 A1
10. Central Buttress 7 or 10b ★
11. Face in the Crowd 6
12. Wild Onions 7

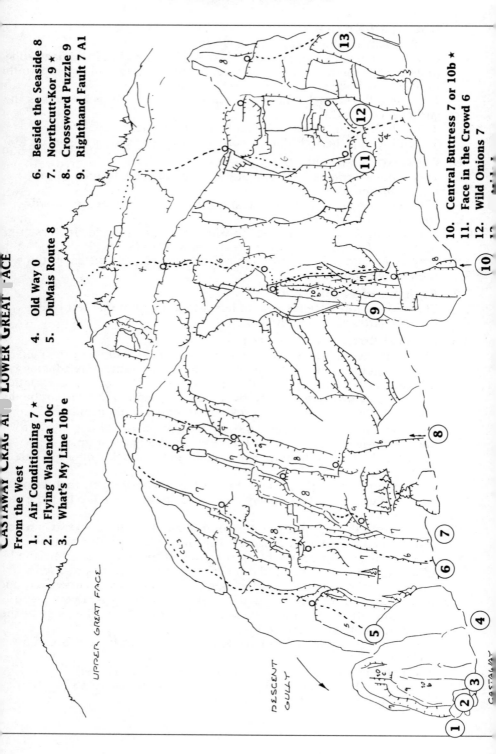

11. Face in the Crowd   6
FA: Kimball, 1980.
A series of right-facing flake/dihedrals lie right of the central buttress.
Right of these and nearer the southwest buttress is a large recessed
area capped by horizontal roofs. This route ascends slabs along the left
side of the recess but right of a large right-facing dihedral.

12. Wild Onions   7
FA: Kimball and Wroblewski, 1981.
This route climbs through the recess and takes on the roof band. Begin
right of a mossy gully/dihedral, the bottom of which is dotted with
green lichen. Climb to the highest of some tree-covered ledges and
belay. Climb up and right along flakes, follow a crack through the roof,
and belay just above (7). Continue more easily to the top of the face.

13. Outside Lane   8
FA: Kimball and Anne Tarver, 1979.
This route ascends the southwest buttress. Begin at the right side of the
buttress. Climb to the crest of the ridge and belay. Continue up to the
highest ledge and belay. Climb a thin crack through the middle of the
headwall (8).

Highlander Rock *is the next feature south from the Lower Great Face. It has
a single known route.*

14. Highlander   7
Begin at the far left side of the slab and follow a flake/crack to a roof
that is passed on the left.

ILY MOUNTAIN AND

AST PORTAL

he forested slopes of Lily Mountain rise to the west of Highway 7 about six iles south of Estes Park. On the south ridge of the mountain and visible om the highway, a picturesque group of crags rises above Lily Lake. A num- er of routes have been completed here, most of which are mediocre. owever, at least one feature, The Fin, offers some distinguished climbing.

HE FIN

he Fin is an isolated tower near the south end of The Lost Plateau, a flat rea surrounded by domes and buttresses near Lily Lake. To reach The Fin, ark at Lily Lake (across the highway from the Bald Pate Inn) and walk the orth shore to the west end of the lake. Leave the trail and hike north rough open forest. Find a footpath that leads up a gully between two large uttresses and follow it directly to The Fin and The Lost Plateau. To descend om the top of The Fin, scramble down the southeast corner.

1. **Northeast Face   9 TR**
   Begin to the left of a right-facing corner about 30 feet left of the pronounced north arête. Continue up the face to the top. Use long slings to
   rig a toprope from two bolts on top the crag.

2. **Edge of Time   9+ ★**
   This face climb ascends the left (northeast) side of the striking north
   arête of **The Fin**. Two bolts, two knifeblades, and two cruxes.

3. **West Face   12 ★**
   The vertical west face features a challenging route protected by seven
   bolts.

AST PORTAL

 has been said: "In Colorado, water doesn't run downhill, it runs toward oney." Highway 66 terminates at a small reservoir at the east end (portal) of e Alva B. Adams Tunnel, which transports water from Grand Lake on the est side of the Continental Divide to Lake Estes on the east side (case in oint). An isolated and unusual rock tower called Cottontail Crag resides on small plateau a short way south of the reservoir.

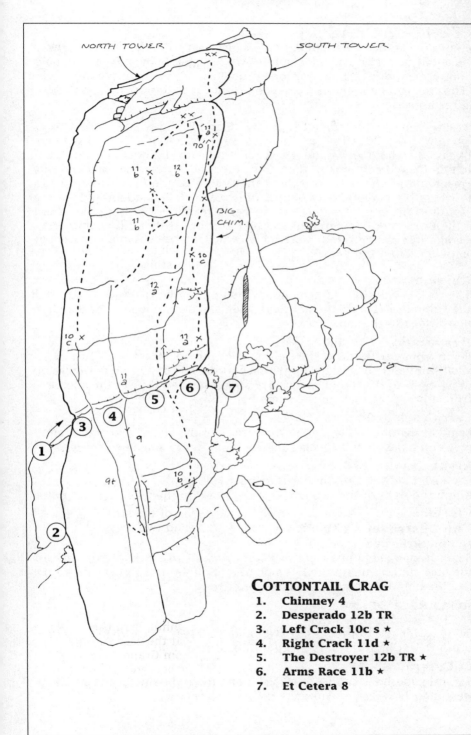

COTTONTAIL CRAG

1. **Chimney 4**
2. **Desperado 12b TR**
3. **Left Crack 10c s ★**
4. **Right Crack 11d ★**
5. **The Destroyer 12b TR ★**
6. **Arms Race 11b ★**
7. **Et Cetera 8**

COTTONTAIL CRAG

Cottontail Crag is located about 0.3 mile southwest from the end of Highway 66. It is about 80 feet high and is split down the middle by a deep chimney. The climbs, most of which are toprope problems, are very steep and on good rock. The crag can be seen on the skyline from the road but is not visible during the approach.

Approach. From the junction of Highway 36 and Highway 34, go west through downtown Estes Park on Highway 36. Turn left at a traffic light and continue on 36 (Moraine Avenue) to its junction with Highway 66 (Hwy. 262). Veer left on 66 and continue to the end of the road. Park at the east end of a small reservoir. From the south side of the lake, hike southwest about 0.25 mile to where the national park boundary is reached. Pick up a trail here that leads south to the crag. It also is easy to begin from the farthest west camp-site in the Estes Park Campground and hike southwest through open forest to the crag. This campground is privately owned, so be cool and don't gener-ate complaints from campers.

1. Chimney 4
The rock is split by a large chimney that offers the easiest way to reach the summit. Begin on the northeast side and scramble up into the chimney. Bridge to the top.

2. Desperado 12b TR
Begin from a pedestal at the right side of the northeast face. Turn a small roof and go straight up the face to the left of a groove. Higher up, move right to the top of the groove and easier terrain. Set the anchor from a bridge of rock on the summit.

3. Left Crack 10c s ★
Begin at the northwest side of the crag. Jam the left of two cracks and face climb past a bolt (hanger may be missing) to a shallow corner.

4. Right Crack 11d ★
FA: Mike Caldwell and Topher Donahue, 1987.
Climb the right of the two cracks, then work up the face past two bolts. Lower off.

5. The Destroyer 12b TR ★
FA: Bill Nicholson (?), 1990.
Begin from a ledge just right of *Right Crack*. Turn a roof (10b), work up the face, and battle up the left side of a blunt arête (12b near the top). Use the bolt anchor at the top of *Right Crack*.

6. Arms Race 11b ★
FA: Tim Hansen (TR), 1989
Begin as for the *Destroyer* but after about 30 feet, move right onto the south face. Climb the very steep wall past four bolts.

7. Et Cetera 8 - 11
Several good lines can be toproped along the right side of the south-west face; however, anchors are difficult to set up.

FERN CANYON

The name Fern Canyon does not appear on topographic maps of Rocky Mountain National Park; however, the name is in common use and represents about two miles of terrain between the west end of Moraine Park and the confluence of Fern Creek and Spruce Creek with the Big Thompson River. The Fern Lake Trail wanders up this forested canyon and reveals a fairly impressive line of cliffs to the north. The climbing history here is brief, likely because most of the routes pale in quality next to those at Lumpy Ridge or in the high peaks, and though the approach is casual, it is not along the way to any of the big peak climbs. Thus, relatively few climbers see these crags. The area is best known for an ice climb called *Jaws* and a buttress called Rock of Ages, but interesting routes have been completed on several other features. The formations are listed from left to right (west to east) along the north side of the canyon.

Fern Lake Trailhead. Take Highway 36 into Rocky Mountain National Park, and after about two miles, turn left on Bear Lake Road. Drive another two miles and turn right (west) on the road to Moraine Park Campground. After about a half mile, turn left onto another road and follow it to the Fern Lake Trailhead (at the west end of the road).

Fern Lake Trail. The first significant landmark along the trail is Arch Rocks, giant boulders that tower over the trail at about 1.3 miles. There also is a designated campsite just beyond the rocks on the north side of the trail. The Pool is at about 1.8 miles, where the Fern Lake Trail crosses the Big Thompson River and begins its climb southwest to Fern Lake. The trail continues beyond Fern Lake and climbs up Odessa Gorge to a high point beneath Notchtop Mountain, then descends eastward to Bear Lake.

THE LOST WORLD

The Lost World is a group of domes and buttresses on the mountainside north of The Pool. The Orange Arête, a spectacular out-leaning prow, is the highest feature of the group. At its left is The Colossus, a dome with its east side sheared away. A steep, narrow chute descends from the base of the Orange Arête and opens into a talus gully that separates two lower domes: Moot Point Apron is at left, and Gnome Dome is on the right.

Approach. To reach The Lost World, hike the Fern Lake Trail to The Pool. Turn north and scramble up steep talus through a narrow gap in a cliff band, then hike north to the west end of a marsh. From the northwest side of the marsh, scramble up the talus gully that leads between Moot Point Apron and Gnome Dome.

THE LOST WORLD From the South

MOOT POINT APRON

   Welcome to the Jungle 9
   Yosemite Slab 10a(?) ★
   Wandering Star 6

GNOME DOME

4.   **Night of the Unicorn 8 or 10a ★**
5.   **Goblins Slab 5**

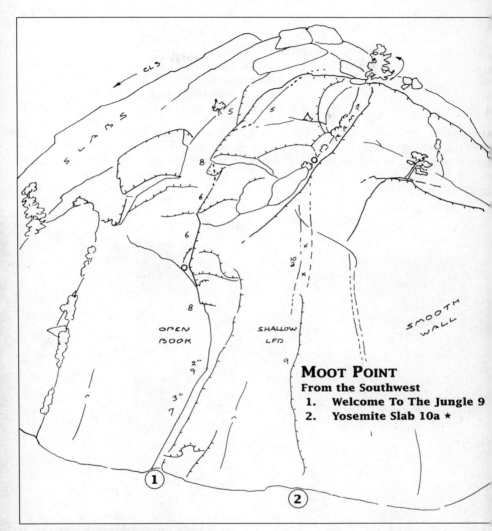

MOOT POINT
From the Southwest
1.   **Welcome To The Jungle 9**
2.   **Yosemite Slab 10a ★**

MOOT POINT APRON

Moot Point Apron is the rounded dome on the left side of the talus gully. It features two good routes on Yosemite-like granite. To return to the base from the top of the dome, walk a short way west, then friction-hike down easy slabs.

1. Welcome To The Jungle   9

FA: Richard Rossiter, Gene Ellis, and Bonnie Von Grebe, 1993. SR to a #4 Friend.

Identify a curving open book dihedral at the left side of the south face.
1. Climb the dihedral past some ferns and a steep constriction (crux), then continue up flakes and cracks to a tiny ledge (9, 130 feet).

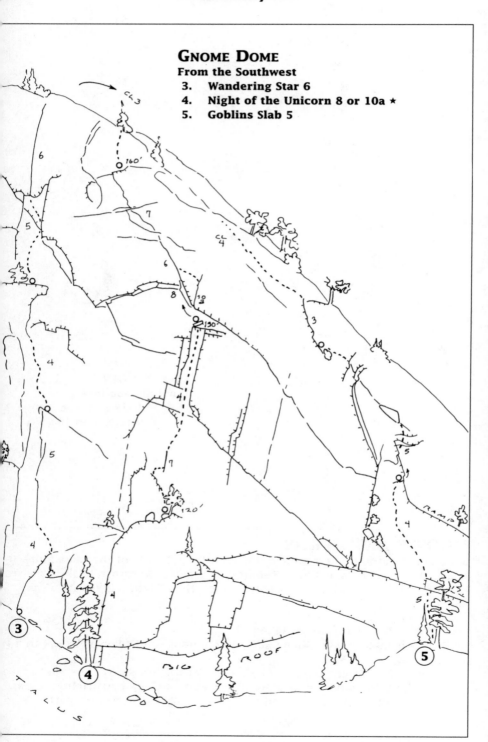

GNOME DOME
From the Southwest
3. **Wandering Star 6**
4. **Night of the Unicorn 8 or 10a ★**
5. **Goblins Slab 5**

2. Climb straight up a thin crack, undercling left around a roof, then work up and right and belay in a gully (8, 130 feet).

2. Yosemite Slab   10a(?) ★
FA: unknown; name is given as a convenience.
This attractive route ascends a shallow left-facing dihedral and slab a short way right of *Welcome To The Jungle.* The slab above the dihedral i protected by two quarter-inch bolts with Leeper hangers.

GNOME DOME

Gnome Dome is the large, rounded buttress across the talus gully to the eas of Moot Point Apron. It is reminiscent of The Pear at Lumpy Ridge and offers interesting climbing with fine views of the peaks above Odessa Gorge. To escape from the summit, scramble north along a ledge system for about 400 feet (cl3) to the base of the Orange Arête. Descend a steep, narrow gully pas a constriction (4) to the broad talus gully that leads back to the bottom of the west face. It also is possible to descend the wooded gully along the southeast side of the dome.

3. Wandering Star   6
FA: Gene Ellis and Hector Galbraith, 1994.
This route ascends the left side of the west face. Begin about 60 feet left of a big overhang. Two pitches wander up the face via discontinuous cracks that are easy but slightly difficult to protect. The third pitch gains a steep hand crack that is followed to the top of the dome. This last pitch is a beauty.

4. Night of the Unicorn   8 or 10a ★
FA: Gene Ellis, Richard Rossiter and Bonnie Von Grebe, 1993.
This route ascends the middle of the west face and passes through a broad A-shaped roof high on the wall.
Begin from a large Douglas fir tree at the left end of a big overhang.
1. Climb an easy crack and traverse right to belay on a ledge with a pir tree (4, 120 feet).
2. Work up and left for 40 feet, then crank right and climb a thin crack Above the crack follow easy rock to belay beneath the right side of a conspicuous A-shaped roof that is visible from the talus (7, 130 feet).
3a. Climb through the apex of the roof and follow a thin crack up a beautiful slab to a small ledge (8, 160 feet).
3b. Climb the difficult crack directly above the belay to the same fate (10a).
4. Climb an easy slab to the top of the dome (cl4, 60 feet).

5. Goblins Slab   5
FA: Hector Galbraith and Gene Ellis, 1994.
This route ascends the right side of the Gnome Dome, passing through a roof before reaching easy terrain. Begin behind a large pine several hundred feet right from *Night of the Unicorn.*
1. Wander up the slab to a belay stance just left of a right-facing dihedral.

2. Step around into the dihedral and turn a roof at its top (crux). Run out the rope and belay in a shallow corner with a bush.
3. Scramble up the slab to the top of the dome.

ROCK OF AGES

Rock of Ages sits high on the slope above the Arch Rocks campsite. It is a large formation with good potential for new routes. The small buttress at lower left, usually referred to as the Rock of Ages, is easily recognized by a smooth and steep south face covered with pale green lichen. However, the dauntless individuals who developed the original routes did not limit the name to this feature. Above this 200-foot buttress is a vertical cliff with a sheer, flat south face (and no routes). Immediately west of the buttress is a small, steep amphitheater of reddish rock that has two known routes. To the east is a very impressive buttress with the route *Every Pitch Tells A Story*. Down to the right is a sprawling apron with several large roofs and the route *Got to Get Out of This Place*.

1. Desolation Angels   11 s
FA: Alec Sharp and John Allen, 1981.
This route ascends the red dihedral and square roof toward the left side of the amphitheater. It is the farthest left route on the formation.
1. Ascend a ramp and traverse left to the bottom of the dihedral (6).
2. Climb the dihedral and roof at its top (crux).

2. Nameless Demons   10a ★
FA: Alec Sharp and Pete Brashaw, 1981.
Climb the large, left-facing dihedral at the right side of the amphitheater in two short pitches, each of which is 10a.

3. Days of Heaven   10d ★
FA: Alec Sharp, Dan Hare, and Pete Brashaw, 1981.
This steep crack climb ascends the left side of the main buttress and is perhaps the best route in Fern Canyon. It was originally begun with the first pitch of *Center Dihedral,* whereas a harrowing traverse left was made from the first belay. The dihedral above was climbed on a subsequent outing.
Begin from the top of a large, detached block at the bottom of the south face.
1. Work left from the top of the block, stand up on a horn, and gain a left-angling groove (10a) that is climbed up and left (9) to a ledge.
2. Face climb up to a tiny pine tree, hand traverse left along a flake, and make a difficult move into a hand crack on the left. Jam the crack for about 25 feet and belay at a stance along the left edge of the face (10).
3. Jam a spectacular tapering hand crack to the top of the face (10d).

4. Center Dihedral   10d
FA: Dan Hare and Alec Sharp, 1981. SR to a #4 Friend.
This route climbs the conspicuous right-facing dihedral that splits the upper wall.
Begin from the top of the big detached flake beneath an obtuse left-facing dihedral with an obvious jug at the bottom.

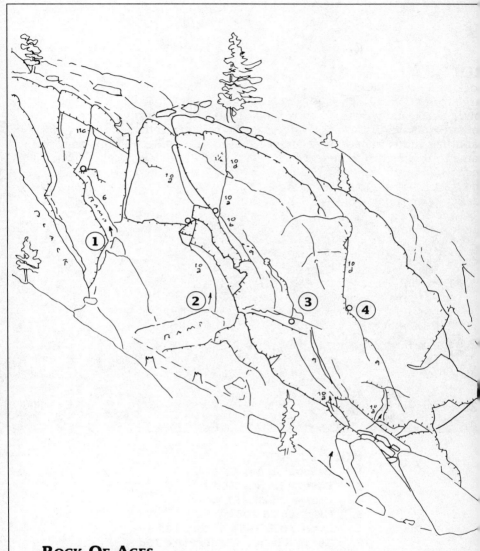

ROCK OF AGES
From the Southwest
1. **Desolation Angels 11 s**
2. **Nameless Demons 10a ★**
3. **Days of Heaven 10d ★**
4. **Center Dihedral 10d**

ROCK OF AGES

1. **Desolation Angels 11 s**
3. **Days of Heaven 10d ★**
4. **Center Dihedral 10d**
5. **Original Sin 10d**
6. **Every Pitch Tells A Story 10d s ★**
7. **Got to Get Out of This Place 10d**

1. Grab the jug, crank over the roof (10a), and climb to the top of the dihedral. Move right to a crack and climb to a belay stance at the base of the main dihedral (9).
2. Climb the strenuous dihedral to the top of the face (10d).

5. Original Sin   10d
FA: Alec Sharp and Randy Leavitt, 1981.
Climb the right-leaning, right-facing dihedral about 100 feet down to the right from the big blocks beneath *Days of Heaven*. Rappel 75 feet from a tree.

6. Every Pitch Tells A Story   10d s ★
FA: Alec Sharp and John Allen, 1981.
This route ascends the imposing buttress at the right side of the forma⁣tion.
1. Climb a ramp out into the center of the wall and belay at the bottom⁣ of a right-leaning, right-facing dihedral (10a).
2. Climb the dihedral, then move left to belay (10d).
3. Climb a right-leaning arch, then move left and work up a bulging wa⁣ with good holds and adequate pro (10b/c).

7. Got to Get Out of This Place   10d
FA: Alec Sharp, 1981.
To the right of the *Every Pitch* buttress is a sprawling apron distin-guished by several large overhangs. This route takes the upper left of the roofs. Climb in from the left and follow a crack out through the right side of the roof.

8. Red Rover   11a
FA: Scott Kimball and Hidetaka Suzuki, 1984.
This route is on a reddish cliff about a half mile west from the Fern Lake Trailhead. Look for a clean crack system just left of a deep gully.
1. Jam a fist crack over a bulge and belay at a stance (10a, 70 feet).
2. Make an awkward move right into the next crack system (crux). Beware of a loose flake. Follow the crack to the top.

ORANGE CRUSH WALL

bout 20 minutes west from the Fern Lake Trailhead, locate a dome-shaped
uttress with an orange lichen streak running down a disjunct left-facing
ihedral system. The wall is about 400 feet high and is the left of two promi-
ent buttresses separated by a vague gully/dihedral. Descend from the top
f the wall via a rocky gully to the west. The following route description is
ased on a topo sent to me in the mail that did not list the first-ascent party.

Orange Crush   9 or 10a

This route climbs the most obvious feature on the wall: the dihedral
with the orange lichen streak. From the Fern Lake Trail, hike up to the
base of the wall and begin below an ear-like flake some 90 feet off the
ground.
1. Climb a "hidden" chimney/crack to the "ear" (8+), then traverse up
and left to belay in the main dihedral.
2. Climb the left-facing dihedral past a small roof to a ledge with some
bushes and belay (8).
3. Climb a two-inch crack (9), then work up and right to belay beneath a
smooth wall.
4a. Work up and right and climb an easy crack (5) to the top of the wall.
4b. Work up and right from the belay, but before reaching the easy
crack, climb up and left along a thin crack with a dead tree and gain the
top of the wall (10a).

ERN CANYON ICE CLIMBS

1. Jaws   WI4 ★
This is a popular and spectacular frozen waterfall about one mile up
the Fern Lake Trail on the north side, just before Arch Rocks. It can be
done in one long lead. The left column is usually the easiest. Rappel 50
meters from a large tree.

2. Windy Gulch Cascades   WI2
Moderate ice will be found in a gulch above the trail on the north, about
a third of a mile from the trailhead.

FALL RIVER CANYON

Fall River Canyon runs west-northwest from Estes Park and could be likened to Boulder Canyon west of the city of Boulder. There are fewer crags here and perhaps none of greater quality than those in Boulder Canyon, but the setting is more grand, and Fall River crags, such as Deer Mountain Buttress and McGregor Slab, present greater vertical relief with routes up to six pitches long. In either case, the topography consists of steep forest slopes, sparse on the north and dense on the south, with a dispersion of granitic slabs and buttresses. The climbing is varied and interesting.

Highway 34 climbs the first seven miles of the valley, then escapes to the south at Horseshoe Park. The more rugged Fall River Road continues up the canyon to Fall River Pass on the Continental Divide. The crags are listed from from east to west along the south side of the canyon, then west to east along the north side.

DEER MOUNTAIN BUTTRESS
Deer Mountain Buttress sits high on the north slope of Deer Mountain (elev. 9,937 ft.), due south across Fall River Canyon from McGregor Slab. It is a cold place to climb on any but a warm summer day. The 600-foot, north-facing buttress is wider than it is tall and has two distinct faces divided by a narrow prow. At least one route is said to have been completed on the northeast face but most of the activity has been on the greater northwest face. The classic route for the crag is the *Nun Buttress,* which ascends the prow. At the base of the prow is a pinnacle called the Praying Nun. From the notch behind the Praying Nun, a long ledge called Stagway cuts across the northwest face about 150 feet above the talus.

Approach. There are three options for reaching the crag, all of which are fairly strenuous:

Approach A. This is the shortest route. From Estes Park, drive west on Highway 34 until about one mile from the Fall River Entrance to Rocky Mountain National Park (a short way past Fall River Estates) and turn left on Fish Hatchery Road. Drive past Harmony House, turn left, and park. Hike directly up the steep slope to the crag (1400 vertical feet).

Approach B. From Aspen Glen Campground inside Rocky Mountain National Park, follow a trail to the north until it bends westward, then bushwhack directly up to the buttress.

DEER MOUNTAIN BUTTRESS
From the Northwest

2. Forrest Solo 10b/c or 5.7 A3
3. Nun Buttress 8 ★
4. De-Range-O Direct 9
5. Pathfinder 9
6. Rectangle Wall 8
7. Center Left Face 10c ★

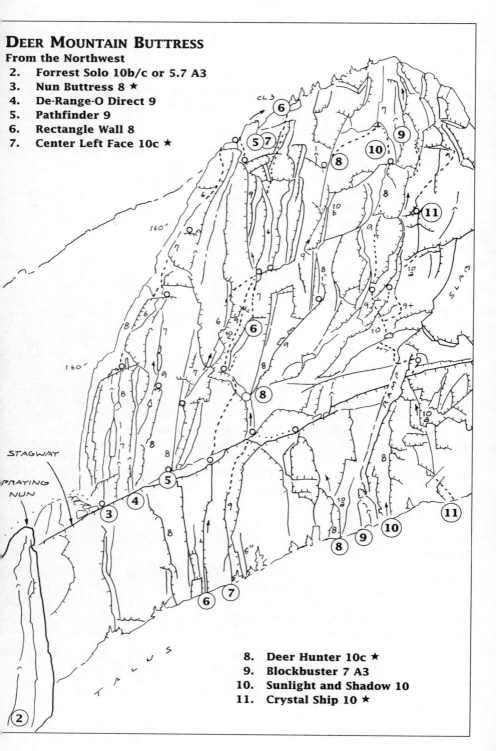

8. Deer Hunter 10c ★
9. Blockbuster 7 A3
10. Sunlight and Shadow 10
11. Crystal Ship 10 ★

Approach C. From Deer Ridge Junction (the western intersection of Highway 34 and Highway 36), hike the Deer Mountain Trail (summit trail) until roughly level with the low point of the crag (the farthest north switchback), then leave the trail and contour east to the bottom of the buttress.

Descent. From the top of the buttress, hike down a talus field on the west side.

Praying Nun. The following two routes ascend the spire at the base of the prow that splits the north face of the buttress. To escape from the summit, rappel north from a block.

1. **Praying Nun   3**
   FA: Tom Hornbein.
   Scramble up into the notch on the south side of the spire and climb easy rock on the east face.

2. **Forrest Solo   10b/c or 5.7 A3**
   FA: Bill Forrest, 1966.
   Angle in from the north and climb two 80-foot pitches up the overhanging west side of the spire.

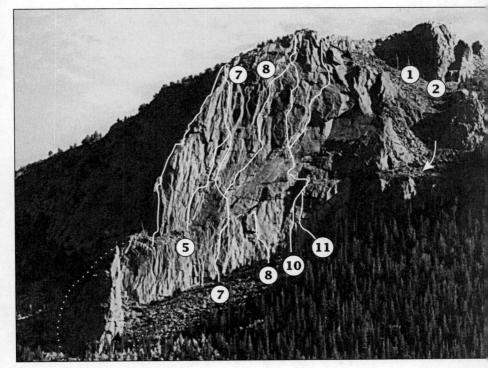

DEER MOUNTAIN BUTTRESS

1. **Praying Nun 3**
2. **Forrest Solo 10b/c**
5. **Pathfinder 9**
7. **Center Left Face 10c ★**

8. **Deer Hunter 10c ★**
10. **Sunlight and Shadow 10**
11. **Crystal Ship 10 ★**

Main Face. *The following routes ascend the central prow and the large north-west face to the right.*

3. Nun Buttress 8 ★

FA: Bob Culp and Roger Raubach, 1965.
This classic ascends the prow of the buttress that divides the crag into two faces. Begin in the notch behind the Praying Nun.
1. Climb an excellent hand crack in the right side of the flat prow and continue through a flared section (8) to a good belay ledge (160 feet).
2. Climb a hand crack in a left-facing dihedral (7) and continue up discontinuous cracks to belay from a horn (160 feet).
3. Work up and left to the crest (6) and continue on easier terrain to a belay.
4. An easy pitch leads to hiking terrain.

4. De-Range-O Direct 9

FA: Rick Austin and Steve Phipps, 1973.
This route follows the first good line right of the prow.
1. An initial pitch over poor rock can be climbed to *Stagway* (9) or traverse out right from the notch behind the Praying Nun.
2. Follow a good crack system about 30 feet right of the prow and belay at a stance (8).
3. Take the left of two dihedrals, turn a small roof, and continue up and left to join the *Nun Buttress* route (9).

5. Pathfinder 9

FA: Scott Kimball and Casey Swanson, 1978.
This line follows cracks and corners about 120 feet to the right of the prow but to the left of a slab with a thin, vegetated crack (see *Rectangle Wall,* Walter Fricke).
1. Climb an undesignated lower pitch or traverse onto Stagway from the notch.
2. Climb up and around a loose spike (8), then follow a good crack to a broken area.
3. Work up and right over a small roof (7) and continue to a belay at the bottom of a clean, right-facing dihedral.
4. Climb the dihedral – the last pitch of *Center Left Face* (9).

6. Rectangle Wall 8

FA: Layton Kor and Bob Culp, c. 1965.
This route takes a crack line to the right of *De-Range-O.* It is shown in Walter Fricke's guide going up the center of a slab to the right of *Pathfinder;* Kimball's guide has it to the left. Your best bet, once on Stagway, is to locate the wide crack and roof described under pitch two.
1. Climb a chimney to Stagway (6, 100 feet) or traverse in from the notch.
2. Jam a three-inch crack for about 25 feet, turn a roof (crux), and work up the face to belay in a shallow chimney.
3. Climb the chimney and scramble to the top.

7. Center Left Face 10c ★

FA: Bob Bradley and Rick Petrillo, 1967. FFA: Scott Kimball and Carl Harrison, 1979.

This is an interesting route up the middle of the northwest face.
Begin at the bottom of the face by a cairn, one flake system left of a
weathered, loose cleft.
1. Climb a right-facing white flake and continue in the same system to
Stagway (9).
2. Climb the right side of a broken buttress and belay.
3. Climb up and left toward a right-leaning, white and orange lichen-
covered slot. Undercling around a bend in the dihedral (10c), pass a
small roof with two fixed pins (9), and belay at left.
4. Step back right, climb a wide crack (8), work up and left, then climb
finger crack in a long, clean, right-facing dihedral (9).

8. Deer Hunter 10c ★
FA: Scott Kimball and Carl Harrison, 1979.
This demanding route ascends the center of the wall and shares a shor
pitch with *Center Left Face.* Begin near a cairn about 50 feet left of a
prominent ramp that angles up and right to Stagway.
1. Make tenuous moves over white rock to reach a thin crack (8+). Do a
difficult lieback (10), then hand traverse left and climb the right side o
a massive flake to Stagway.
2. Go left and climb the broken right-facing system as for *Center Left Fac*
3. Climb up and right along a steep ramp (8 s) and continue with a lon;
vegetated crack the diagonals up to the right (9). Belay at the base of a
clean, one-inch crack.
4. Climb the crack and angle left to a roof at the top of a dihedral. Han
traverse left and step around the left side of the roof (9), then follow a
orange-lichened, right-facing dihedral with a thin flake on the right to ;
good stance (10c).
5. Work up and slightly right over easier rock to the top (7).

9. Blockbuster 7 A3
FA: Gary Garbert and Bill Forrest, 1966.
This is an old aid route to the right of the center of the wall.
1. Reach *Stagway* via the obvious ramp that slants up to the right.
2. Climb straight up crossing *Crystal Ship* twice and belay at the base (
a slab.
3. Climb through the big roofs as for *Crystal Ship* but stay left and follow a dihedral system to easier rock near the top.

10. Sunlight and Shadow 10
FA: John Harlin, Rick Derrick, and Scott Kimball, 1980.
Begin at the right side of the wall about 30 feet right of the ramp that
slants up to Stagway.
1. Start up the face between rose-colored rock and dark lichen. Follow
crack and left-facing dihedral up past the left side of the overhangs an
belay on Stagway (8).
2. Climb up, then down across the top of the ramp, hand traverse left,
and gain an arching crack with a large bush. From the bush, angle up
and left across the slab (10b/c) to the bottom of three small dihedrals.
Angle up and left across the corners (9) to a shallow, zigzag, right-facing dihedral in the middle of a higher slab.

3. Follow the dihedral through an A-shaped roof, lieback up another corner and belay on a ledge at right (9).
4. Climb a crack up to a roof that is turned on the right and follow easier terrain to the top (7).

1. Crystal Ship   10 ★
FA: Tim Hansen and Scott Kimball, 1980.
This compelling route ascends the right side of the northwest face. Begin about 50 feet to the right of *Sunlight and Shadow* below a large roof.
1. Undercling left along a sharp flake, then work up and left to a tiny stance above a roof. Climb straight up through a left-facing flake, turn a two- foot roof (10b), and continue up to a belay on Stagway (150 feet).
2. Climb across the top of the ramp, hand traverse left, and gain an arching crack that leads to a large bush. From the bush, angle up and left across the slab (10b/c) and reach the right of three small dihedrals. Work up the corner and belay in a flake at left.
3. Follow the dihedral as it curves to the right and make some thin moves (10a) to reach the bottom of an impressive hand crack. Follow the crack to a belay stance.
4. Follow a system of left-facing dihedrals to the top (8).

1A. Overboard   9+
FA: Steve "The Crusher" Bartlett and Fran Bagenal, c. 1990.
Begin from the top of the difficult moves above the bush. Work right, then straight up the face via knobs to regain the main line at the second belay (9+).

AINBOW ROCK
ainbow Rock is the smaller buttress a short way west from Deer Mountain ttress.

1. Lonesome Tonight   8
FA: Scott Hall and Skip Daniel, 1987.
This route is said to begin 100 feet left of *Rainbow Bridge* at a large pine tree that grows from the base of the rock.
1. Make a few unprotected moves (6) to reach a crack system, then continue up to a friction mantle (8) and belay at a flake (150 feet).
2. Jam a hand crack (6).
3. The final pitch joins *Rainbow Bridge.*

2. Rainbow Bridge   5
FA: Chip Salaun and Doug Allcock, 1980.
Hendrix Lives!
Begin this pleasant route at the lower west corner of the buttress.
1. Climb a crack with small trees in a low-angle slab, continue up a fractured wall (crux), and belay on a shelf.
2. Work up the exposed ridge to easier terrain (4).

McGREGOR MOUNTAIN

McGregor Mountain (10,486 feet) is the massive exfoliation dome north across Fall River Canyon from Deer Mountain and west across the Black Canyon from Sundance Buttress. It is densely forested but for some small, black slabs on its eastern slope and a few steep buttresses on its southwest slope, the latter of which includes the popular McGregor Slab.

McGREGOR SLAB

McGregor Slab is the broad, beehive-shaped buttress on the southwest slope of McGregor Mountain about three-quarters of a mile northeast of the Fall River Entrance to Rocky Mountain National Park. The 700-foot slab of the south face is broken by numerous dihedrals that arch toward the center from either side. The right side of the south face is particularly complex making it somewhat difficult to identify individual routes, many of which have common pitches. Descriptions vary somewhat from one guide book to another. But if you get lost, never fear: all dihedrals lead to the top of the mountain! Due to the relatively low angle of the slab, the hardest route, *Lubrication*, weighs in at only 9 vs and most of the lines are rated 7 or 8. So what the hell, mix and match!

The routes *Up, Overhang, Lubrication,* and *Direct* were first climbed by Bob Bradley and Paul Mayrose between 1960 and 1962. *Left Standard, Right Standard, Climbing with the Camel Man,* and *Scramble* are also early vintage, but the first-ascent parties are not known. The routes *Miss Direct, Mr. Direct, Incorrect, Rag Head, Camel Jockey,* and *Double Hump* are from a topo submitted by Peter Hubbel.

Approach. Drive west on Highway 34 and park at the National Park Village. Hike up to the highest level of the National Park Resort. Find a distinct footpath that climbs the grassy slope to the north and passes just east of two water tanks. After about 100 yards, another trail branches left at a cairn. Follow this trail (indistinct at first) northwest up the steep hillside and, after about a 30 minute pump, arrive at the base of the wall in the vicinity of the route *Up*. Branch off to the right earlier to reach *Lubrication* and routes on the right side of the wall.

Descent. From the north side of the summit, make a short rappel to reach hiking terrain or walk off the east side to reach a gully.

1. **Left Standard 3**
   Locate a right-facing dihedral system a short way down and left from the sandy bench at the beginning of the route *Up*. The initial dihedral has a beautiful stunted pine about 25 feet off the ground. Where the second pitch veers right it is also possible to climb straight up. Five pitches in either case.

2. **Up 8 ★**
   Begin a short way up and right from *Left Standard,* at some sandy benches and locate a right-facing dihedral system with a small pine and a shrub near its bottom.

1. Climb to a ledge on the left (7).
2. Move left and climb another right-facing corner (8); move right and belay.
3. Climb up to a roof and hand traverse to its right end, then follow a right-facing dihedral until forced to belay.
4. Continue up the corner and belay a on ledge with trees (5).
5 and 6. Follow another corner system to the top of the dome.
It also is possible to follow the initial dihedral system up and right to join *Overhang* in the middle of its second pitch (8).

3. Overhang   7 ★

From the sandy benches at the beginning to *Up*, scramble up a ramp to the right and set the belay at some scrub trees beneath a conspicuous flake in a right-facing dihedral system.
1. Climb over the flake and belay in the dihedral (7).
2. Continue up the dihedral as it curves right and join *Lubrication* (7).

4. Lubrication   9 vs ★

This is the most famous (and feared) route on McGregor Slab. It has several variations. Begin some 200 feet down and right from *Overhang*. Scramble up a ramp on the right, then back left to a high ledge with a Douglas fir tree.
1. Climb a beautiful slab past two bolts to a flake/ledge with a tree (8).
2a. Step out left and climb straight up past a smooth bulge, then follow a water groove up and left to a ledge (9, no pro).
2b. Move straight left along a dike, then climb the wall to the left end of the water groove (7, no pro).
2c. Go straight right into a left-facing dihedral (*Direct*), climb up about 50 feet, then traverse back left along a ledge to rejoin the line (7).
3. Climb up through the overlap, then follow a flake system up and left and belay at its top (7).
4. Pass another roof band on its left or right (left being standard) and continue up the face to belay on a small ledge with a tiny tree (6).
5. Follow a groove up and right, then climb a shallow corner to belay on a horizontal dike (6).
6. Work up and right, pass an easy roof, and belay at a tree (5). Scramble to the top.

A. Lube Direct   (9 vs) ★

This is probably the best version of the route.
1. Climb a beautiful slab past two bolts to a flake/ledge with a tree (8).
2. Climb through the crux as described above and start up the water groove, then break right and climb along flakes to a ledge. Move right and belay beneath a beautiful left-facing dihedral with one or two fixed pins (9 vs).
3. Climb the dihedral for about 60 feet, then work up and left beneath an arch until it is possible to climb up to a narrow ledge. This may be the original third pitch of *Direct*.
4. Wander up the face for a full rope length as for *Direct* (6).
5. Follow a dihedral/groove up and left to a pie-shaped slab. Climb along the right side of the pie and turn the roof at its top (8), then work up and left to join the route *Up*.

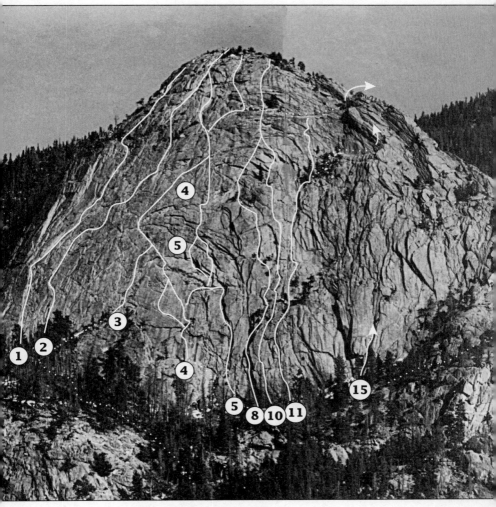

McGregor Slab
South Face

1. **Left Standard** 3
2. **Up** 8 ★
3. **Overhang** 7 ★
4. **Lubrication** 9 vs ★
5. **Direct** 7 ★
6. **Miss Direct** 7
8. **Indirect** 7 ★
10. **Climbing with the Camel Man** 8 ★
11. **Right Standard** 6 ★
15. **Scramble** 0

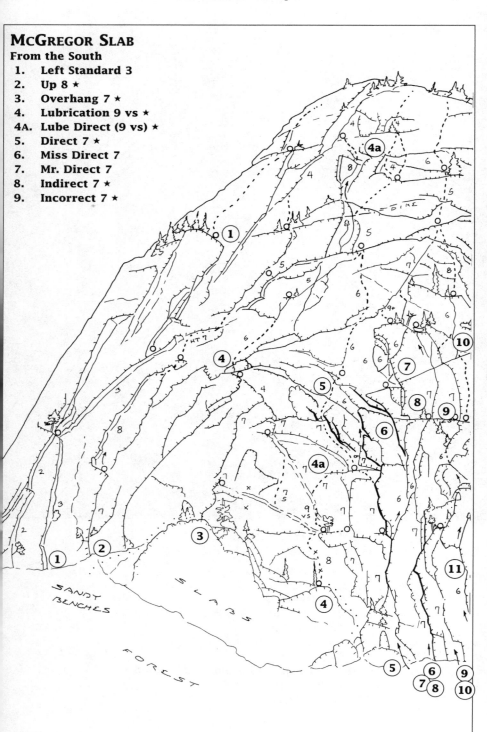

McGregor Slab

From the South

1. **Left Standard 3**
2. **Up 8 ★**
3. **Overhang 7 ★**
4. **Lubrication 9 vs ★**
4A. **Lube Direct (9 vs) ★**
5. **Direct 7 ★**
6. **Miss Direct 7**
7. **Mr. Direct 7**
8. **Indirect 7 ★**
9. **Incorrect 7 ★**

10. **Climbing with the Camel Man 8 ★**
11. **Right Standard 6 ★**
12. **Rag Head 8**
13. **Camel Jockey 7**
14. **Double Hump 8**
15. **Scramble 0**

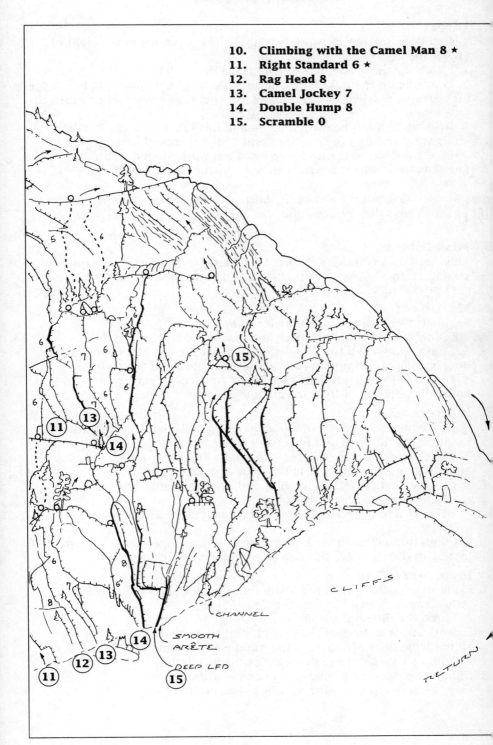

5. Direct   7 ★

Begin at the smaller of two left-facing corner systems to the right of
Lubrication.
1. Climb the dihedral system to a stance on the left (7).
2. Continue up the flake/dihedral to a big ledge (7). Note that this ledge
may also be reached by climbing the next corner system out to the left
(see topo).
3. Work up and left beneath a roof band until it is possible to climb
straight up through the overlaps and gain a marginal belay (7).
4. Face climb up to the next overlap, then work up and left to join
Lubrication. It also is possible to work up and right to join Indirect.

*he following three routes ascend the large, black-streaked dihedral to the
ght of Direct, but they diverge after the first belay.*

6. Miss Direct   7

This route is a variation of *Direct.* Begin as for *Indirect,* then climb the
second pitch of *Direct.* Thereafter, take the option on the right where
ever possible.

7. Mr. Direct   7

Begin 40 feet right of *Direct* (as for *Indirect*).
1. Climb the dihedral and belay at a small tree (7).
2. Climb straight up the dihedral system on the left and belay on the
long horizontal ledge that runs across the middle of the wall (6).
3. Follow flakes up and left, then break right in a clean corner and join
Indirect at the top of its third pitch (6).

8. Indirect   7 ★

Begin about 40 feet right of *Direct* in a large, black left-facing dihedral.
1. Climb the dihedral and belay at a small tree (7).
2. Work straight up over flakes and ramps and belay on the long horizontal ledge that runs across the middle of the wall (6).
3. Climb a shallow left-facing dihedral, then continue in a left-leaning
crack to a ledge with trees (7).
4. Work up and left, then follow a diagonal crack to a ledge beneath an
arch (7).
5. Climb through the arch and continue up to a ledge with a large tree (7).
Escape to the right or continue directly up slabs to the summit.

9. Incorrect   7 ★

Begin in a shallow crack and corner system about 25 feet right of
Indirect as for *Climbing with the Camel Man.*
1. Climb the dihedral and belay on a ledge with trees (7).
2. Work straight up over flakes and ramps and belay on the long horizontal ledge that runs across the middle of the wall (6).
3. Climb a conspicuous left-arching dihedral until it is possible to break
right at a groove and finish in the crack of the *Camel Man* (7). One also
may continue up and left and join *Indirect* at the belay.

4. Do the crux pitch of the *Camel Man* or climb a diagonal crack from the left end of the lower ledge as for *Indirect*. Belay on a small ledge beneath an arch in either case.

5. Climb through the arch and belay on a ledge with a big tree. Escape to the right or continue straight up slabs to the summit.

10. Climbing with the Camel Man 8 ★

Begin in a shallow left-facing flake system about 25 feet right of the large black corner of *Indirect*.

1. Follow the flake and crack system to a ledge with a small tree (7).

2. Work up and right along flakes and ramps and belay on a long ledge just right of a left-arching, left-facing dihedral (4).

3. Climb a long crack to the right of the arch and belay on a ledge with a large fir tree (6).

4. Climb through a series of arches and overlaps to a ledge beneath an arch (8).

5. Climb through the arch and belay on a ledge with a big tree. Escape to the right or continue straight up slabs to the summit.

11. Right Standard 6 ★

This popular route begins in a prominent left-facing dihedral system about 25 feet right of the *Camel Man.*

1. Climb the dihedral to where it forms a shallow roof to the left, then work up and right to a ledge with trees (6).

2. Move up and right along flakes and belay at a large block on a long horizontal ledge system (5).

3. Climb straight up into a left-facing dihedral and follow it to a big ledge with trees (6).

4. Climb the slabs and overlaps above or scramble off to the right.

12. Rag Head 8

Begin in the next dihedral to the right from *Right Standard* and join that route after one pitch.

13. Camel Jockey 7

1. Begin from a slab at the base of the wall and climb a series of small left-facing corners to a ledge with a large tree (7).

2. Work up and right over easy ground and belay at the right end of a long horizontal ledge system in the middle of the wall.

3. Climb a left-leaning dihedral and belay on a ledge with trees (6). Climb the slabs above or scramble off to the right.

14. Double Hump 8

Begin in a prominent left-facing dihedral just right of a curtain-like flake/roof with down-pointing spikes of rock. Proceed as shown in the topo.

15. Scramble 0

This is an old route that apparently begins in a large dihedral with a hanging block just left of a very clean and attractive arête. Climb the dihedral to a good ledge with a pine tree. Climb straight up either of two shallow corners to a ledge with a small tree. Two more pitches up easy corners lead to the walk-off ledge.

Mighty Dog   11d
FA: Mike Caldwell and Dan Ludlam, 1986.
Jam a thin hand-and-finger crack through a big roof above McGregor Mountain Lodge on Fall River Road. Mike Caldwell writes, "Changing management at the lodge has limited access, but it is worth getting shot for!"

CASTLE MOUNTAIN
Castle Mountain (8,834 feet) is the large hill to the south of Lumpy Ridge. Its summit is 1.6 miles southwest of Batman Rock. It is sparsely forested and features two notable crags, Castle Rock and Window Rock.

Approach. The easiest approach is to drive west on Highway 34 from its eastern junction with Highway 36. Continue past McGregor Avenue (Devil's Gulch Road) to a point about 150 yards east of the junction with the business route of Highway 34. Castle Rock (left) and Window Rock are clearly visible to the north. Walk through a break in a barbed wire fence and hike up a gully for about 300 yards. Look for a 100-foot ponderosa pine beside an enormous boulder from which it is an easy hike up the hillside to the base of Window Rock. To reach Castle Rock, continue to the west. One also may reach Castle Rock by hiking up a dirt road that begins across the highway from the Deer Crest Motel.

Castle Mountain Road is a sort of steep driveway on the north side of Highway 34, about two miles west of McGregor Avenue. The following two routes, as well as several others of unknown origin and difficulty, are located on the hillside above the end of Castle Mountain Road. FA: Mike and Tom Caldwell, 1990.

1. Midlife Crisis   11b ★
This and the following route are on the west-facing wall of a corridor a few hundred yards up and right from the turnaround at the top of Castle Mountain Road. This is the left of the two lines. Three bolts.

2. Orgasmatron   12d ★
This is the route on the right. Four bolts.

CASTLE ROCK
From Highway 34, Castle Rock (8,669 feet) appears to the left (west) of Window Rock and is the higher of the two. Approach as described above. All routes are on the west and south sides. To escape from the summit, hike the ridge to the north, then spiral around to the west.

1. Castle Left   9
Walk uphill beneath the west face to a point short of a reddish section capped by a roof. Climb two cracks, move right to a flake, and belay (8). Climb a finger crack in a dihedral (9).

2. Fortunate One   9
Hike up along the bottom of the west face to some large blocks and scramble up onto the highest one on the right.

1. Climb up to a roof and jam a hand crack through its right side (9).
2. Climb a black, knobby face to the left of a dihedral (7).

3. Prow   7+ ★
Begin from the bottom of the impressive prow that forms the right margin of the west face.
1. Climb a left-facing dihedral and continue to a ledge with a large leaning block (7). It also is possible to climb an attractive dihedral that begins at the low point of the west face.
2. Work straight up the face above the block (7).

Toprope   11c
Climb a vertical finger crack in a 30-foot boulder to the east of the northeast corner of the crag.

WINDOW ROCK
The long, narrow spine of Window Rock culminates in an airy summit overlooking the Great Divide and Lumpy Ridge. An unlikely hole through its midsection gives the rock its name.

Approach as for Castle Rock. To descend from the summit, rappel 70 feet from the northwest corner or scramble down the south ridge to a notch, then down ledges to the northwest. Routes are described counterclockwise beginning from high ground at the north end of the crag.

1. Seams to Me   7 A3
FA: Keith Lober and Aaron Walters, 1977.
Climb a crack system just right of the northwest arête. Pass a bolt, then traverse out to the left of the arête on aid and nail up a seam in the overhanging wall.

2. Mystery Achievement   10 A2
FA: Tim Hansen and Randy Joseph, 1983.
Begin with *Seams to Me* but continue straight up the crack system.

3. Chockstone Chimney   8
Begin about 30 feet right of the northwest arête at the bottom of a chimney. The upper part of the chimney is a perfect 12-inch slot.

The following three routes ascend the buttress between Chockstone Chimney and a distinct, curving alcove on the right.

4. Sunshine Daydream   10d ★
FA: Lawrence Stuemke and Mike Lorentti, 1992. Rack: mid-range stoppers plus QDs.
Follow a line of four bolts up the left side of the buttress. Crux is above the first bolt.

5. Sunshine Face   9 ★
FA: Stuemke and Lorentti, 1992. Rack: 4 QDs.
Step off from a boulder and follow a line of four bolts up the center of the buttress. The crux is getting to the first bolt. Lower off from a bolt anchor.

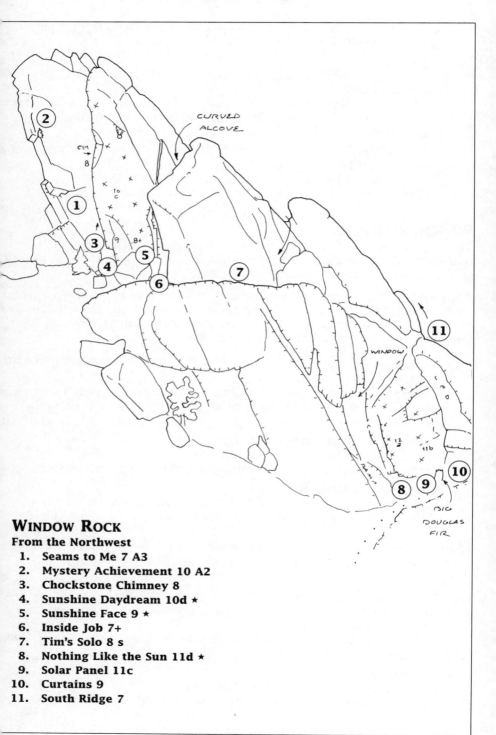

WINDOW ROCK
From the Northwest

1. **Seams to Me 7 A3**
2. **Mystery Achievement 10 A2**
3. **Chockstone Chimney 8**
4. **Sunshine Daydream 10d ★**
5. **Sunshine Face 9 ★**
6. **Inside Job 7+**
7. **Tim's Solo 8 s**
8. **Nothing Like the Sun 11d ★**
9. **Solar Panel 11c**
10. **Curtains 9**
11. **South Ridge 7**

6. Inside Job   7+

Begin toward the right side of the buttress just inside the opening of a curved alcove. Follow cracks to the top.

Note: Anchors for three projected routes have been set in the curving alcove and on the small buttress at its right.

7. Tim's Solo   8 s

Begin right of the alcove but left of the walk-off ledges at the base of a small face. Climb unprotected via knobs and rugosities.

The following three routes ascend the wall to the right of the "window."
Scramble in from the left. For no apparent good reason, someone has marked
the approach (all of 30 feet long) with orange spray paint.

8. Nothing Like the Sun   11d ★

FA: Stuemke and Lorentti, 1992.
Begin just right of the short gully that leads up into the window. Make difficult moves to get started and climb the arête past four bolts. The second clip-in is hairy.

9. Solar Panel   11c

FA: Stuemke and Lorentti, 1992.
Begin just left of a large Douglas fir tree and take a wandering line up the center of the face past four bolts.

10. Curtains   9

FA: Scott Kimball and Liz Lehmann, 1977.
Begin at a large Douglas fir tree and climb the left-facing dihedral that bounds the right side of the face.

11. South Ridge   7

Begin about 100 feet up and left from the low point of the rock. Follow cracks and short sections of face to the summit.

The following routes are located along the east face.

12. Over Anxiety   10a s

FA: Tim Hansen and Scott Kimball, 1983.
Begin a short way down and left from the window. Climb a wide crack to reach a small, arching corner. Climb the corner and an exposed face on the right.

13. Hill of Beans   10a

FA: Hansen and Kimball, 1983.
Climb the short, clean, wide crack to the left of the window.

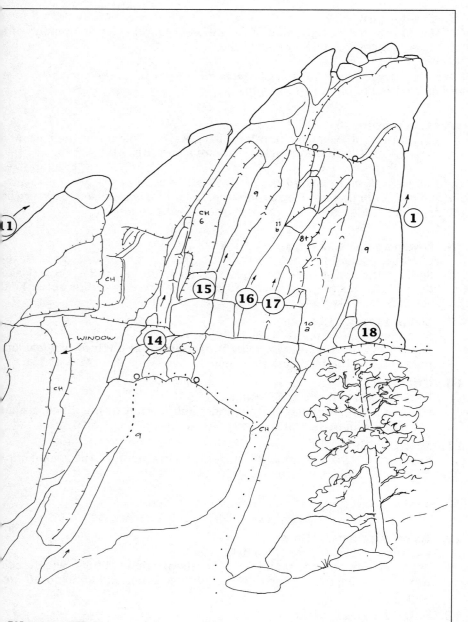

WINDOW ROCK
From the East
1. Seams To Me 7 A3
11. South Ridge 7
14. Old Way 6
15. Skylight 9
16. Window Pain 11b/c
17. Church Bells 10a ★
18. Northeast Ridge 9

The following routes lie to the right of the window and are reached via a larg ramp. It is possible to climb up from the bottom of the ramp or to traverse in to the routes from the right — a roped pitch in either case.

14. Old Way 6
Climb in from below the window or traverse in from the right. Climb a chimney with some old pitons. Two pitches.

15. Skylight 9
FA: Kimball and Hansen, 1983
This route ascends the right-leaning corner system to the right of *Old Way*. Traverse left to a stance at the top of the ramp (9), jam up a chimney and fist crack, then lieback up the dihedral (9).

16. Window Pain 11b/c
FA: Hansen and Kimball, 1983.
Look for a right-leaning crack and corner system that leads to the left side of a small roof.
1. Traverse in from the right and jam a short, vertical hand crack to the right side of a ledge (10a).
2. From the left side of the ledge, climb the right-leaning finger and hand crack through the left side of the roof (crux).

17. Church Bells 10a ★
FA: Kimball and Hladick, 1983
This route takes the crack just right of the second pitch of *Window Pair* Do the first pitch of *Window Pain* (10a), then climb the crack on the right (8+).

18. Northeast Ridge 9
Begin just left of the northeast corner of the crag.
1. Climb a shallow, left-facing dihedral and a thin, diagonal crack to a ledge (9).
2. Traverse left (easy) and climb the south ridge to the summit.

The author on Pear Buttress, The Right Book. Photo: Greg Carelli

LUMPY RIDGE

Lumpy Ridge is one of America's great rock climbing areas. The scenic and forested ridge spans about four miles on an east-west axis and is graced with numerous domes and buttresses of excellent granite. The tallest crag on the ridge, also the highest in elevation, is Sundance Buttress, the summit of which is about 10,000 feet above sea level. Most of its routes are seven or eight pitches long where the average route on Lumpy Ridge is two to four pitches. The longest approach (also Sundance Buttress) is about two miles; the shortest is about 50 yards (Little Twin Owls). The climbing is characterized by a great variety of cracks and chimneys, but very good bolt-protected face climbs have been done on some features. The Book area sees a lot of activity during the summer, but by almost any comparison, the ridge still is uncrowded and an air of tranquility and expansive natural beauty prevails.

The most strategic parking location is the Twin Owls parking area. This is reached by driving one mile north on Devils Gulch Road (McGregor Avenue) from downtown Estes Park. At the first, sharp rightward bend in the road, continue straight into McGregor Ranch and drive to the end of the road. If the parking lot is full, it also is possible to park at the Gem Lake Trailhead another half mile to the east along Devil's Gulch Road, however, this is less convenient.

A large sign at the west end of the parking area lists wildlife closures and other restrictions. Camping is not allowed at Lumpy Ridge. The use of piton and bolts is permitted; however, battery-operated drills are prohibited under a regulation designed to keep motorized equipment, such as chain saws, dirt bikes, and outboard motors, out of the backcountry. Toilets and drinking water are available except during winter.

TRAILS
Trails lead to all of the popular crags. Please help protect the ground cover and plant life by using these trails where they have been developed. There are three trailheads at the Twin Owls parking area.

Black Canyon Trail. This is the left (south) of two trails that proceed to the west from the Twin Owls parking area. Use this trail to reach all crags from The Book westward. Maintained approach trails branch right from this trail The Book, The Pear, and Sundance Buttress.

Batman Rock Trail. This is the right (north) of two trails that proceed westward from the Twin Owls parking area. A right branch after about 50 yards leads to the Little Twin Owls. The Lumpy Ridge Trail branches left a short way further. The main trail leads to Checkerboard Rock. To reach Batman Rock, a right branch must be taken after about a half mile.

Lumpy Ridge Overview

1. Sundance Buttress
2. Sundance Needle
3. The Parish
4. Thunder Buttress
5. Observatory Dome
6. The Citadel
7. Sunshine Buttress
8. The Pear
9. Lens Rock
10. The Bookend
11. The Book
A. Left Book
B. Bookmark
C. Bookmark Pinnacle
D. Binding
E. Right Book

LUMPY RIDGE OVERVIEW

12. **Batman Rock**
13. **Lightning Rock**
14. **Batman Pinnacle**
15. **Checkerboard Rock**
16. **Skyline Rocks**
 A. **Little Twin Owls**
 B. **Christmas Crag**
 C. **Fan Rock**
 D. **Rock Two**
 E. **Twin Owl Glacier**
 F. **Rock One**

17. **Twin Owls**
18. **Gollum's Arch Rock**
19. **Triangle Rock**
20. **Pacman Crag**
21. **Crescent Wall**
22. **Fin City**
23. **Out West Crag**

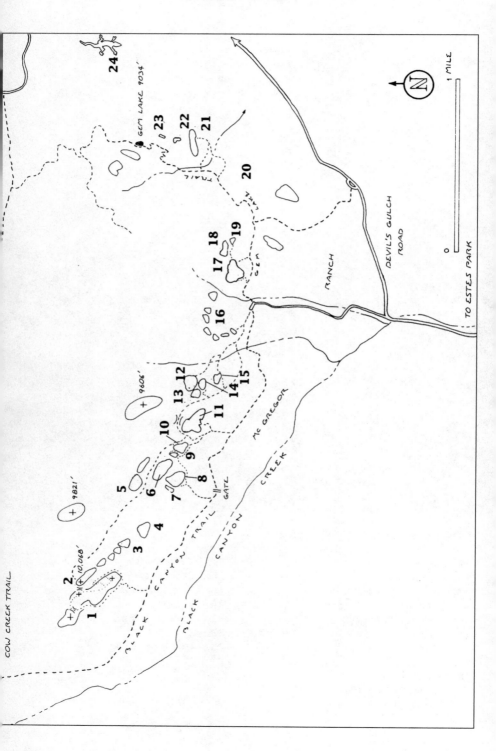

LUMPY RIDGE OVERVIEW

1. Sundance Buttress
2. Sundance Needle
3. The Parish
4. Thunder Buttress
5. Observatory Dome
6. The Citadel
7. Sunshine Buttress
8. The Pear
9. Lens Rock
10. The Bookend
11. The Book
    A. Left Book
    B. Bookmark
    C. Bookmark Pinnacle
    D. Binding
    E. Right Book
12. Batman Rock
13. Lightning Rock
14. Batman Pinnacle
15. Checkerboard Rock
16. Skyline Rocks
    A. Little Twin Owls
    B. Christmas Crag
    C. Fan Rock
    D. Rock Two
    E. Twin Owl Glacier
    F. Rock One
17. Twin Owls
18. Gollum's Arch Rock
19. Triangle Rock
20. Pacman Crag
21. Crescent Wall
22. Fin City
23. Out West Crag
24. Alligator Rock

Skyline Trail begins with the Batman Rock Trail but branches left after about 75 yards. It climbs up past the west side of Lightning Bolt Rock and gains the sandy saddle behind The Book, then descends into the forested gully between the Left Book and the Bookend. Here, one may hike down to the Bookmark Trail or continue westward on the Skyline Trail, which passes north of the Bookend and contours along the ridge, eventually leading to the summit of Sundance Needle. This is a very old trail, sometimes difficult to follow. Its builder is not known.

Gem Lake Trail. This trail proceeds from the east end of the Twin Owls parking area. It travels east and north to a tiny lake on the crest of Lumpy Ridge, then continues north to join the Cow Creek Trail about one mile west of its trailhead (4.5 miles). Use the Gem Lake Trail to reach the Twin Owls area, Crescent Wall, and Out West Crag.

SUNDANCE BUTTRESS

Sundance Buttress is the big rock at Lumpy Ridge. The main wall faces southwest toward the Diamond on Longs Peak, and by comparison, it is nearly as large a feature. It is also the highest of the popular crags on the ridge, which becomes apparent during the long uphill approach. Where commanding vistas are standard fare at Lumpy Ridge, the 800-foot south face of Sundance provides the ultimate in panoramic climbing. There are many excellent routes, most of which follow long, vertical crack systems in beautiful granite. Most of the routes are Grade III, but some of the harder routes on the Southeast Buttress are Grade IV.

Climbs are described from left to right across the West Slab, the broad South Face (which actually faces southwest), the Southeast Buttress, and the North Slab (which faces east). The West Saddle, a low point west of the true summit, separates Sundance Buttress from Sundance West, the most remote feature of the group, upon which no climbs are recorded. The Southeast Buttress culminates in a summit that is separated from the main ridge by a notch called the East Saddle. A convenient descent goes down a gully to the northeast from this saddle. To the north across a forested gully from the main buttress is The Needle, a large rock that, due to its lack of continuous features, is seldom climbed.

Approach. Hike the Black Canyon Trail for about two miles until directly beneath the Southeast Buttress of Sundance. Watch for a cairn and a path that branches off on the right. This path leads to the base of the crag in the vicinity of the route Mr. President and two large flakes that lean against the wall.

Descent. There are three ways to descend from the summit ridge of Sundance without rappelling:

Descent A. West Saddle (cl2). From the false summit, hike northwest over the true summit and down to the West Saddle (see above), then follow a long, easy gully down to the south to return to the bottom of the West Slab. About two-thirds of the way down, the gully is divided by a rib of rock – take the right (west) branch in the gully.

Sundance Buttress

3. **Cajun Capers 7** ★	21. **The Guillotine 10b** ★
7. **English Opening 9** ★	23. **Kor's Flake 7+** ★
9. **Eumenides 8** ★	31. **Turnkorner 10a** ★
16. **Mainliner 9** ★	38. **The Nose 10a** ★

Descent B. North Side (cl3). From an indistinct point east of the false sum mit and perhaps 150 feet up the ridge from the top of *Mainliner,* enter a dirt gully that drops down to the northeast. Follow a series of left-facing dihe- drals (looking down) and sloping ledges that lead down and left (north) for several hundred feet, then traverse left across a slab for about 150 feet and downclimb a short step into the forested gully between Sundance Buttress and The Needle. If the correct line is found, the descent is not difficult. If you get screwed up, rappel from trees into the forested gully. Once in the gully, follow a faint path down to the bottom of the Southeast Buttress and the base of the crag.

Descent C. East Saddle (4). From the East Saddle, downclimb or rappel the steep gully that descends to the northeast, then hike down the broad, forest ed gully below the North Slab to arrive at the base of the crag.

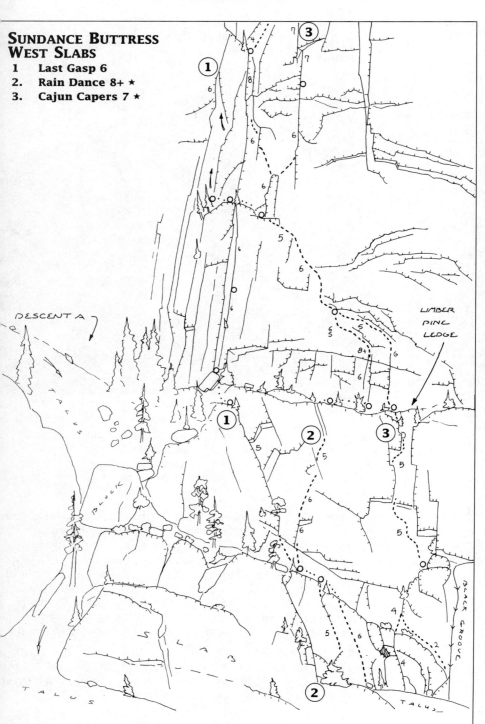

SUNDANCE BUTTRESS WEST SLABS

1   Last Gasp 6
2.   Rain Dance 8+ ★
3.   Cajun Capers 7 ★

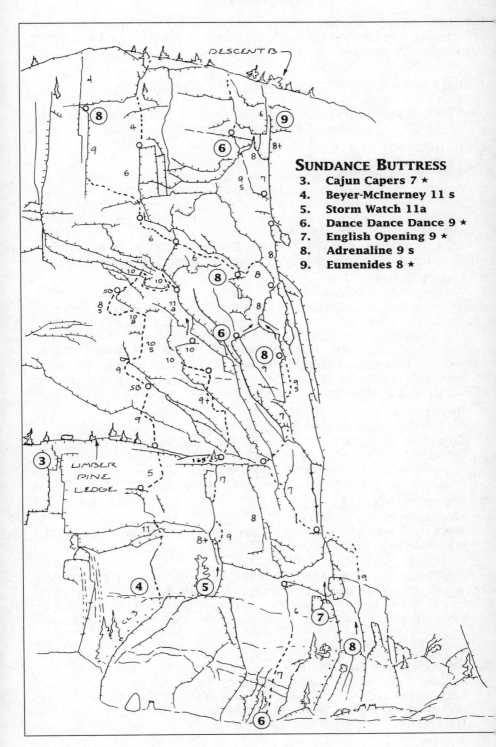

SUNDANCE BUTTRESS

3. **Cajun Capers** 7 ★
4. **Beyer-McInerney** 11 s
5. **Storm Watch** 11a
6. **Dance Dance Dance** 9 ★
7. **English Opening** 9 ★
8. **Adrenaline** 9 s
9. **Eumenides** 8 ★

Lumpy Ridge

West Slab. The following five routes ascend the broad West Slab, the farthest west continuous feature on the southwest face of Sundance. Use Descent A to return to the beginning of the routes.

1 Last Gasp 6
FA: Chip Salaun.
This line begins just right of *Rain Dance,* then works up and left to the long right-facing dihedral at the west margin of the wall.

2. Rain Dance 8+ ★
FA: Richard and Joyce Rossiter, tandem solo, 1984.
This route is of the same quality as *Cajun Capers* and, in fact, shares its fourth pitch. Begin at the farthest west ground at the bottom of a large right-facing dihedral. Move up and right onto a clean slab and climb to a ledge. A long pitch up another beautiful slab brings one to Limber Pine Ledge. Move the belay to the right and continue as shown in the topo. The crux is just above Limber Pine Ledge. Finish in the steep dihedrals up and left from the flake/pillar on *Cajun Capers* (8).

3. Cajun Capers 7 ★
FA: Chip Salaun and Aaron Walters, 1979.
This is a long friction climb on excellent rock that angles up and left across the expansive West Slab. Note that there are two finishes: the right, known as *Coonass Direct* (7), is the best option. To find the beginning of the route, hike west along the base of the wall about 500 feet past the Eumenides Dihedral area and locate a large, black-streaked groove. It is actually not possible to hike much beyond this point without dropping down around a slabby buttress.

4. Beyer-McInerney 11 s
FA: Pat McInerney and Jim Beyer, 1990.
This route takes the right side of the West Slab beginning just right from the black-streaked groove of *Cajun Capers.* Scramble up and right in a smaller groove and begin from the left side of a ledge with two trees. The crux is the roof on the first pitch. See topo.

5. Storm Watch 11a
FA: Jim Beyer, solo, 1990.
Begin from the right side of the ledge with two trees mentioned in the preceding route. See topo.

r routes beginning here and east through the Mainliner area, the most expe-
ient escape from the ridge crest is probably Descent B. Note that the top of
escent B is nearly straight across the crest to the northeast from the top of
e route Eumenides, just east of the false summit. Descent A also is reason-
le.

6. Dance Dance Dance 9 ★
FA: Michael Covington and Billy Westbay, 1973.
This interesting route takes the left side of the Eumenides Slab but is drawn right into the dihedral of *English Opening* high on the face. Begin 100 feet or so to the left of *English Opening* at a slab with a broad band

of light-colored rock. Friction up the slab just right of some shallow corners and head for a large left-facing dihedral and the east end of Limber Pine Ledge.

7. English Opening 9 ★
FA: George Hurley and Dave Carlson, 1971.
This is one of the better moderate routes on Sundance Buttress. The line follows a continuous left-facing dihedral system to the top of the crag. There is more than one crux section. *Eumenides* offers the more aesthetic finish. Begin about 200 feet left of the Eumenides Dihedral. Scramble up a grungy left-facing corner and belay on a large flake beneath a black roof.

8. Adrenaline 9 s
FA: John Marrs and Chris Anne Crysdale, 1983.
This route obviously has some good climbing but it is not well-known. The line wanders about the Eumenides Slab intersecting *English Opening* and *Dance Dance Dance,* then breaks left on a long traverse and heads for the top.
Begin in the first left-facing dihedral right of *English Opening.* The last two pitches, which do not show in the topo, continue left between two roofs until, on the seventh pitch, a clean, left-facing dihedral is reached The pitch continues up the corner and up a sharp left-facing flake (9) to finish with slightly run-out face climbing.

Eumenides Dihedral. The following routes begin in the Eumenides Dihedral, the massive, left-facing corner system that forms the right margin of the West Slab.

9. Eumenides 8 ★
FA: George Hurley and Walter Fricke, 1970.
This is a fairly popular route, steep and sustained with lots of climbing in the 7 and 8 range. Begin in the actual corner of the huge dihedral and work up to some overlaps where the route moves out onto the broad slab on the left. The crux is probably the beginning of the third pitch unless the right version of the roof on the fifth pitch is taken.

10. Slim Pickin's 10a ★
FA: Chip Salaun and Scott Kimball, 1978.
This route takes the crack system just right of *Eumenides* in the right wall of the dihedral. Begin with a left-facing dihedral that turns into a chimney. The route is continuously interesting and on good rock. The third pitch (crux) is exceptionally good.

11. Progression 10 ★
FA: Doug Snively and Cito Kilpatrick, 1980.
This route takes the middle system in the right wall of the dihedral. Begin in the farthest right system but veer left from the *Hurley-Neri* in finger-and-hand crack. The crux is a thin, white dihedral on the second pitch but there is another difficult dihedral on the fourth pitch; an easi er alternative takes cracks to the right (8).

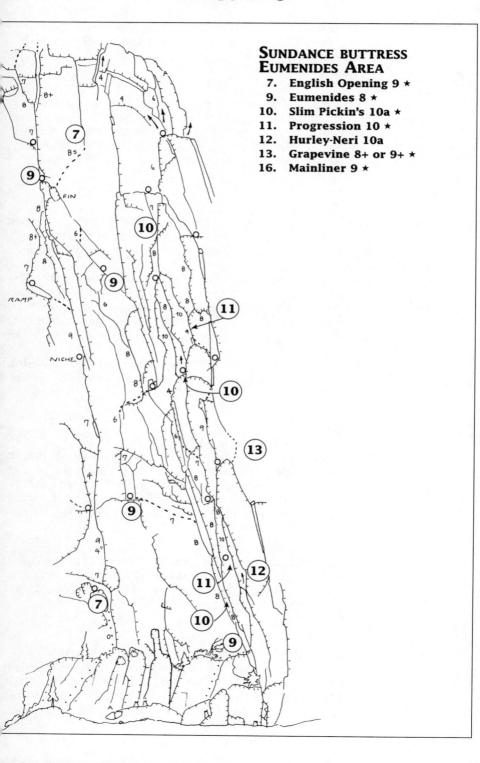

SUNDANCE BUTTRESS
EUMENIDES AREA
7. English Opening 9 ★
9. Eumenides 8 ★
10. Slim Pickin's 10a ★
11. Progression 10 ★
12. Hurley-Neri 10a
13. Grapevine 8+ or 9+ ★
16. Mainliner 9 ★

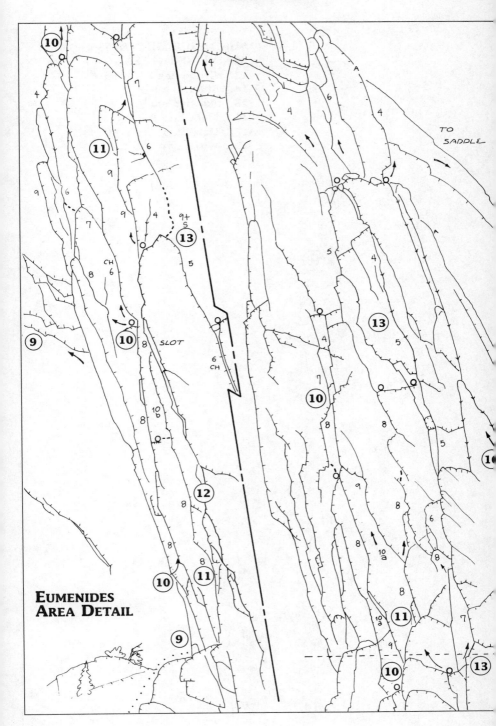

EUMENIDES
AREA DETAIL

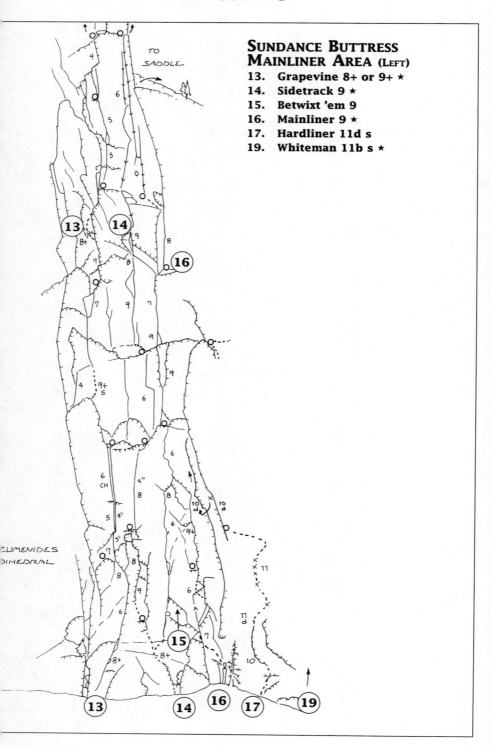

SUNDANCE BUTTRESS MAINLINER AREA (LEFT)
13. **Grapevine 8+ or 9+** ★
14. **Sidetrack 9** ★
15. **Betwixt 'em 9**
16. **Mainliner 9** ★
17. **Hardliner 11d s**
19. **Whiteman 11b s** ★

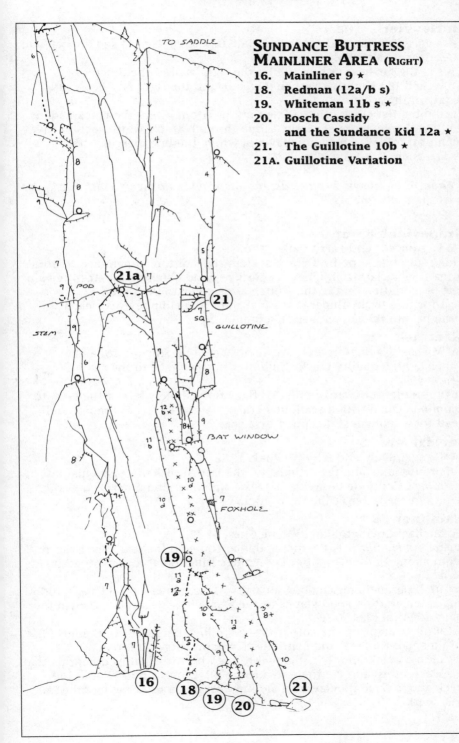

12. Hurley-Neri   10a
FA: George Hurley and Mike Neri, date unknown. FFA: Mike Caldwell and
Mick Scarpella, 1988.
This is the farthest right route on the right wall of the dihedral.
1. Ascend the slightly overhanging crack on the right and belay at a
ledge on the arête.
2. Climb a fist crack (9) to a fixed nut (a Titon) where the crack widens
and overhangs more severely. Climb through an off-width section (five-
inch pro) followed by a bombay slot where the line merges with
Progression.

South Face. *The following routes ascend the broad and steep South Face, also
known as the Guillotine Wall.*

13. Grapevine   8+ or 9+ ★
FA: Layton Kor and Larry Dalke, 1965.
This route takes the first crack system right of the Eumenides Dihedral.
It features a classic chimney and lots of good climbing on steep terrain.
The 9+ variation on the third pitch adds spice to the route.
Begin with a tricky finger crack just right of a chimney that leads
straight into the Eumenides Dihedral.

14. Sidetrack   9 ★
FA: Michael Covington, Billy Westbay, and Doug Snively, 1975.
This is a high-quality crack climb up the steep face to the right of
Grapevine.
Begin just left of a small pillar or flake immediately left of the start to
Mainliner. Open with a scalloped crack that angles up to the left and
head for a reddish slot capped by a roof.

15. Betwixt 'em   9
FA: Doug Snively and Billy Westbay, 1982.
This route jams and face climbs up the latticework of cracks just left of
Mainliner. Continue between (betwixt) *Mainliner* and *Sidetrack*, eventual-
ly to join the latter at the third pitch.

16. Mainliner   9 ★
FA: Michael Covington and Wayne Goss, 1972.
Queue up! *Mainliner* is the most popular route on the crag. Use Descent B.
Begin about 100 feet right of Eumenides Dihedral at a very broad inside
corner.
1. Climb parallel cracks along a narrow flake, move a bit left, and follow
varied terrain to a good stance above a small left-leaning corner in the
main dihedral (8, 150 feet).
2. Climb straight up the corner (9+) or follow cracks out to the left (6),
turn a small roof (8), and continue to a good ledge (160 feet).
3. Climb a crack up into a channel formed by two shallow dihedrals that
face each other and continue to a ledge (9). Climb a pod (9) and the
crack above (7) and belay on a sloping ledge in a right-facing dihedral
(160 feet).

4. Climb the dihedral for about 60 feet, then crank left to a large shelf (optional belay) and continue up easy terrain to a ledge beneath a flared slot (8, 150 feet)

5. Climb straight up the slot and belay on a big ledge (6, 150 feet). One also may exit right after about 100 feet and scramble to the East Saddle and Descent C.

6. Step right and climb an easy right-facing dihedral to the ridge crest or go left and climb easy slabs to the same fate (cl4, 100 feet).

17. Hardliner 11d s
FA: Jim Beyer and Pat McInerney, 1990.
Begin about 25 feet right of *Mainliner* as for *Redman*. Climb up to the left and smaller of two left-facing, left-leaning flakes and head for some bolts. Five bolts plus some fixed wires.

Descent C is recommended for the following routes unless otherwise noted.

18. Redman 12a/b s
FA: Malcolm Daly, Randy Joseph, and Bill Feiges, 1983.
Begin about 20 feet left of *Whiteman*. Face climb past a fixed stopper, then undercling and lieback along a left-facing flake (crux). From the top of the flake, climb straight up past a bolt and continue to the belay on *Whiteman*.

19. Whiteman 11b s ★
FA: unknown. FFA: John Long and Lynn Hill, 1980.
Classic. This continuously difficult, two-pitch climb begins with a series of overlapping flakes about 60 feet right from the broad inside corner of *Mainliner*. The second pitch tackles a long right-left flip-flop dihedral with the crux near the top. Continue with the alternate finish to *The Guillotine*. The bolts on this climb, like many at Lumpy Ridge, are old, rusty quarter-inchers that should be replaced with modern gear designed for rock climbing.

20. Bosch Cassidy and the Sundance Kid 12b ★
FA: Topher Donahue, Mike Donahue, and others, 1988.
This was reported to be an excellent, three-pitch face climb up the narrow buttress between *The Guillotine* and *Whiteman*. The fixed protection on the route was completely destroyed by some bozo who apparently believed that everyone must do first ascents according to his specifications. The route is listed with the hope that it might be replaced. See topo.

21. The Guillotine 10b ★
FA: Jim Disney and Dean Moore, 1962. FFA: John Bryant, 1964.
This classic route has a little bit of everything and should not be missed. High on the wall is a large, rectangular inset with some sharp, overhanging blades of rock at its top – The Guillotine. Begin about 100 feet to the right from *Mainliner* at a clean, flared finger crack that usually has water seeping from its bottom. This crack is the crux of the route; the remainder is a piece of cake by comparison.

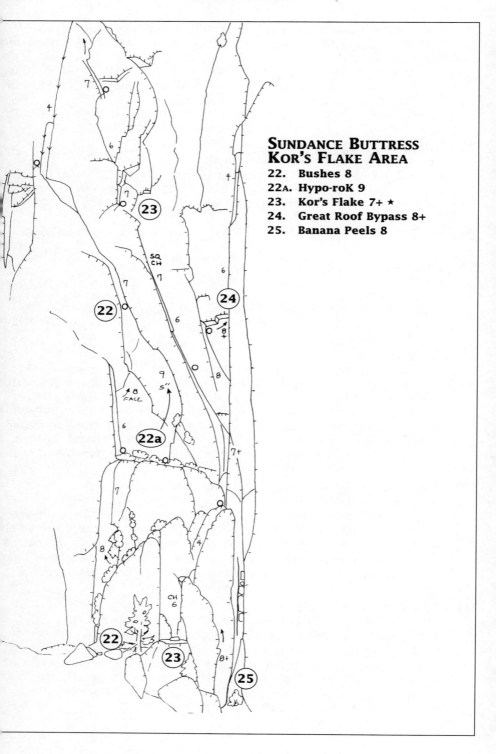

SUNDANCE BUTTRESS
KOR'S FLAKE AREA
22. **Bushes 8**
22A. **Hypo-roK 9**
23. **Kor's Flake 7+** ★
24. **Great Roof Bypass 8+**
25. **Banana Peels 8**

21A. Guillotine Variation

Climb out the back of the Bay Window on the left via an 8+ squeeze, then work up and left to the top of a pillar and back right (7) into a hand crack (see topo).

22. Bushes 8

This seldom climbed route begins about 12 feet right from *The Guillotine* and joins that route after three pitches.

22A. Hypo-roK 9

FA: Chip Salaun and Aaron Walters, 1977.

This route ascends the underside of the *Kor's Flake* feature, lending the name. Climb the first pitch of *Bushes,* then move right on a ledge to the base of a crack that leads into the main event. Be prepared for a five-inch crack.

23. Kor's Flake 7+ ★

FA: Layton Kor and partner, 1950s. SR to a #4 Friend.

This area classic is the earliest known route completed on Sundance Buttress. It ascends the long diagonal flake to the left of *Banana Peels.* From the top of the approach trail, turn left and hike around to the left side of a large pedestal, then cut back right to its top. Begin with a narrow chimney capped by a chockstone.

1. Climb the chimney and exit right under the chockstone, then go straight up for another 50 feet and belay in an area of ledges (6, 120 feet).
2. Go straight up easy terrain and follow a left-leaning dihedral (7+) to the ramp formed by a long, diagonal flake. Work up the ramp and belay at some small flakes (7+, 155 feet).
3. Climb the ramp/dihedral past a wide section and belay on a slab at its top (7, 155 feet). A 30-foot squeeze chimney can be gracefully avoided by stemming the dihedral (8).
4. Traverse up and left across the slab and climb a short right-facing dihedral to a roof. Crank left around the roof, do a tricky traverse left, and follow a crack to a good ledge (7+, 120 feet).
5. Climb a left-facing dihedral, turn a roof on the left, and follow flared cracks to a ledge with some loose rocks (6, 145 feet).
6. Scramble up a big slot and belay from a tree (cl4, 100 feet). Traverse right to the East Saddle and use Descent C.

24. Great Roof Bypass 8+

FA: Bob Culp and T. Haig, early 1960s. FFA: Jim Erickson and Luke Studer, 1973.

Begin as for *Kor's Flake* but continue up a steep dihedral to a roof that is passed on the right.

25. Banana Peels 8

FFA: Mike Neri and Jim Heiden, 1976.

Climb the deep chimney between *Bonzo* and *Kor's Flake* that marks the west margin of The Southeast Buttress.

The Southeast Buttress towers above the entrance to the Black Canyon like a guardian of the high peaks. It is distinguished by several ancient aid lines and two great classic routes: Turnkorner and The Nose. The approach trail tops out near the bottom left side of the buttress. Note the two massive flakes that lean against the wall between Mr. President and The Nose. The left and smaller is dubbed the Lesser Flake; the right is the Greater Flake.

26. Chain of Command   11a ★

FA: (via *Bonzo*) Randy Ferris and Mike Caldwell, 1987; of first pitch, Mike Caldwell and Janet Neath, 1991. SR (sparse) with six QDs.
This route ascends the wall to the right of the *Banana Peels* chimney via three pitches of bolt-protected face climbing.
1. Climb the face immediately left of the *Bonzo* dihedral (four bolts, 10a).
2. From the top of the dihedral, follow bolts up the left side of the wall and crank right to a bolt belay at a ledge (10c).
3. A short pitch goes up to another ledge (11a). Rappel or continue with *Mr. President*.

27. Bonzo   10a ★

FA: Scott Kimball and Al Rubin, 1983.
From the bottom of the *Banana Peels* chimney, make steep face moves up and right and climb a steep, right-facing dihedral to a bolt anchor. It also is possible to climb in from higher up in the chimney (9+).

28. Mr. President   10d ★

FA: Layton Kor and Steve Komito, early 1960s. FFA: Jeff Lowe and Ron Matous, 1979.
This intense route follows the flared chimney and bulging crack/corner between the chimney of *Banana Peels* and the left of the two big flakes that lean against the wall. The crux bulge on the second pitch is deceptive and slightly hard to protect. Top out at the East Saddle.
An aid line appears to go up through the roof to the left of the Lesser Flake. Look for a bolt under the roof and another higher up above a ledge.

29. Laura Scudders   11b s ★

FA: Jeff Lowe and Charlie Fowler, 1979.
Begin at the left side of the Lesser Flake.
1. Climb the first pitch of *Turnkorner Direct* (9+).
2. Angle up and left along a groove and some flakes and belay on a small ledge as for *Mr. President* (9).

SOUTHEAST BUTTRESS OF SUNDANCE BUTTRESS

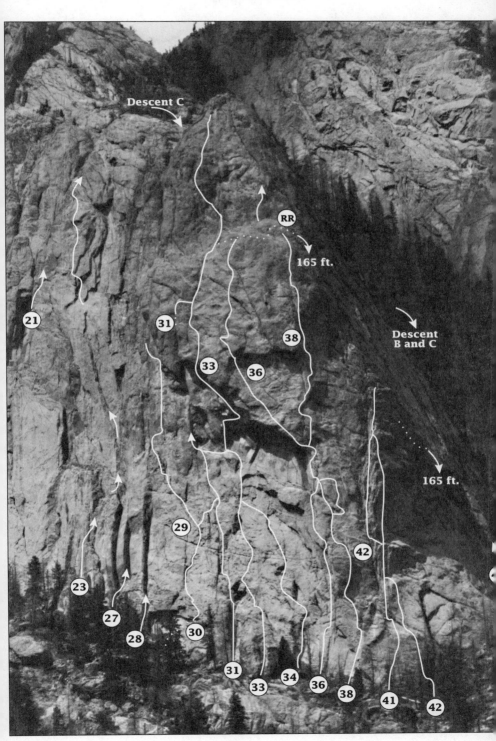

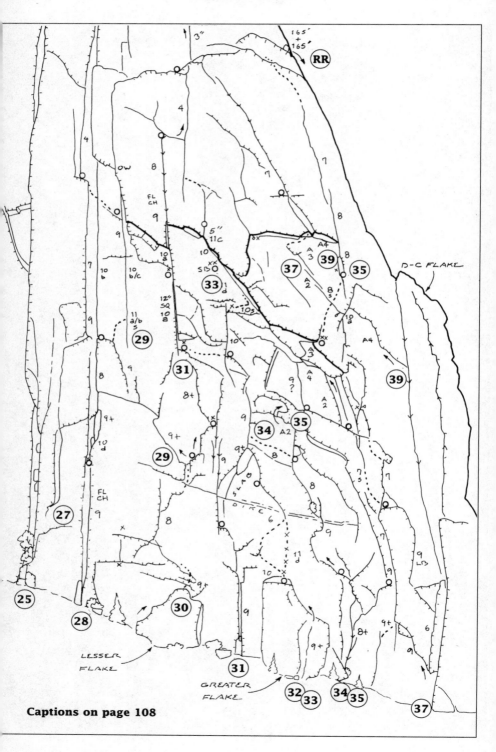

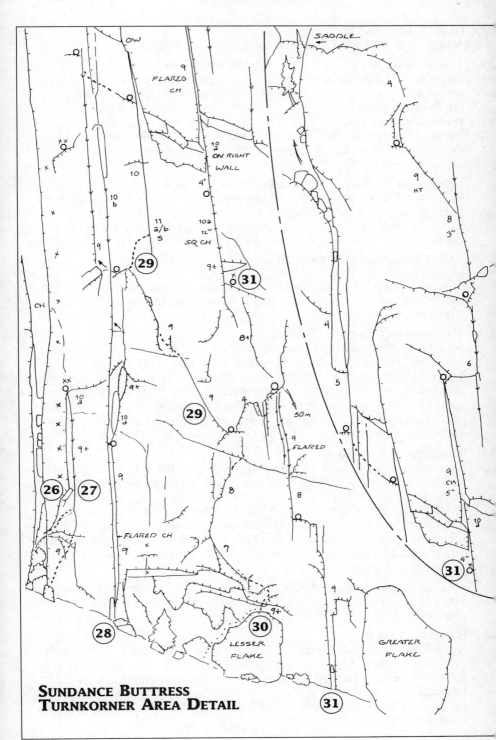

SUNDANCE BUTTRESS
TURNKORNER AREA DETAIL

3. From the right end of the ledge, climb straight up for 20 feet and pull right into a thin crack. Climb the continuously difficult crack past a bulge (11b s) to a ledge beneath a large roof and belay.
4. Traverse left and follow an easy crack to the East Saddle. It is not known if anyone has ever climbed the scaly off-width through the roof.

29A. Laura Scudders Variation
FA: Jim Brink and Paul Hayliger, 1983.
From the top of the third pitch, take a thin crack out across the right wall of the dihedral at the big roof (10) and join the finish to *Turnkorner.*

30. Turnkorner Direct   10b s ★
FA: Ray Jardine, George Hurley, and Chris Walker (IV 5.8 A3+), 1969.
FFA: Scott Woodruff, Mike Gilbert, and Dan Hare, 1970s.
Begin by climbing the left side of the Lesser Flake to its top. Turn the roof via jugs at right (TCU, 9+), then work up and left into a shallow right-facing corner. Climb the corner and continue past its top to a belay ledge. Work up and right to join *Turnkorner* at the top of its second pitch, or go left and climb *Laura Scudders.*

31. Turnkorner   10a ★
FA: Layton Kor and Jack Turner (IV+ 5.8 A3), c. 1962. FFA: Royal Robbins and Bob Boucher, c. 1964. FA (of two upper pitches): Richard and Joyce Rossiter, 1984. SR plus two #3.5 and #4 Friends.
This spectacular route is a must for the wide crack aficionado. The climb begins with the right-facing corner between the two large flakes that lean up against the wall. The fourth and fifth pitches are the most difficult and follow a wide crack through the massive upper roof.

32. Big Flake   9 A3
This little-known route climbs the Greater Flake and the wall above to join precipitation on its third pitch. *Icarus* free-climbs the bolt ladder above the flake.

33. Icarus   11d s ★
FA: Jeff Lowe and Sandy East, 1980; pitch 1a, Lowe and Charlie Fowler. This very challenging route begins with Big Flake, then works up and left through increasingly difficult terrain and turns the main roof 30 feet right of *Turnkorner.*
1a. Climb cracks on the main wall behind the left side of the Greater Flake and belay on top (10b/c).

Randy Joseph on Bosch Cassidy and the Sundance Kid. Photo: Randy Joseph Collection

1b. Climb a shallow corner up the right side of the Greater Flake and belay on top (9+).

2a. Clip the first bolt of a bolt ladder, then traverse up and left to a flake, up and right into a left-leaning dihedral, and belay on a ramp beneath a left-leaning dihedral (10b/c).

2b. Climb straight up past five bolts and belay on the ramp (11d).

3. Climb through an apex/roof and jam a finger crack to the bottom of a right-facing dihedral (9+).

4. Climb a hand crack up the dihedral, turn a roof, and clip a bolt (placed after the first ascent), then make a hairy traverse right to the big left-leaning roof/dihedral (The Great Roof). Climb a crack of varied width past a pinch (crux) and belay from two bolts (11d).

5. Work up and left, then jam an wide crack (four to five inches) through the Great Roof and belay above (11c).

6. Continue up the wide flared crack, then traverse left into *Turnkorner* (7

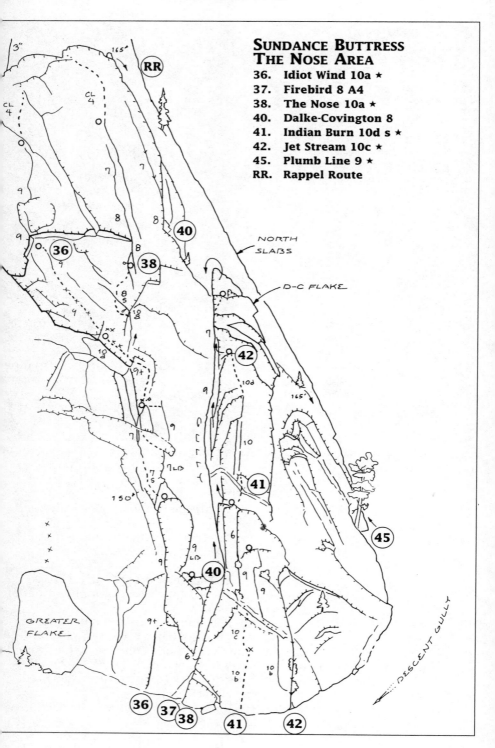

SUNDANCE BUTTRESS
THE NOSE AREA

36. **Idiot Wind 10a** ★
37. **Firebird 8 A4**
38. **The Nose 10a** ★
40. **Dalke-Covington 8**
41. **Indian Burn 10d s** ★
42. **Jet Stream 10c** ★
45. **Plumb Line 9** ★
RR. **Rappel Route**

34. Under the Big Top   10b ★

FA: Scott Kimball and Carl Harrison, 1980.

Begin with the first two pitches of *Precipitation* (9), but belay before the
A2 section.

3. Traverse left on "boiler plate" flakes to a vertical hand crack that is
jammed to a belay at the bottom of a right-facing dihedral (9).

4. Traverse left to join *Turnkorner* (7).

35. Precipitation   9 A2

FA: Layton Kor, Tom Fender, and Joe O'Laughlin (IV 5.8 A2), 1964. Rack
as for *Firebird.*

Begin with a steep groove about ten feet right of the Greater Flake.
Continue up and left via face climbing and cracks (9) with a short sec-
tion of A2 to a ledge beneath the Great Roof. Turn this roof as for
Firebird (A3) but skirt an upper roof via a hand crack on the right (8).

36. Idiot Wind   10a ★

FA: Ed Webster and Pete Athans, 1986.

This excellent route parallels *The Nose* on the left.

Begin at a thin crack between *Precipitation* and *Firebird.*

1. Climb a 40-foot finger crack, then veer right into the crack of *Firebird*
and follow it to the top of the flake (9+ s, 150 feet).

2. Work out left and climb the face (7, no pro) to a V-groove. Continue
up the groove, then follow a crack right to the bolt belay on *The Nose*
(8, 60 feet).

3. Climb up to a roof and traverse left around a small right-facing dihedral as for *The Nose,* then continue left past two bolts and belay from a
two-bolt anchor above empty space (10a, 70 feet).

4. Friction up and left past three bolts, climb a short finger crack, and
belay in slings (pin and bolt) beneath the left end of upper roof of
Firebird (9, 100 feet).

5. Turn the roof on the left and follow a flared crack to a stance (optional belay), then continue more easily to the large terrace at the top of
The Nose (9, 150 feet).

Rappel from the east end of the upper terrace or continue as for
Turnkorner.

37. Firebird   8 A4

FA: Larry Dalke and Cliff Jennings (IV 5.8 A4), 1967. SR plus an assortment of pins up to one-half inch.

This ancient aid line begins just left of *The Nose.* It follows a left-facing
dihedral system for three pitches, then takes on the two great roofs on
the buttress via difficult aid including a pendulum beneath the first roof.

38. The Nose   10a ★

FA: Filip Sokol, Dick Erb, and Jock Jacoba (IV 5.8 A3), 1970. FFA: Duncan
Ferguson and Chris Reveley, early 1970s.

This classic route follows a series of disjunct cracks and dihedrals up
the center of the Southeast Buttress. The crux is a slightly run-out, left-
ward traverse on the fourth pitch. The free version avoids the original
fifth pitch through the upper roof (A3) by skirting right as for
Precipitation.

SUNDANCE BUTTRESS NORTH SLABS

40. Dalke-Covington 8
41. Indian Burn 10d s ★
43. Covert Action 8
44. Lichentology 9+ s
45. Plumb Line 9 ★
RR. Rappel Route

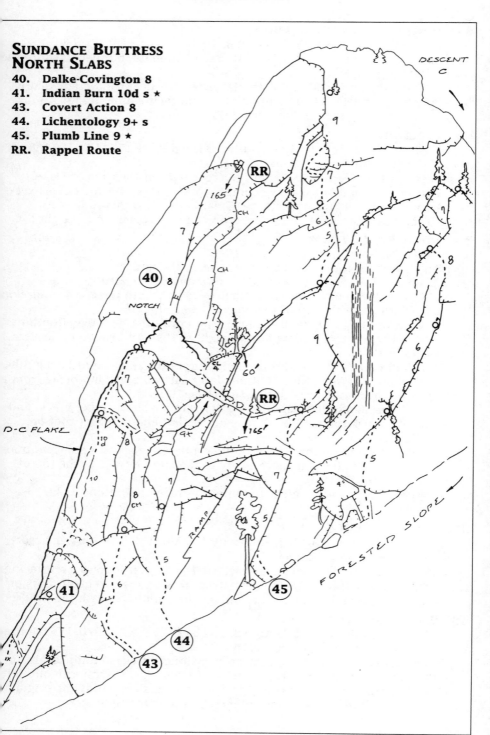

Begin just left from the low point of the crag at an indistinct left-facing corner, or begin with *Firebird* a few feet to the left.

1. Climb the corner, then work up and left to belay at the bottom of a huge flake (6, 85 feet).

2a. Climb a right-facing dihedral with a wide crack along the right side of the flake and belay at its top (9, 75 feet).

2b. Traverse left into *Firebird* and jam a steep flared crack to the top of the flake (9).

3a. Climb a right-facing dihedral to a roof, then go up and left to a belay with two bolts in a flared corner (8, 80 feet).

3b. From the roof, work up and right to a hand crack, climb to near its end, then traverse left to the bolt belay (9).

4. Work up and a bit right to a roof, make an airy traverse left around a corner, then climb straight up to a stance in a right-facing corner (9+, optional belay). Continue up the corner to a seam with a fixed wire, then crank left around a bulge (crux). Work up and right across a blank slab (8 s) and belay in a flared crack with a bolt (10a, 160 feet).

5. Climb to the top of the crack, step right, and follow another crack up steep terrain to a sloping shelf (8+, 150 feet).

6. Angle up and left and follow blackened rock to a large terrace (6, 100 feet).

7 and 8. Climb two moderate pitches to the top of the Southeast Buttress (6) or traverse left and do the finish to *Turnkorner* (9). Or do *The Nose Rappel.*

RR. The Nose Rappel Route

From the east end of the upper terrace, rappel 50 meters from slings to the top of a pillar. Downclimb 35 feet to a long ramp that descends from the Dalke-Covington Flake and scramble 80 feet north to the lowest tree. Rappel 50 meters to the ground at the start to *Plumb Line.* This is labeled RR on photos and topos.

39. Curve Grande 7 A4

FA: Steve Shea and Dick Jimmerson (III 5.7 A4), 1969. SR plus a selection of thin pitons.

Climb the first 350 feet of the *Dalke-Covington* route, then aid left along an arching roof and climb up to the belay beneath the upper roof on *The Nose.* Aim left toward the center of the roof (A4), then straight up (A1) to gain a long, left-facing corner.

The Dalke-Covington Flake. The following routes ascend a large pinnacle at the southeast corner of Sundance Buttress. It is set off from the main wall by a prominent gully along its left side; the right side merges with the North Slab.

40. Dalke-Covington 8

FA: Larry Dalke and Michael Covington, 1965.

This old route climbs the gully along the left side of the Dalke-Covington Flake. From the top of the gully, it follows a flared crack up the main Southeast Buttress to the right of *The Nose.*

41. Indian Burn   10d s

FA: Jack Roberts and Bret Ruckman, 1988.

This route begins in the middle of the slab between the *Dalke-Covington* gully and *Jet Stream*. Look for a bolt more than halfway up the initial slab. The line crosses *Jet Stream* at the second belay, then follows steep cracks right of the arête for a long pitch (crux). Join *Jet Stream* for the last pitch.

42. Jet Stream   10c ★

FA: Scott Kimball and Carl Harrison, 1980.

This route ascends the southwest arête of the Dalke-Covington Flake. Begin with a short, steep crack (crux) about 150 feet around to the right from the bottom of the gully that separates the flake from the main buttress. Work up and left to the arête, which is climbed to the top (9). To escape from the top of the flake, scramble down a ramp to the north to the lowest tree and rappel 50 meters to the ground. One also may finish with the final pitches of *Dalke-Covington*.

The North Slab. *This is the broad, 600-foot wall to the right of the Southeast Buttress and above the forested descent gully (the wall actually faces east). It is bounded on the left by the Dalke-Covington Flake and on the right by the steep gully of Descent C.*

43. Covert Action   8

FA: Larry Dalke and Michael Covington, 1965.

Around to the right of the Dalke-Covington Flake is a massive right-facing dihedral with a deep chimney. Climb a clean slab to reach the chimney.

44. Lichentology   9+ s

FA: Scott Kimball and Greg Child, 1979.

Climb the bulge and right-facing dihedral to the right of the obvious chimney of *Covert Action*.

45. Plumb Line   9 ★

FA: Jim Pettigrew and Michael Covington, 1976.

This route begins several hundred feet up the forested descent gully from the bottom of the Southeast Buttress and takes a direct line to the left of the long, black water streaks in the middle of the slab.

Begin with a small, clean arête at the right side of an arching roof.

1. Climb the arête up to the corner of the roof and continue up to belay on a ledge beside a small tree (7).
2. Traverse up and right into a left-facing flake system and climb this feature to its top (9). Belay out to the left.
3. Work up and around the right side of a bulge and belay beneath a right-facing dihedral capped by a roof (6).
4. Start up toward the roof but cut left before reaching it (7). Move back right into the crack system higher up and jam to a belay by a small tree (9).
5. Easier climbing leads to the top of the Southeast Buttress.

46. In the Rough 8
FA: Scott Kimball and Michael Covington, 1977.
Begin several hundred feet up the forested descent gully and about 100
feet right of the arête described under *Plumb Line.* This is to the right
of the black water steaks in the middle of the slab and a short way right
of a 20-foot-high inset.
1. Climb an easy slab and belay at a tree (5).
2. Work up and right along a ramp and belay from pins (6).
3. Climb to the end of a crack, then continue up the face and belay on a
grassy ramp (8).
4. Climb a left-facing flake/dihedral and belay on a ledge with a big
Douglas fir (7).
5. Traverse right into the gully of Descent C. End of game.

CATHEDRAL GROUP
To the east of Sundance Buttress is a series of crags varying greatly in shape
and size that is seldom visited by climbers. The highest of these, The Needle,
is also the highest point at Lumpy Ridge (10,068 feet above sea level). Though
routes have been completed on most of the features, not all of them are
described in this book. The Needle, for example, has a single route up its
southeast ridge but it is more of a mountaineering project than a rock climb.
The Parish and Thunder Buttress probably are the more interesting of the lot.

THE PARISH
The Parish sits due east of Sundance Buttress and across a wooded gully to
the northeast from Thunder Buttress. Features of note are a rounded south
arête and a steep west-facing wall above a gully. To the left of the gully is a
200-foot spire or buttress with a single route.

Approach. Hike the Black Canyon Trail past Thunder Buttress until The
Parish comes into view. Leave the trail and hike cross-country to the base of
the wall. To descend from the summit, hike north, then go west and downclimb into the gully that borders the west face. A short rappel completes the
descent. One also may hike down around the east side of the crag.

1. Shake-N-Flakes 9
FA: Doug Snively and Scott Kimball, 1976.
This route ascends the spire across the gully to the west.
1. Climb a chimney on the east side and exit via a left-angling flake,
then follow a vertical crack to a belay.
2. Continue with cracks left of a chimney.

2. Rain Maker 8
FA: Larry Bruce and Molly Higgins, 1976.
Begin near a large tree up in the gully toward the left side of the west-
facing wall.
1. Follow a system of three brushy cracks.
2. Work right of a red roof and continue to the top of the wall.

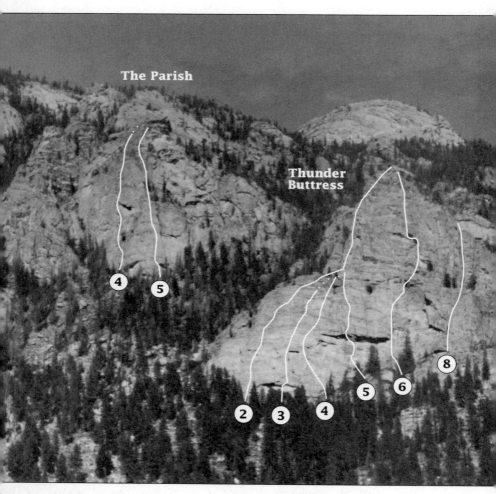

THE PARISH

4. Mad Raven 8
5. Parish Route 7

THUNDER BUTTRESS

2. Thunder Buttress Route 7+
3. Straight Arm 9+
4. Three's Company 7 ★
5. Seconds of Pleasure 10b/c
6. Wounded Knee 9
8. Southeast Ridge 7

3. Chimney Sweep   7
FA: Kimball and Lynn Albers, 1976.
Begin about 100 feet up the gully and follow a wide crack up the face.

4. Mad Raven   8
FA: Michael Covington and Dan McClure, 1976.
Begin a short way up the gully below the west face.
1. Climb directly up to a large roof, pass the roof via a chimney at left, and belay on a ledge with a tree.
2. Pass another roof on the left and head for the summit.

5. Parish Route   7
FA: Kimball and Covington, 1976.
This route ascends the attractive, rounded arête that forms the right margin of the west face. Three pitches.

THUNDER BUTTRESS

Thunder Buttress is the large, south-facing formation about one-quarter mile east-southeast from Sundance Buttress.

Approach via the Black Canyon Trail. Continue about a half mile past the gate below The Pear, then hike through open forest and meadows with downed aspen to the base of the broad south face. To escape from the summit, downclimb a ridge to the north (class 4) and hike down around either side of the crag.

1. Twenty Two Ticks   6
FA: Lynn Albers and DeeDee Hampton, 1979.
Follow the left edge of the south slab and join the *Thunder Buttress Route*

2. Thunder Buttress Route   7+
FA: Kimball and Covington, 1976.
Begin at the left side of the south face just left of a low roof band.
Climb up through banded black rock and work up the clean slab for two pitches. Two more pitches up the steep headwall lead to the summit. A roof near the top of the third pitch is the crux.

3. Straight Arm   9+
FA: Kimball and Harrison, 1982.
Begin beneath the lower roof.
1. Climb up to the roof and pass it just right of center with a mantle onto a fin (9+).
2. Head up the slab, pass a smaller roof on the left and belay near the ridge crest.

4. Three's Company   7 ★
FA: Kimball, Wroblewski, Yuri, 1979.
Begin up to the right from *Straight Arm* at a point almost level with the lower roof.
1. Follow a faint rib up and left onto the slab and belay out to the left from the big roof.
2. Climb straight up the slab and belay on a ledge after about 150 feet.
3. Climb more easily up to big ledges at mid-face. Join Thunder Buttress route or walk off.

4A. Two's a Crowd   8 s
FA: Estabrook and Knight, 1989.
This is an alternate first pitch. Begin 50 feet or so up to the right, directly beneath the big roof. Climb up to a black band and follow it up and left. Continue up a face with a good crack to reach a small right-facing dihedral. Climb the dihedral (8, no pro) and traverse 15 feet left to belay.

5. Seconds of Pleasure   10b/c
FA: Kimball and Wylie, 1981.
Locate a large overhang near the center of the south face. This route turns the roof to the left of center at a double section.

6. Wounded Knee   9
FA: Anne Tarver and Bob Bradley, 1979.
This line has one feature in common with its namesake in Boulder Canyon – an off-width crack through a roof high on the climb.
1. Climb a crack that passes the right margin of the central roof band (7).
2. An easy pitch leads to a belay in a large left-facing dihedral.
3. Climb the dihedral, then jam an offwidth crack through a roof (9).
4. An easy pitch leads to the summit.

7. East But West   7
Too much like real life. This route apparently follows a right-trending crack system to the right of *Wounded Knee* to the big ledge at mid-face, then crosses *Wounded Knee* and climbs the left side of the headwall. Kimball's guide reports, "Take the headwall (where the rock is not good quality), just right of the dihedral forming its left margin." Good luck.

8. Southeast Ridge   7
FA: Bob Bradley and Norman Harthill, c. 1965.
Begin at the right side of the south face.
1. Climb a chimney in a large left-facing corner and belay on a big ledge.
2. Climb a clean, left-facing dihedral to the ridge crest.
3 and 4. Follow the crest to the summit.

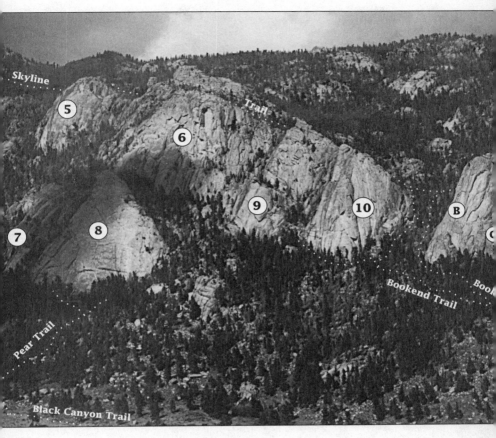

THE PEAR GROUP

5. **OBSERVATORY DOME**
6. **THE CITADEL**
7. **SUNSHINE BUTTRESS**
8. **THE PEAR**
9. **LENS ROCK**
10. **THE BOOKEND**
11. **THE BOOK**
A. **LEFT BOOK**
B. **BOOKMARK**
C. **BOOKMARK PINNACLE**

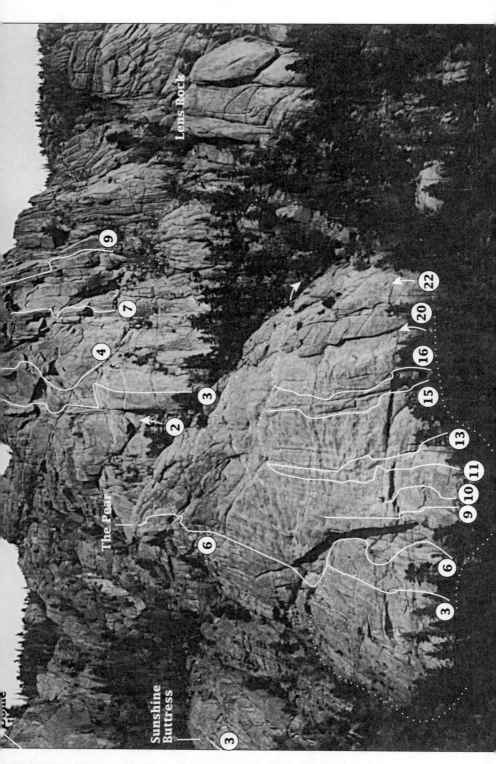

THE PEAR GROUP

SUNSHINE BUTTRESS
3. Brown-Haired Lady 7 s ★

THE PEAR
3. La Chaim 7 s ★
6. Chrome-Plated Semi-Automatic Enema Syringe 7 ★
9. Root of all Evil 9+ ★
10. Sweet Sabrina 9+
11. Good Timing 10a ★
13. Slippage 9+ s ★
15. The Whole Thing 10b s ★
16. Fat-Bottomed Groove 10d s ★
20. Right Dihedral 9 ★
22. Fading Light 7 s

THE CITADEL
2. Sanitarium 8
3. Picadilly Circus 10c
4. Candyland 10b/c ★
7. Heart of Norway 10b s ★
9. Sunset Dihedral 9

im Hansen on Heart of Norway, The Citadel. Photo: Randy Joseph

THE PEAR GROUP

The Pear Group is a cluster of crags across a wooded fully to the west of the Bookmark, which includes Observatory Dome, The Citadel, Sunshine Buttress, The Pear, Lens Rock and The Bookend. All of these features can be accessed from the trail that leads to The Pear, but The Bookend and perhaps Lens Rock are more easily reached from the trails described under The Book.

OBSERVATORY DOME

Observatory Dome sits high on the hillside to the northwest of The Citadel. It may be identified by a long, square rib (the telescope slot) that runs the height of the south face and forms a right-facing dihedral. Approach by hiking up through the woods to the west of Sunshine Buttress or via the path to The Pear. The easiest descent from the summit is to hike down along the west side.

1. **Dance of the Heavens 6**
   FA: Jim Detterline, Pete Detterline, and Williams Sarmiento, 1992.
   This three-pitch route is to the left of the central rib.
   1. Climb a flake/crack system and belay on a small ledge with a tree (6, 130 feet).
   2. Climb a hand crack to a large ledge (6, 150 feet).
   3. Move right into a chimney system and continue to the summit (5, 100 feet).

2. **Telescope Gate 6**
   FA: Keith Lober and Harry Kent, mid 1970s.
   Climb the long, right-facing dihedral formed by the prominent, vertical rib. An alternate finish takes the roof at the top of the dihedral (10a).

3. **Observatory 6**
   FA: Bradley and Mayrose, 1963.
   Climb two pitches of cracks and slabs out to the right from the big dihedral.

THE CITADEL

The Citadel is the broad and complex buttress to the northeast of The Pear. Approach as for The Pear, and take the right branch in the trail, then hike up around the right side of the buttress. To reach routes on the right side of the south face, hike up into the gully to the left of Lens Rock, then cut back to the west along a ledge system. To escape from the summit, scramble down slabs to the north, hike east through the woods to the top of the gully between The Citadel and Lens Rock, then hike down the gully to the forest slope.

1. **Shortstop 7**
   FA: Michael Covington and Dick DuMais, 1975.
   This route wanders up the left side of the south face. Begin with a right facing dihedral. Avoid any major obstacles by passing them on the left

2. Sanitarium   8
FA: Michael Covington and partner, 1974.
Walk up and left from the bottom of the rock, then scramble up a gully to where it steepens into a dihedral.
1. Follow the crack in the corner, then step left into a wide groove and belay at its top (8).
2. Jam a crack to the left edge of the roof band, then undercling and lieback out a left-arching, left-facing dihedral to easy ground (8).

3. Picadilly Circus   10c ★
FA: Billy Westbay and Michael Covington, 1975.
Scramble up the gully as for *Sanitarium* but stop to belay at two pines.
1. Move out right on friction and follow a finger crack in a low-angle slab, then work straight left into a right-facing dihedral with a wide crack (8), and belay above its top.
2. Move left, then up and right across a slab to belay beneath a large roof (7).
3. Climb either of two cracks that pierce the roof (10c), then climb a flake and steep right-facing dihedral that lead to the top.

4. Candyland   10b/c ★
FA: Scott Kimball and Gary Sapp, 1984.
Begin down to the right from the preceding route. Scramble up a gully into the middle of the face and belay beneath a bulging wall with a left-angling crack.
1. Jam up the crack and belay at a good stance (10b/c).
2. Follow a steep, lichenous crack that trends left, then curves up and right. Turn a small roof and arrive near the right end of a large over-hang. Squeeze through a hole and belay on a ledge (9).
3. Walk right on the ledge to a bolt. Climb the face up and right past a shallow rib (9), then work up the face to the top (7).

5. Uproot   8 A3
FA: Neri and Johnson, 1977.
This route ascends the wall to the right of *Candyland.* Aid a thin crack, angle to the right corner of the roof, and pick up a left-angling crack. Join *Candyland.*

6. It Went Straight Up the Middle   9 A2
Follow a dihedral and crack system up the center of the wall to the summit.

7. Heart of Norway   10b s ★
FA: Tim Hansen and Randy Joseph, 1983.
This route ascends the huge green dihedral that culminates in a mas-sive domed ceiling to the right from the middle of the face. Approach from the right and walk out to the left end of a ledge system beneath a dark rotten overhang.
1. Turn the initial roof on jugs (10b). Jam up a steep crack toward a sec-ond roof, then work right to a spike (9). Follow a finger crack up and left on the slab above the roof (9) and belay on a good ledge.

2. Work right (10a s) into the massive right-facing dihedral that leads to the domed roof and lieback to its top. Rappel (double ropes are necessary).

8. Sanctuary 10 A3
This is thought to be the oldest route on The Citadel, but its history is unknown.

Begin from the ledge 50 feet right of *Heart of Norway.* Climb the rotten overhang free (10) or on aid, then follow a crack in the right wall of the dihedral to the domed roof. Exit to the right.

9. Sunset Dihedral 9
FA: Neri and Johnson, 1977.

Begin up and right from *Sanctuary* beneath a right-facing dihedral.

1. Ascend the dihedral (8+) and belay on the left side of a ledge.
2. Traverse left into a steep crack that trends left for a long lead. Pass a block on the right near the top of the crack (9).

SUNSHINE BUTTRESS
This is the small buttress just northwest of The Pear. The south face of the buttress is characterized by a large, left-facing dihedral. Approach as for The Pear, but hike west once at the bottom of the south face. To descend from the summit, scramble down the gully next to The Pear. All routes by Carl Harrison, 1980.

1. Silver Streak 8
Begin on a bench up and left from the low point of the crag, to the left of the huge dihedral and below a white dike.

1. Undercling around a roof, then follow the dike up the slab to the base a slot (7, 150 feet).
2. Climb the slot and a steep bulge to a belay on a ramp (8, 140 feet).
3. Scramble up the ramp and climb a steep dihedral with a large block above it (6, 100 feet). One also may climb straight up from the belay past a bush and traverse right around the arête to easy terrain.

2. Heroes 8
Begin in a finger crack to the right of *Silver Streak* and to the left of the big dihedral.

1. Follow the discontinuous crack for about a rope length and belay at the base of the headwall.
2. Work to the left of a short, wide crack and join *Silver Streak* at the ramp of pitch two (7).

3. Brown-Haired Lady 7 ★
Begin to the right of the large dihedral that splits the middle of the south face.

1. Work up a water groove past the left edge of a roof band, then follow a crack to a ledge with a large pine tree (6).
2. Face climb 20 feet, move left into a crack, and follow it to a large ledge (6).
3. Climb an arête to easier terrain and the summit (7).

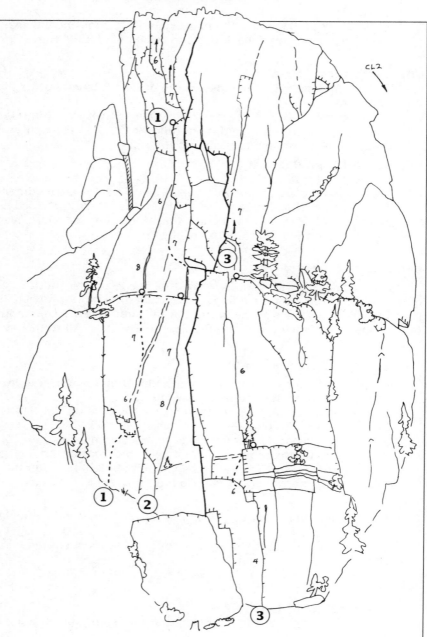

SUNSHINE BUTTRESS

1. **Silver Streak 8**
2. **Heroes 8**
3. **Brown-Haired Lady 7 ★**

THE PEAR

The Pear is the broad, pear-shaped buttress seen nearest the Black Canyon Trail after passing through the gate about 1.3 miles west from the Twin Owls parking area. It is well-known for its expansive granite slabs and excellent friction climbing. However, on most of the harder climbs, the protection is disheartening. Bolts are sparse and typically small diameter junk from hardware stores. The result is that these otherwise great routes are very seldom climbed.

Approach via the Black Canyon Trail. After about 1.3 miles, pass through a gate in a fence and continue on the trail a short way. Branch off to the right at a cairn and follow a pleasant path to a junction where branches lead to the right or left sides of the south face.

Descent A. For routes along the left side of the south face, one may walk off to the left after two pitches or continue to the summit.

Descent B. To descend from the summit, scramble down to the southeast, first along a ramp to the right of the crest, then back along the crest until it is easy to escape onto the forested slope. One also may rappel 75 feet north from bolts at the summit or 60 feet from bolts a short way down the east ridge.

Descent C. To escape from routes to the right of *Batrachian Dihedral,* scramble up and off to the right after two or three pitches.

1. **Platinum Stethoscope   7**
   FA: Bradley and Mayrose, 1960s.
   Climb right-facing dihedrals along the far left side of the south face. Two pitches.

2. **A Pig with Earrings   6 s**
   FA: Bob Bradley et al, 1984.
   Begin just right of the dihedrals at the left edge of the face and wander all the way to the summit.

3. **La Chaim   7 s ★**
   Rack up to a #2.5 Friend.
   Begin in a groove just left of *Neko's Route* or lieback up the left side of the boulder and cut left.
   1. Climb to the top of a flake, then follow a white dike to a belay in a blocky area.
   2. Climb a beautiful, thin crack and finish at the walk-off ledge.

4. **Neko's Route   7 ★**
   Begin beside a large block about 50 feet left of the *Batrachian Dihedral*
   1. Lieback up along either side of the block and work up shallow corners to the first belay on *Chrome-Plated.*
   2. Move left, then climb the face just left of the *Chrome-Plated* dihedral

5. **Finger Tripping   10a**
   FA: Quinn McCleod and Luke Luktemeyer, 1984.
   Begin down and left from *Chrome-Plated.* Climb the smooth slab past three bolts (new) and belay as for that route. Continue to the walk-off ledge via slab with another bolt just right of the *Chrome-Plated* dihedral.

eff Lowe on Between The Sheets, The Bookmark. Photo: Randy Joseph

6. Chrome-Plated Semi-Automatic Enema Syringe   7 ★
FA: Bob Bradley and Paul Mayrose, 1969.
This very popular route ascends the slab and right-facing corner to the left of the big Batrachian Dihedral, then shoots for the summit.
Begin at a groove/dihedral that leads into the Batrachian Dihedral.
1. Start up the groove, but at the first opportunity, climb up and left via flakes and short corners to a stance in a right-leaning, right-facing dihedral (7).
2. Climb the dihedral to the right end of the walk-off ledge and belay after a rope length (7).
3. Move the belay along the ledge if necessary and climb to the top of a flake that forms a short left-facing dihedral. Turn a bulge on the right t escape the upper Batrachian Dihedral (7). Move up and right into a left-facing slot (possible belay) and climb straight up the face (5) to belay on a big ledge (160 feet).
4. Climb a shallow left-facing dihedral to a roof, crank right (7), and belay on a ledge (70 feet).
5. Turn a small roof and gain a right-facing dihedral that is followed to the summit (7, 75 feet).
The last two pitches are from *Slippage* and can be done as one. Two other possibilities for finishing this route exist to the left of the line described (see topo).

7. Batrachian Slab   6
FA: Bob Culp and Steve Komito, 1967.
Climb the enormous left-facing, left-arching dihedral that splits the south face, and finish with *Chrome-Plated.*

8. Root Of All Evil   9+ ★
FA: Jim Erickson and Art Higbee, 1973; alternate start, R. Rossiter, 1991
Begin with a crack that is just right from the bottom of the Batrachian Dihedral.
1. Climb the crack to its end and continue up the face to a square-cut roof with a bolt (8). Jam a crack through the roof (9+) and belay on a sloping stance. One also may begin around to the right and climb a beautiful slab up to the roof (7 or 8).
2. Follow the crack up to easier ground (8).

9. Sibling Rivalry   9+ ★
FA: Topher and Nemonie Donahue, 1988.
Climb the first pitch of *Root Of All Evil* and belay above the bulge. Move out left and climb the left edge of the slab past four bolts to a bolt anchor. Rappel 80 feet to the tree right of the first belay, then 85 feet t the ground, or better, rappel over the edge of the Batrachian Dihedral and arrive at the base of the wall: 165 feet.

10. Sweet Sabrina   9+
FA: Ed Webster and Robert Anderson, 1990.
Climb up the middle of the broad slab past two bolts and a small roof (7 Aim for the pine tree and turn the main roof at a short right-facing corne with a pin and a bolt (9+). Belay at the pine tree and rappel. The route could continue up a shallow dihedral to the lower angled slabs above.

THE PEAR

1.   **Platinum Stethoscope 7**
3.   **La Chaim 7 s ★**
4.   **Neko's Route 7 ★**
5.   **Finger Tripping 10a**

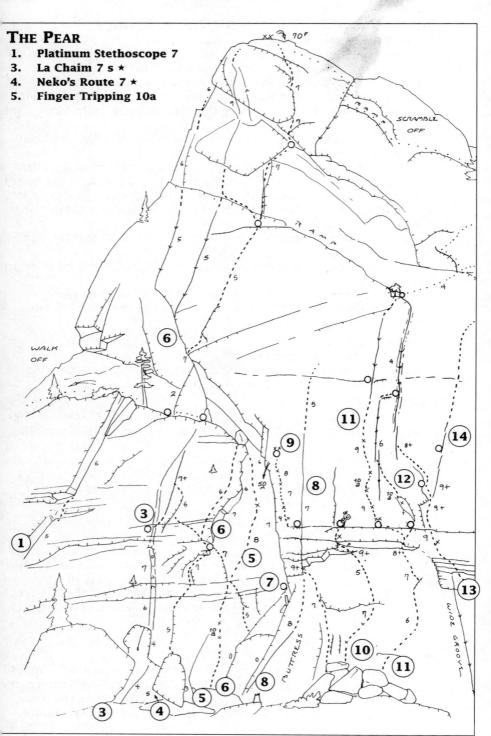

6. **Chrome-Plated Semi-Automatic Enema Syringe 7** ★
7. **Batrachian Slab 6**
8. **Root Of All Evil 9+** ★
9. **Sibling Rivalry 9+** ★
10. **Sweet Sabrina 9+**
11. **Good Timing 10a** ★
12. **Trippage 10a** ★

13. **Slippage 9+ s** ★
14. **Graceful Dancer 9+ s** ★
15. **The Whole Thing 10b s** ★
16. **Fat-Bottomed Groove 10d s** ★
17. **Destination Unknown 11b s**
18. **Weight Loss Clinic 11b s**
19. **Heavenly Journey 10b vs**
20. **Right Dihedral 9** ★
21. **Northern Lights 11a s** ★
22. **Fading Light 7 s**
23. **Gina's Surprise 4**

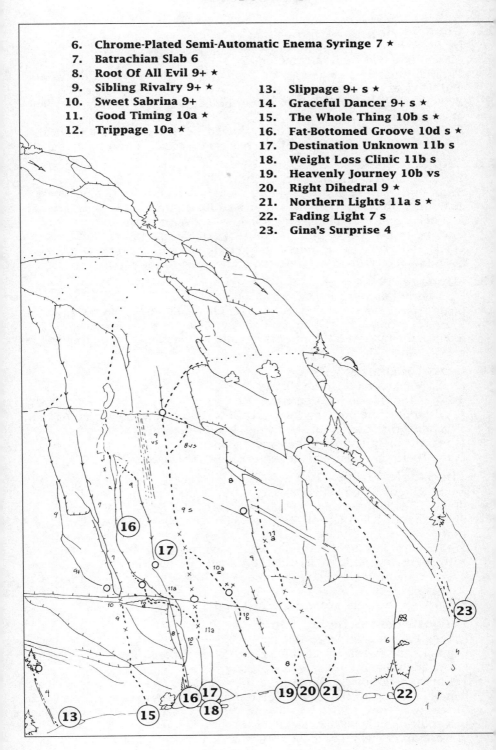

11. Good Timing   10a ★
FA: Ed Webster and Gene Ellis, 1990.
Classic face and friction climbing.
1. Climb the slab and roof as for *Trippage* (8+), move left on the ledge, and belay at two bolts.
2. Work up and slightly left past four bolts (10a), gain a crack, and belay at a good stance.
3. Continue up the crack and belay at a tree. Scramble up and right, then down the east ridge to a point where a ramp leads off into the trees.

12. Trippage   10a ★
FA: Doug Snively and Bernard Gillett, 1988.
Begin to the left of *Slippage* and to the left of a large groove or recess.
1. Wander up a slab (7), turn a roof near its right edge (8+, #1.5 Friend), and belay on a ledge beneath a shallow groove (needs a bolt anchor).
2. Work up the groove past two bolts (10a), then go up and left to gain a crack. Follow the crack to its end, go right to another crack, and belay.
3. Follow the crack to easy ground and escape to the right.

13. Slippage   9+ s ★
FA: Layton Kor and partner, c. 1965.
Begin from a pine tree 50 feet up a slab beneath a break in the roof.
1. Work up past a bolt, over a bulge, and belay in a shallow groove.
2. Work up and left (still interesting) and gain a crack that is followed to easy terrain.

14. Graceful Dancer   9+ s ★
FA: Ed Webster and Lauren Husted, 1984.
Belay at the tree as for *Slippage.*
1. Climb past the bolt and into a shallow right-facing corner as for *Slippage.* From the top of the corner, work right into a thin and sustained incipient crack and belay at a stance (9+).
2. Continue up easier terrain and escape to the right.

15. The Whole Thing   10b s ★
FA: Bob Bradley and Paul Mayrose, 1969. FFA: Mark Hesse and Larry Bruce, 1974. SR to a #2.5 Friend.
Begin about 30 feet left of *Fat-Bottomed Groove* beneath a notch in the roof.
1. Climb up past a bolt to the notch (9) and power over horizontal holds with a bolt and piton to a sandy-bottomed trough (crux).
2. Continue up the trough (7) or move left into a thin crack that leads to a belay ledge (9+).
3. Work up to easier ground and exit to the east.

16. Fat-Bottomed Groove   10d s ★
FA: Scott Kimball and Carl Harrison, 1979.
Begin up and left from the thin crack of *Destination Unknown* beneath a left-facing dihedral with a wide, black groove.
1. Climb the groove straight up to the right side of a roof (8) or take a hand/fist crack on the right (10c). Hand traverse left along a flake beneath the roof, pass the overhang about 15 feet out (crux), and belay in a solution hole with a chickenhead.
2. Work up the white dike (9) until it is easy to exit right.

17. Destination Unknown   11b s
FA: Tim Hansen and Randy Joseph, 1983. SR to a #2.5 Friend.
A very demanding route.
1. Jam a finger-tip crack just right of *Fat-Bottomed Groove,* work up and left to a hand crack (11a), crank past the right side of a roof (11a), and belay in a crack.
2. Climb the crack (9) and follow a dike to easier terrain.

18. Weight Loss Clinic   11b s
FA: Mike Caldwell and Dan Ludlam, 1985. SR to a #3.5 Friend.
Begin with the finger crack of *Destination Unknown.*
1. Climb the crack, pass one bolt, and belay from a three-inch crack after about 60 feet.
2. Work straight up past four bolts (10) and take a 60-foot runout (9) to reach a ledge with a good crack (see topo).

19. Heavenly Journey   10b vs
FA: Billy Westbay and George Hurley, 1974. SR to a #2.5 Friend.
Begin about 15 feet left of *Right Dihedral.*
1. Jam a flared crack to near its end (9+), move right and up to a horizontal groove (10b), and belay a bit higher at two funky, one-quarter-inch bolts.
2. Friction up and left (10a), then straight up the slab for 160 feet to a ledge with a good crack. There is no pro at all on this sustained pitch, however, one may work a little further left and clip the last two bolts on *Weight Loss Clinic.* There was a piton about two-thirds of the way up but it was snapped off by a 130-foot leader fall.

20. Right Dihedral   9 ★
FA: Filip Sokol and Jim Sharp, 1968.
This route ascends the prominent left-facing dihedral along the right side of the south face.
1. Work in from the slab on the left (8) and follow the corner to a small stance (9, 150 feet).
2. Climb to the top of the dihedral and exit right (7).

21. Northern Lights   11a s ★
FA: Tim Hansen and Scott Kimball, 1983.
Ascend the steep slab immediately right of the *Right Dihedral.* One long pitch with three bolts.

22. Fading Light   7 s
Climb up into an apex about 25 feet right of *Northern Lights,* then follow a fading crack and rounded arête to easier ground.

23. Gina's Surprise   4
FA: Chip Salaun and Gina Wilson, 1978.
This is a pleasant route along a dike on the southeast shoulder of the crag.

LENS ROCK

1. Hunkidori 9+
2. Tennis Shoe Tango 6
3. Arch Crack 6
4. The Spectacle 9 s
5. Ellipse 12a ★
6. Optic Nerve 9 vs
7. The Frame 8 ★

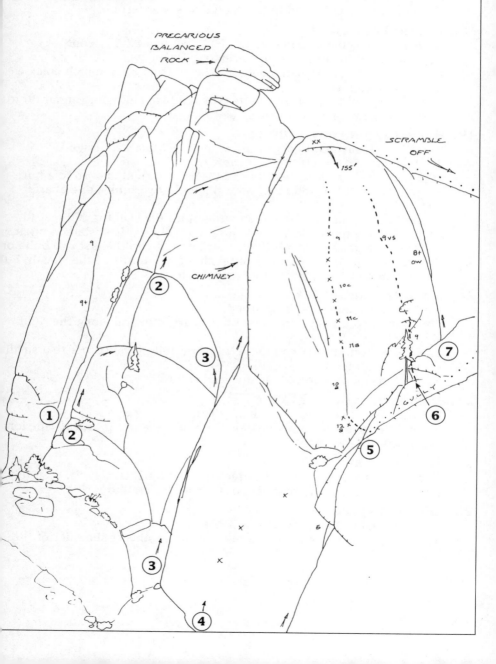

The following routes ascend the steep north face beneath the summit of The Pear. They are on the north face directly beneath the summit and on the south-facing wall just across a gap to the north.

24. Larry Day Memorial   12b/c (TR)
FA: (?) Bernard and Robert Gillett, 1987.
Climb the very steep, 70-foot face directly below the summit.

25. Dextrous Digits   9+
Climb discontinuous cracks just right of *Jam On It* and join that route near the top.

26. Jam on It   9 ★
FA: (?) Bernard and Robert Gillett, 1987.
Jam a hand crack a short way left from the summit.

The following routes are on a south-facing wall just north of The Pear.

27. Devil's Lake Revisited   8 ★
FA: Bernard Gillett, c. 1987.
Ascend excellent rock along a thin crack opposite *Dextrous Digits*.

28. No Woman No Cry   9
FA: Bernard Gillett, c. 1987.
Climb the crack across from *Jam on It*.

LENS ROCK

This small crag sits a short way west of The Bookend and is easily identified from the Black Canyon Trail by The Lens, a 50-meter, elliptical face at the upper right of the formation.

Approach. Follow the trail to The Bookend and continue west beneath its south face. For routes on The Lens, it is probably easier to scramble up behind this feature from the gully between Lens Rock and The Bookend, which is also the easiest descent from any route. One also may climb straight up to The Lens from the bottom of the rock via a chimney in the right side of the south face (4).

1. Hunkidori   9+
FA: John Harlin and partner, 1988.
Climb the vertical crack in the east-facing wall just left of *Tennis Shoe Tango*.

2. Tennis Shoe Tango   6 ★
FA: Chip Salaun, solo, 1979.
Climb in from a chimney at the left side of the face and jam straight to the summit. It is easiest to traverse off to the right just below the summit block.

3. Arch Crack   6
FA: Chip Salaun, solo, 1979.
Begin at a chimney beneath the left side of the Lens. Ascend the chimney, then jam out left in the arching crack and join *Tennis Shoe Tango*.

4. The Spectacle   9 s
FA: Todd Swain, Rick Guerrieri, and Andy Brown, 1992.
Below The Lens is a compelling, rounded buttress.
1. Begin with a left-facing flake and continue up and right past two bolts (crux). Run it out to the third bolt and belay at the bottom of a chimney.
2. Ascend the chimney to reach the notch behind the summit (balanced rock).

5. Ellipse   12a ★
FA: Joyce and Richard Rossiter and Rob Woolf, 1988. Rack: RPs, stoppers, #0.5 Tricam or TCU, and about ten QDs.
Sustained face and friction climbing with good pro. Begin in a gully near the low point of The Lens. Crank up and left past two bolts (crux) and follow a seam to where it fades (10a), then climb the beautiful, rounded arête to the top. A second crux (11c) is encountered near the fourth bolt (160 feet, eight bolts). As an alternate finish, one may move left from the third bolt and ascend an attractive dihedral, but it is disappointingly easy (7).

6. Optic Nerve   9 vs
FA: Doug Snively and Bernard Gillett, 1988.
This is a good route with bad pro. For those climbing at the level of its grade, it is best toproped. Begin 50 feet down and left from *The Frame*, beside a small tree. Go up a short finger crack (9), up right to a flake, then friction straight up to the top (9 vs).

7. The Frame   8 ★
FA: Chip Salaun, 1979.
This is a 100-foot offwidth crack at the upper right side of The Lens.

THE BOOKEND
The Bookend is the easternmost feature of The Pear Group and is just across a wooded gully from the from The Bookmark. It has many fine routes on its south and east faces.

Approach. Start out on the Black Canyon Trail. After about one mile, just after the trail enters Rocky Mountain National Park, take a path that branches right. Stay left at two signed junctions and arrive at the southeast corner of the crag after about a 20-minute hike. To escape from the summit, scramble down an easy gully to the north, then hike back around to the east and south.

1. Pancake Stack   8
This route climbs the south face of a distinct pinnacle at the west end of The Bookend. Scramble up (fourth class) to where the rock steepens and belay.
1. Ascend a left-facing dihedral with a small roof (8) and continue upward until a blank section forces the route to the right. Belay at the right margin of the face.
2. Continue up the southeast corner via flakes (8) to the summit.

THE BOOKEND

1. Pancake Stack 8
6. Bombay Chimney 8
8. Pinch 8
9. Corinthian Column 9 ★
11. Sun King 10d or 12a ★
12A. Knight's Gambit Variation 10d

17. Orange Julius 9 s or 10b ★
22. Handbook 9 ★
24. Climb of the Ancient Mariner
25. Sorcerer 8+ s ★
26. Treebeard 7

2. Pain Pain So Good   11d
FA: Hidetaka and Mishiko Suzuki, 1983.
Begin with the *Pancake Stack* and climb to the base of a very steep, zigzag finger and hand crack in the west side of The Bookend. Jam it.

3. Chemise Demise   10b/c
FA: Salaun and Laird, 1979.
Begin with the *Pancake Stack* and belay at the bottom of an awesome, left-leaning offwidth crack in the west wall of The Bookend. Jam the crack to a good belay (five-inch pro). Traverse right, then go straight up to the summit.

4. No Bozos   10c
FA: Mike Caldwell and Pat Barlow, 1986.
This route goes up the southwest corner of The Bookend.
1. Climb up a vertical, crystalline fist crack on the west side of the buttress that turns into a hand and finger crack (crux). From the end of the crack, make an improbable move right to a jug and belay from pins.
2. Continue up the southwest buttress via face climbing (one bolt) and thin cracks (10b).

5. 12a   (?)
Locate a line of bolts and pins a short way left of *Bombay Chimney.*

6. Bombay Chimney   8
FA: Filip Sokol and Del Monte, 1968.
This route ascends the fourth and farthest left chimney on the south face.

7. Unknown Chasm   7
This is the third major chimney left of the Foxhead.

8. Pinch   8
This is the second major chimney left of the Foxhead.

9. Corinthian Column   9 ★
FA: Chip Salaun and Carl Harrison, 1979.
This route ascends the column at the left of *Sicilian Defense.* Begin just left of that route in a crack with a squaw current bush.
1. Work in from the right and start the crack above the bush. Jam up the flared hand crack and belay at the base of a chimney (9).
2. Climb the chimney and belay on a good ledge (9).
3. Move left on the ledge to the edge of the *Pinch* chimney. Climb a hand crack, exit right via sharp flakes to the face of the column, and continue to another good ledge (8+).
4. Start on the left and work up and right to a crack that is followed to a big ledge (9). Scramble to the summit.

0. Sicilian Defense   9
FA: George Hurley and Bill Forrest, 1971.
Route finding is not a problem here. A couple yards left of *Knight's Gambit* is a long, deep chimney.

1. Sun King   10d or 12a ★
FA: Matt Smedley, Dave Larsen, and Bill Anderson, 1990. Rack up to one inch plus a #6 Hex or equivalent.

Begin at a thin, left-facing flake between *Knight's Gambit* and *Sicilian Defense*. Work up the steep, difficult face past four bolts to a flake, then hand traverse right to a bolt anchor.

2. Rappel or climb a very difficult second pitch protected by bolts.

12. Knight's Gambit   9+ ★
FA: Scott Kimball and Chip Salaun, 1979.
Begin in the chimney at the left of the Foxhead.
1. Start up the chimney, then undercling left and jam a nice hand crack. When the crack fades, move back right to the chimney (9+).
2. Continue up to an overhang (9+) and traverse right to belay.
3. Follow disjunct grooves straight up to a stance in a deep crack system (8).
4. Do the last pitch of *Sicilian Defense* (7).

12A. Knight's Gambit Variation   10d
A variation to the first pitch of this climb is shown on the topo. It has two bolts and finishes at the bolt anchor on *Sun King* (10d).

The Foxhead is a small pinnacle at the lower east side of the south face.

13. Gunk-Lumpy   8
This obscure line goes up the south face of the Foxhead pinnacle. To escape from the top of the Foxhead, downclimb the gully between the pinnacle and the main wall on the east.

The following routes ascend the east side of The Bookend.

14. Pineapple Juice   11b ★
FA: Matt Smedley, Dave Larsen, and Bill Anderson, 1990.
Begin ten feet left of *Strawberry Shortcake* and work up into the chimney between the Foxhead and The Bookend. Crank right into a line of five bolts on the arête and climb up to the first belay on *Orange Julius*. Rappel 140 feet or finish *Orange Julius*.

15. Strawberry Shortcake   10c
FA: George Hurley and Earl Wiggins, 1977.
Climb the first crack right of the Foxhead chimney straight up to the first belay on *Orange Julius*.

16. Tarantula   11a
FA: Scott Woodruff and Dan Hare, 1975.
Begin with a crack just right of *Strawberry Shortcake*, climb up and right along an overhanging flake, then turn a roof and join *Orange Julius*.

17. Orange Julius   9 s or 10b ★
FA: the route was named by Mike Yokell and Joe O'Laughlin, who made an ascent in 1970, but it may have been climbed by Larry Dalke and Wayne Goss, who in 1966 nailed straight up the Orange Julius Flake (III 5.9 A2).
Identify a large, left-facing dihedral capped by a roof at the southeast corner of the crag.

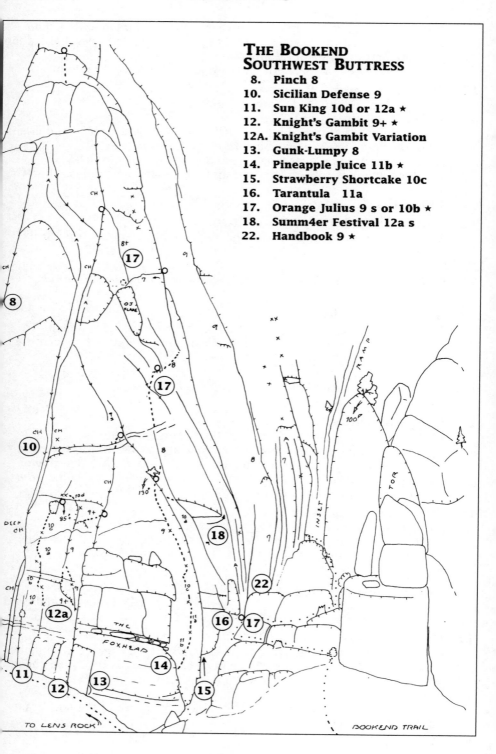

THE BOOKEND
SOUTHWEST BUTTRESS

8. Pinch 8
10. Sicilian Defense 9
11. Sun King 10d or 12a ★
12. Knight's Gambit 9+ ★
12A. Knight's Gambit Variation
13. Gunk-Lumpy 8
14. Pineapple Juice 11b ★
15. Strawberry Shortcake 10c
16. Tarantula 11a
17. Orange Julius 9 s or 10b ★
18. Summ4er Festival 12a s
22. Handbook 9 ★

Begin in a niche behind a block.

1. Climb straight up the dihedral, go left under the roof (10b), and belay beneath a tree in a crack. One also may angle left across the face to reach the left side of the roof (9 s).
2. Work up and right to belay beneath a hanging, lichenous flake (the Orange Julius) (8).
3. Traverse straight right to the edge of the face (8 s) and ascend a wide crack (7) to a belay stance.
4. Make a long hand traverse left to the arête and belay (7).
5. Ascend a thin crack to a pedestal (8 s), step left, and power up a flared, wide crack to a big ledge (7).
6. Jam a short crack and unrope after 50 feet.

18. Summer Festival   12a s
FA: Hidetaka and Mishiko Suzuki, 1983.
Climb the offwidth slot through the right side of the roof on the first pitch of *Orange Julius*.

19. Rejoice   11c/d s
FA: Steve Muehlhauser and Sarah Spalding, 1983.
Begin just right of the *Orange Julius* dihedral.

1. Ascend a deadend groove past a bolt to get up on the main wall and belay in the crack of *Hot Licks* (11c/d s). One may avoid this pitch via *Hot Licks*.
2. Veer right and work up the steep face past three bolts (about 20 feet apart) and belay as for *Hot Licks/Orange Julius* (10d).
3. Traverse right and ascend a large right-facing dihedral about ten feet left of the *Hot Licks* offwidth (9+).

20. Hot Licks   9 ★
SR plus an extra #3.5 or 4 Friend.
This route ascends the slab to the left of *The Great Dihedral*.

1. Do the first ten feet of *The Great Dihedral* and stem up into a steep crack on the left. Gain the face and belay higher up as the crack widens (8, 150 feet).
2. Jam the crack until it fades and continue up the face (9) to join the third pitch of *Orange Julius*.
3. Traverse right into *The Great Dihedral* and jam a conspicuous offwidth crack in a southeast-facing wall (8).

21. The Great Dihedral   7
FA: Filip Sokol and Steve Pomerance, 1968.
This route ascends the huge dihedral/chimney that separates the crag into north and south features. Three pitches. Begin from the left end of the grassy ledge of *Handbook*.

22. Handbook   9 ★
FA: Scott Woodruff, Dan Hare, and Brad Gilbert, 1974.
This route ascends the crack and corner system just left of *Labor of Lust*.
Begin on a grassy ledge up and right from the start to *Orange Julius*.

1. Climb a wide crack and belay on a sloping stance after about 70 feet (7).

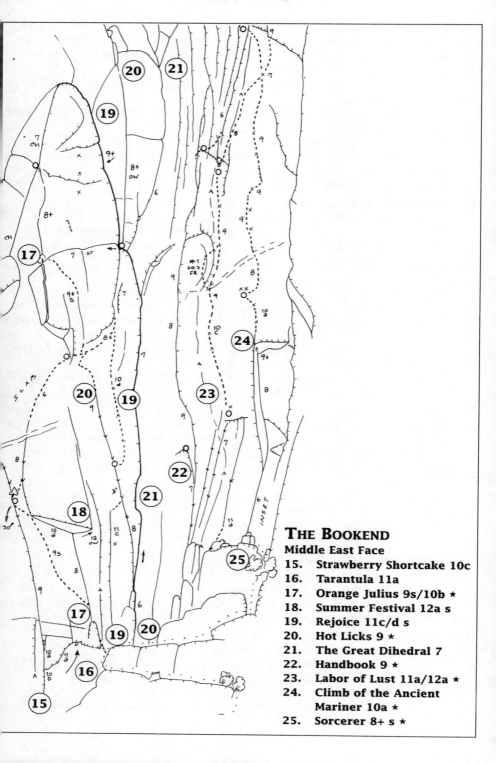

THE BOOKEND
Middle East Face

15. **Strawberry Shortcake 10c**
16. **Tarantula 11a**
17. **Orange Julius 9s/10b** ★
18. **Summer Festival 12a s**
19. **Rejoice 11c/d s**
20. **Hot Licks 9** ★
21. **The Great Dihedral 7**
22. **Handbook 9** ★
23. **Labor of Lust 11a/12a** ★
24. **Climb of the Ancient Mariner 10a** ★
25. **Sorcerer 8+ s** ★

2. Jam up the steep left-facing corner and belay at a good stance after about 120 feet (9).

3. Switch to a crack on the right and work up to join the last pitch of *Sorcerer* (6).

23. Labor of Lust   11a or 12a vs ★

FA: Randy Joseph and Bill Wylie, 1981; of alternate start, Hidetaka Suzuki.

This route ascends the 300-foot, rounded arête to the right of *Handbook*. Begin up and right from *Orange Julius.*

1a. Climb two parallel, flared cracks up to a good stance with a bolt (7).

1b. Begin from the same ledge as *Sorcerer* and climb a very difficult thin crack on the left wall of the alcove (12a).

2. Lead straight up the arête past two one-quarter-inch bolts and belay at a flake with slings (11a s, 150 feet). It is possible to get pro in a short dihedral on the left (mid-range Friends) partway up the pitch.

3. Continue up the arête (9 s), angle right past a bolt (7), and climb through *Sorcerer* roof at a finger crack (9). Belay after about 150 feet.

4. Continue up the crack to the top (4).

The original line belayed in the short dihedral on the second pitch, then worked out onto face near the following route.

24. Climb of the Ancient Mariner   10a ★

FA: Richard and Joyce Rossiter and Bonnie Von Grebe, 1991. The dihedral and roof are said to have been climbed by Doug Snively c. 1975. Bring Friends up to a #3 plus six QDs.

The *Mariner* ascends the clean, right-facing dihedral and long, narrow face to the left of *Sorcerer.*

1. Climb the first 40 feet of *Sorcerer,* then break left and stem up a right-facing dihedral (8) that is capped by a roof. Turn the roof (9) and work up a steep slab (10a) to a bolt anchor.

2. Move right and up from the belay and climb the peerless face past six bolts (sustained 8 and 9). Belay at a good stance one crack left from the end of the roof on *Sorcerer.*

3. Move back right above the roof and follow the arête to the summit (6).

25. Sorcerer   8+ s ★

Begin this classic route in the same alcove as the *Mariner.*

1. Climb the left side of the alcove, a sharp-edged corner (7), and a tricky left-facing dihedral to belay at a stance beneath a small roof (8+ s, 165 feet).

2. Continue up the dihedral to a higher roof, then undercling left to a good belay stance on the arête (8). One also may continue straight up the main corner (6).

3. Follow deep grooves up and right to the summit (5).

25A. Sorcerer's Apprentice   9+ ★

Work up and left from the middle of the second pitch along a smaller dihedral (9+), then up and left (7) past the last bolt on *Labor of Lust.* Finish as for the *Mariner.*

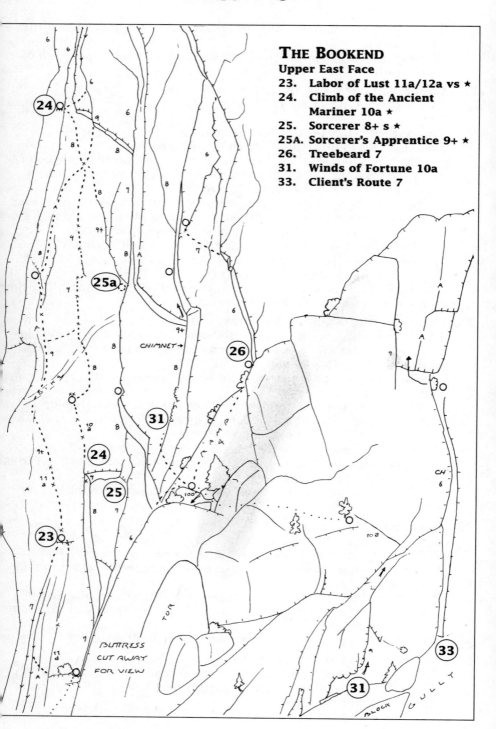

THE BOOKEND
Upper East Face
23. Labor of Lust 11a/12a vs ★
24. Climb of the Ancient
    Mariner 10a ★
25. Sorcerer 8+ s ★
25A. Sorcerer's Apprentice 9+ ★
26. Treebeard 7
31. Winds of Fortune 10a
33. Client's Route 7

26. Treebeard 7

This route ascends the farthest right dihedral system on the southeast face. Begin at the southeast corner of the rock and scramble up into an alcove as for the *Mariner.*
1. Climb the crack on the left side of a wide slot (6), then work up and right to a juniper tree.
2. Work up the ramp along the east face to the base of a left-facing dihedral. Climb the crack in the dihedral until it widens, then work out left on scoops, go around a rib, and belay at a crack (7).
3. Follow the crack up a smaller dihedral that merges with the original line and run the rope out to the top (6).

Lower East Side. The lower east side of The Bookend forms a diagonal cliff band along which several routes have been completed (the names of which are sometimes more interesting than the climbs). To descend from the lower end of the ramp, rappel 100 feet from a large juniper tree to the start of Sorcerer, or climb off from the upper end of the ramp. One also may finish with a route on the upper wall.

27. Paint Hair Around It 11a
FA: Peter Hunt and Bill Robbins, 1983.
The low end of the cliff is punctuated by a tor or free-standing pillar. Climb the wide crack on the west side of the tor.

28. Hard Parts 10b
FA: Kimball and Rayton, 1983.
Begin from a ledge at the southeast corner of the tor. Climb a finger crack in a dihedral, traverse left, make a long reach left to a flake, and continue to the top of the tor.

29. Pollywog Slab 8
FA: Kimball and George, 1984.
Begin just right of *Hard Parts.* Ascend an unpleasant chimney followed by a clean slab. The key hold on the slab is a raised area shaped like a pollywog. Finish with a steep crack.

30. Guano with the Wind 8
FA: Kimball, Rayton, Rzonca, 1983.
Begin a few feet left of *Winds of Fortune.* Crank over the roof via a square jug, go up the face, left around a bulge, and finish with a fist crack.

31. Winds of Fortune 10a
FA: Kimball and Joe Hladick, 1979.
The main southeast face of The Bookend is guarded by an offset cliff band. This route begins at a level spot about 200 feet up and right from the tor mentioned in *Hard Parts.*
1. Climb a hanging flake and the vertical wall above, hand traverse right, then jam up a left-angling finger crack to reach the top of the cliff band (10a). Scramble across ledges to a juniper tree near the base of a large, left-facing dihedral with a roof halfway up.

2. Work up the dihedral into a deep recess, jam out the top (9+), and belay after a short distance.

3. Work up and left in a thin crack and run the rope out to the summit.

32. Static Cling   11 vs
FA: Wilford and Joseph, 1982.
This route takes the steep wall to the left of *Client's Route.* Work up the face to a stance beneath a roof. Lieback against dubious flakes to the left of the roof. Continue more easily to the ramp atop the cliff.

33. Client's Route   7
FA: Michael Covington and partner, c. 1975.
Locate a conspicuous and unattractive right-leaning chimney near the center of the east-facing cliff.

1. Climb the chimney and belay beneath a roof.

2. Work left around the roof and gain the ramp that runs along the top of the cliff band.

3. Follow the next workable crack system to the right of *Treebeard* on the upper wall.

34. Hashish   9
The cliffer you get, the smoker you climb! Begin up to the right from *Client's Route* beneath a left-right flip-flop dihedral that runs past the right end of a long roof.

1. Climb the dihedral (9).

2. Move left, turn a bulge, and follow a dike to a vertical crack that leads to easier ground (9).

35. Well Hung   10b/c
FA: Kimball and Wylie, 1979.
Climb a large dihedral at the northeast extreme of the cliff band.

THE BOOK

The Book is probably the most popular crag at Lumpy Ridge. It is known for its hard, smooth granite as well as for having the best collection of long, clean cracks on the ridge. The Book consists of several distinct features, each presenting a fine assortment of climbs. The westernmost feature is the Left Book, an unsurpassed moderate slab. To its right and dropping down to form the low point of the crag is The Bookmark, featuring great crack climbs. To its right and separated by a cleft is the Bookmark Pinnacle, a smaller buttress crowned by a narrow fin. Up to the right stand two massive ribs separated by deep chimneys. This is the Book Binding area. The Isis Buttress (the right of the two) has several routes as do the chimney walls to either side. The broad south face of The Right Book (commonly referred to as The Book) extends to the east from here and presents such famous routes as *Fat City Crack, Pear Buttress,* and *J Crack.*

General Approach. Hike the Black Canyon Trail west from the Twin Owls parking area and take a prominent but unsigned right branch after about one mile. This point is just east of a sign that indicates entry to Rocky Mountain National Park. Follow the trail up into the trees where individual paths lead from signed junctions to each of The Book's features.

LEFT BOOK

The Left Book includes the entire wall behind and to the west of The Bookmark. The right side of this formation is not terribly attractive but the broad slab to the left is high quality terrain. The major point of identification on the slab is a low roof at the bottom of a long, raised flake. The flake forms two clean dihedrals that face away from each other. Running across the upper wall about 150 feet from the top is a broad bench called Paperback Ledge.

Approach. Take the Bookmark Trail, then hike up along the left side of The Bookmark to the bottom of the Left Book.

Descent. Escape most routes by hiking west along Paperback Ledge, then back down along the west edge of the slab. Escape from the top of the upper headwall by hiking down around the west side.

1. Zingando 6 ★
FA: Chip Salaun, 1978.
If this route were higher angle it would be famous. Begin about halfway up along the left side of the slab.
1. Climb up and sling a horn, then move right into a left-facing corner system (6). Continue up through a roof and belay on a flake with a 12-foot Douglas fir tree.
2. From the left side of the flake, work up into an amazing, right-angling crack and follow it to Paperback Ledge (2).

2. Cottontail 6
Begin up along the left side of the face and follow an undercut, left-facing corner system up to a large, right-facing dihedral. Three pitches.

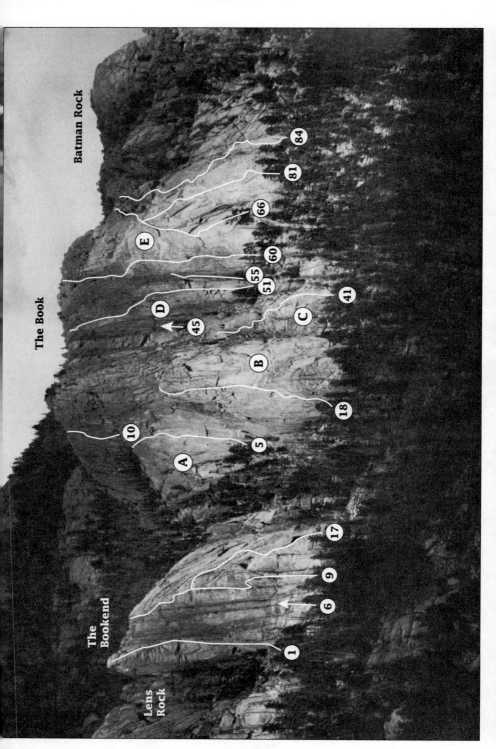

THE BOOK AREA
View from the Southwest

THE BOOKEND
1. Pancake Stack 8
6. Bombay Chimney 8
9. Corinthian Column 9
17. Orange Julius 9 s or 10b ★

A. LEFT BOOK
5. White Whale 7 ★
10. Shake Down 10c

B. THE BOOKMARK
18. Melvin's Wheel 8+ ★

C. BOOKMARK PINNACLE
41. East Side 8+ ★

D. ISIS BUTTRESS
45. Renaissance Wall 12c ★
51. Isis 10a ★

E. RIGHT BOOK
55. Dead Boy 10 ★
60. Osiris 7 ★
66. Fat City Crack 10b ★
81. J Crack 9 or 11c ★
84. Endless Crack 9 ★

3. Manifest Destiny 7 ★
FA: Bob Bradley and Paul Mayrose, c. 1965.
Don't we all?
1. Climb the left-facing system immediately left of *The Dog* and belay on a ledge with boulders (6).
2. Climb a right-facing corner past a roof, go left, then up and right to belay (7).
3. Climb up to a left-angling channel and follow it to Paperback Ledge.
4. Walk off or climb a brushy, left-facing dihedral just left of the fourth pitch of *White Whale* (7).

4. The Dog 7
FA: (?) Bernard and Robert Gillett, 1986.
Begin ten feet left of *White Whale.*
1. Climb a left-facing corner (7) and belay as for *Manifest Destiny.*
2. Continue up the left-facing system past a roof (7); climb a crack on the right (5) or go straight up the slab (6 s) to belay on a pedestal.
3. Climb up and left to a crack with a tiny tree, go up and right to a channel (7), up a crack with an old pin and around the right side of a roof (7).

5. White Whale 7 ★
FA: Dan Hare and Randy McGregor, 1972.
Classic.
1. Climb a fine crack up to the left side of the roof in the center of the lower face and belay at the pine (6).
2. Jam a beautiful crack in the slab left of the raised flake (7).
3. Follow *Hiatus* to Paperback Ledge (7).
4. Walk off or ascend a right-arching wide crack in the headwall (8).

6. Hiatus 7 ★
FA: Dan Hare and Scott Woodruff, 1973. SR to a #4 Friend.
Classic. Begin at the low point of the slab.
1. Follow a thin crack to where it fades, then face climb up to the middle of the low roof and work left to belay at a small tree (7).
2. Ascend the left-facing dihedral along the left side of the raised flake (7, wide), work out left along a shallow corner past a roof, and belay.
3. Climb straight up and stay left of a black water groove (7).
4. Walk off or move right to a topless pine tree and climb straight up through a small, triangular roof (9).

7. Ten Years After 9 s ★
FA: Dan Hare and Clay Wadman, 1983.
A bolder line.
1. Climb a slab directly up to and around the right side of the low roof (9 s).
2. Climb the middle of the raised flake and belay up to the right (6 s).
3. Work up and left under the roofs and ascend a shallow groove to Paperback Ledge (8+ s).

8. Beelzebub 7 s ★
Begin at the low point of the slab, just left of the descent chimney on The Bookmark.

Bonnie Von Grebe ascending White Whale (7) on the Left Book.

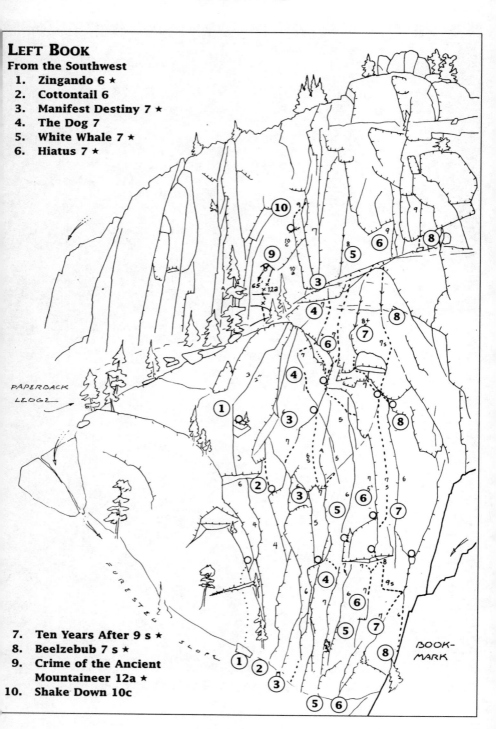

LEFT BOOK
From the Southwest

1. **Zingando 6** ★
2. **Cottontail 6**
3. **Manifest Destiny 7** ★
4. **The Dog 7**
5. **White Whale 7** ★
6. **Hiatus 7** ★

PAPERBACK LEDGE

FORESTED SLOPE

BOOK-MARK

7. **Ten Years After 9 s** ★
8. **Beelzebub 7 s** ★
9. **Crime of the Ancient Mountaineer 12a** ★
10. **Shake Down 10c**

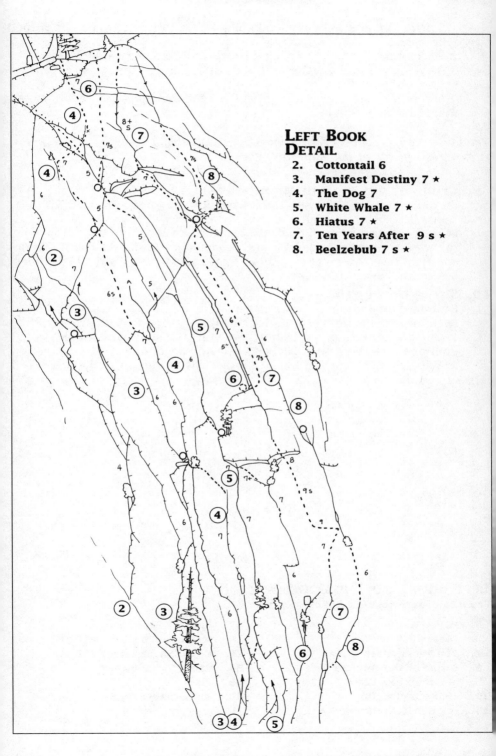

**LEFT BOOK
DETAIL**

2. Cottontail 6
3. Manifest Destiny 7 ★
4. The Dog 7
5. White Whale 7 ★
6. Hiatus 7 ★
7. Ten Years After 9 s ★
8. Beelzebub 7 s ★

1. Friction up and right (6 s) and belay at the bottom right corner of the long flake.
2. Ascend the long, right-facing dihedral and belay near its top (6).
3. Work up and right past a roof, then up a slab to Paperback Ledge (7 s).
4. Walk off or move up and right and ascend a bulging, left-facing dihedral in the headwall (9).

The following two routes begin from Paperback Ledge, the large terrace that runs across the top of the main wall.

9. Crime of the Ancient Mountaineer   12a ★
FA: Mike and Tom Caldwell, 1992. Rack: RPs, stoppers, #1 and 1.5 Tricams, QD.
Begin a short way left of *Shake Down*. Work up and slightly left to a bolt followed by incipient cracks. Place Tri-cams in a horizontal break. Go up and right past two bolts to another thin crack, then up and left to slings on a horn. Lower off 65 feet.

10. Shake Down   10c
FA: Dan Hare and John Warren, 1983.
Begin near the middle of Paperback Ledge beneath a small alcove.
1. Climb a left-facing, left-leaning dihedral (10b) and pass a roof. Continue up a thin crack (10c) and belay on a ledge.
2. Move up and right and follow another left-facing dihedral (9) to easier ground.

LEFT BOOK AND THE BOOKMARK
From the Southwest (on opposite page)

Left Book

Isis Buttress

Bookmark

Bookmark Pinnacle

Flatiron

THE BOOKMARK

This prominent buttress forms the southwest rampart of The Book and presents a great assortment of moderately difficult cracks and dihedrals. Library Ledge, a long horizontal bench, runs across the lower third of the face and offers a belay stance for many of the routes. A small pinnacle called The Flatiron rises up at the bottom center of the south face.

Approach as for The Book (see above) but take a signed left branch in the trail about halfway up the slope.

Descent. To escape from the summit, downclimb (4) or rappel the short north face to the notch, then downclimb the deep chimney that descends to the west (4). This chimney is the lower part of an old route called *Alpinisten* that goes all the way to the summit of The Left Book. FA: Allen Kempers and Ernest Spencer, 1950. One also may downclimb the gully to the east.

11. Bunny Buttress 8

The upper left (west) side of The Bookmark forms a large buttress that rises in two stages to the summit.
Begin this route at an arête to the left of a large, square-cut chimney. Work up and left around a flake, then up the arête to the left of a dihedral.

12. The 37th Cog in Melvin's Wheel 8

FA: Bob Bradley and Paul Mayrose, 1969.
Climb the large, square-cut corner in the west side of The Bookmark. Exit around the left side of a chockstone. Downclimb or finish with a route on the upper buttress.

13. Dead in Bed 10c

FA: Kimball, Harrison, and Hladick, 1984.
Begin just right of the chimney described in the preceding two routes.
1. Climb the buttress via a series of flakes. Make a committing move to a jug (8), then go up and left to belay in a diagonal crack.
2. Work out to the bolt on *Fantasy Ridge,* then go up and right (9) to a belay on a large ledge covered with boulders.
3. Start up *Between the Sheets* (10b), but follow a crack out left and around into a dihedral (10b). Jam a fist crack for 15 feet to where it joins *Sidewinder* (9) and continue to the summit.

14. Sidewinder 9+

FA: (?) Chip Salaun and Carl Harrison, 1979.
Begin as for *Joy and Tribulation* but continue up the wide crack along the west side.
1. Jam away and belay above a bulge after 120 feet (7).
2. Continue up the crack until it is possible to exit via a crack on the right that leads one to a big ledge (8).
3. Climb the third pitch of *Joy and Tribulation* up to the offwidth section, then hand traverse right (9+) to a fist crack and belay at its top (9).
4. A hand crack leads to the top of the spur (6).

15. Joy and Tribulation 9 ★

FA: Paul Mayrose and Danny O'Herrick (II 5.7 A3), 1970. FFA: unknown.
This description is not of the original line but of a popular combination.
The original route apparently finished in the *Alpinisten* chimney.
Hike around the southwest corner of The Bookmark and up to the base
of a long, wide crack.
1. Climb the crack (or face climb in from the left) to where it is possible
to crank around onto the southwest face (8). Stem up a left-facing cor-
ner/groove and belay at a tiny stance where the crack fades.
2. Climb the clean slab past an antique bolt, traverse right to an easy
groove, and belay on the big ledge at its top (9). Move the belay to the
bottom of a square-cut, left-leaning chimney in the west face.
3. Climb the chimney to the top of the spur (8). Scramble east across a
deep groove with a fin in the middle to reach the downclimb.

16. Between the Sheets 11d ★

FA: Bill Wylie and Malcolm Daly, 1981. Rack: double RPs to a #1.5 Friend.
A ferocious thin finger crack. Begin this route from the big ledge
halfway up the west buttress of The Bookmark. Set the belay near the
south end of the ledge.
1. Climb up onto a small pedestal, then work up and left into the crack
and follow it to a bolt belay (11d).
2. Hand traverse straight right to gain the arête (11a) and follow it past
a bolt to the summit area (9).

17. Fantasy Ridge 9 ★

FA: Michael Covington and partner, 1974. FFA: Harry Kent and Keith
Lober, 1976.
Classic. This route is best begun with the first two pitches of *Joy and
Tribulation* (9) but set the second belay at a stance below the big ledge.
One also may climb the next crack system around to the right, which is
apparently the original line (5).
3a. Climb up and right and gain a wide crack in a dihedral. Jam up the
crack and pull right to a ledge beneath a roof (8+). Pass the roof on the
right and follow a crack to its end (9), move up and left to a thin crack,
and follow this until it is possible to traverse right to a belay ledge (9).
3b. Climb out the left side of the roof and jam a thin crack (9) to join 3a.
4. Climb the crack directly above the belay to the top of the spur (9,
tricky at first).
Traverse east across a deep groove with a fin in its middle to reach the
summit and descent.

18. Melvin's Wheel 8+ ★

FA: Bob Bradley and Paul Mayrose (II 5.8 A2), 1965. FFA: unknown.
A classic hand crack. This route originally was called *The 37th Cog in
Melvin's Wheel* but the name was assigned to a different route "by some
guidebook writer," according to Bob Bradley.
Begin just left of The Flatiron at the bottom of the face and scramble up
to a tree to belay.
1. Climb a left-facing dihedral (7), double cracks (8), pass a roof, and
belay on Library Ledge. One also may climb the next crack to the right
(8) as an alternate first pitch.

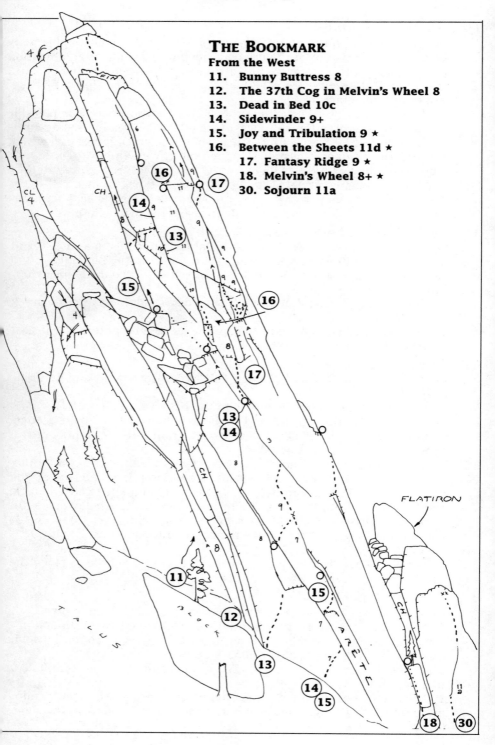

THE BOOKMARK
From the West
11. Bunny Buttress 8
12. The 37th Cog in Melvin's Wheel 8
13. Dead in Bed 10c
14. Sidewinder 9+
15. Joy and Tribulation 9 ★
16. Between the Sheets 11d ★
17. Fantasy Ridge 9 ★
18. Melvin's Wheel 8+ ★
30. Sojourn 11a

THE BOOKMARK

From the South

15. Joy and Tribulation 9 ★
16. Between the Sheets 11d ★
17. Fantasy Ridge 9 ★
18. Melvin's Wheel 8+ ★
19. Stray Shots 10
20. Twiggy Crack 9
21. Skid You Not 11b s/vs
25. Peter's Gate 9+ vs
26. Romulan Territory 10b ★
31. Rusty's Pillar 8 A2

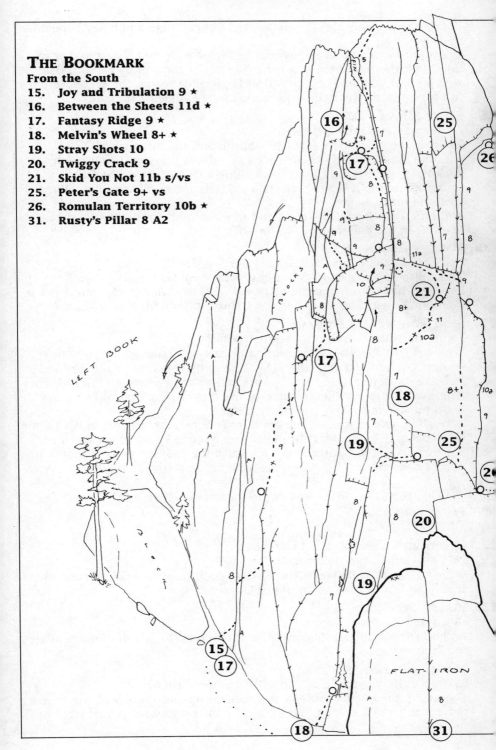

2. Jam the obvious hand crack above Library Ledge and belay beneath a roof (8+).

3. Work up a narrow chimney that becomes wide and flared higher up (8). Climb the right side of a fin at the top of the chimney and finish with a short wall on the right (4). It is possible to run the second pitch a full rope-length and belay where the chimney begins to open.

19. Stray Shots   10
FA: Hansen and Kimball, 1984.
Begin in the notch between The Flatiron and the main wall.
1. Climb the crack right of *Melvin's Wheel* to the belay on Library Ledge (8).
2. Cross to a crack on the left and climb a right-facing dihedral to a roof. Undercling left and turn the roof (crux), then climb a crystalline section (9) to a belay.
3. Climb a crack past the right end of a roof and continue straight up just left of the chimney of *Melvin's Wheel*.

20. Twiggy Crack   9
FA: Scott Kimball and Gary Sapp, 1983.
This route begins a short way right from *Stray Shots* in the notch between the Flatiron and the main wall. Climb a thin crack until it fades, then move right into an easier crack and continue to Library Ledge.

21. Skid You Not   11b s/vs
FA: Aaron Walters and Billy Westbay, 1981.
This difficult route ascends the "bolt-protected" slab to the right of the second pitch of *Melvin's Wheel* (11b). Note that the first 60 feet of the slab are unprotected (9). Most parties climb the second pitch of *Melvin's Wheel* until it is obvious to traverse out right to the first of two bolts.
1. Climb *Melvin's Wheel* to Library Ledge.
2. Work up and right past the bolts (crux above the second) and straight up to belay in a small left-facing corner about 15 feet below a roof.
3. Move up and left with no pro and turn the roof left of center at a difficult finger crack (11a). Continue straight up to the summit.

The following routes begin around on the right side of the south face, to the right of The Flatiron.

22. Coleman's Complex   11b/c s
FA: Keith Lober and Coleman Miller, 1977.
Begin in the gully between The Flatiron and the main wall. Ascend the seam just left of *Inside Straight* to Library Ledge.

23. Inside Straight   9
SR up to a # 4 Friend.
Ascend the left-facing flake, roof, and crack to the left of *Marginal Line* to Library Ledge.

24. Marginal Line   9+
FA: Bob Culp, Wayne Goss, and Cliff Jennings, 1966.
The first pitch of this route is an excellent opener for any of the routes that begin from Library Ledge. Begin up on a sandy ledge just right of

The Flatiron. Climb a difficult flared crack in the main wall (9+ to get started), then follow a right-facing flake up and left to Library Ledge. The original line continued with the crack system of *Melvin's Wheel*.

25. Peter's Gate   9+ vs
FA: Ian Wade and Leonard Sanders, 1970.
A bold venture.
1. Reach Library Ledge via the first pitch of *Marginal Line* (9+).
2. Climb the smooth face to the left of *Romulan Territory;* the crux is a mantle onto a knob about 80 feet out (8, no pro). Traverse right to the crack of *Romulan Territory* and belay as for that route.
3. Start up the corner but move left at the roof band and ascend either of two flared cracks (7).

26. Romulan Territory   10b ★
FA: Scott Kimball and Bill Wylie, 1978.
Even in our own world, sometimes we are aliens.
1. Climb the first pitch of *Marginal Line* to Library Ledge (9+).
2. Ascend the narrow, right-facing dihedral between *Peter's Gate* and *Star Trek*. The crux of the route is in passing a bulge at a right-leaning section of the dihedral.
3. Make difficult moves to get started, then ascend a large right-facing dihedral (8 to 9 with marginal pro) and follow it as it curves right to form a roof. Belay at the right edge of the face. It is possible to climb straight up through the roof where the dihedral bends right (10a).
4. An easy pitch (4) leads to the summit, or one can scramble into the gully and go north to the downclimb.

27. Star Trek   9 ★
FA: George Hurley and Dave Rearick, 1975.
"Boldly go where no man has gone before."
Begin just right of *Marginal Line.*
1. Ascend a brushy slot, then move left and jam nice cracks to Library Ledge (7), or begin with *Marginal Line* (9+).
2. Work up a beautiful slab just left of a right-facing dihedral (6 s), up flakes and seams (9), and right to belay.
3. Climb a flared crack (9) and finish with the last few moves of *Romulan Territory.*

28. Backflip   9 ★
FA: Steve Shea and Dick Jimmerson, 1969; of variation to second pitch, Beth Bennett and Eric Ming, 1979.
This route bears almost no resemblance to the *Backflip* (II 5.7 A2) described in Walter Fricke's original guide to the area but it is a good climb. Begin just left of the gully between The Bookmark and The Bookmark Pinnacle.
1. Jam and lieback up a right-facing flake (8+), move left, and continue to Library Ledge.
2. Follow a right-facing dihedral to a roof, then go straight right to belay at broken flakes (8+), or climb through the roof and merge with *Star Trek* (9+).

THE BOOKMARK

From the Southeast

18. Melvin's Wheel 8+ ★
20. Twiggy Crack 9
21. Skid You Not 11b s/vs
22. Coleman's Complex 11b/c s
23. Inside Straight 9
24. Marginal Line 9+
25. Peter's Gate 9+ vs
26. Romulan Territory 10b ★
27. Star Trek 9 ★
28. Backflip 9 ★
29. Pinnacle Watch 9+

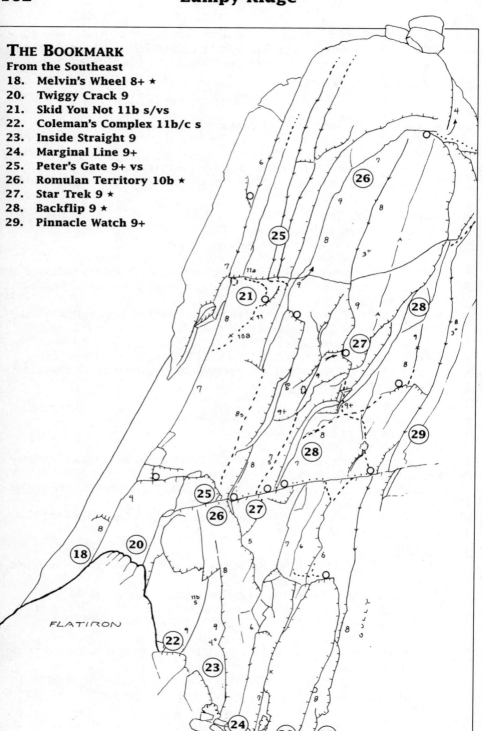

FLATIRON

3. Climb up into a crack with a piton, then up and right to easy ground (9); or step right into a wide flared crack (Pinnacle Watch) and jam up to the same exit (8).

29. Pinnacle Watch   9+
This route takes the farthest right crack system on the south face of The Bookmark. Its description differs in the two editions of the earlier Lumpy Ridge guide. Three versions are shown in the topo – take your pick.

The Flatiron. The following three routes ascend The Flatiron, which is at the bottom of the main south face, just above the top of the Bookmark Trail.

30. Sojourn   11a
FA: Steve Muehlhauser and Sara Spalding, 1983.
This route tackles an incipient crack on the west side of the Flatiron. Unprotected face moves lead into the crack.

31. Rusty's Pillar   8 A2
FA: George Hurley and a client named Rusty, c. 1975.
This route climbs the flared groove in the middle of the south face, just above where the Bookmark Trail tops out. Begin at two small pillars beneath the groove.

32. Rip Stop   9
FA: Kimball and Sapp, 1983.
This route ascends a short red dihedral and the arête at the northeast corner of The Flatiron. Begin across from *Coleman's Complex.*

BOOKMARK PINNACLE
This is the small, isolated pinnacle at the right of The Bookmark.

Approach via The Bookmark and traverse a short way east along its base to reach the pinnacle. It also is easily approached by hiking west along the base of the Right Book. To descend from the summit, make a 75-foot free rappel into the gully on the northeast, then downclimb (0).

33. Northwest Flakes   8
Begin in the notch behind the summit fin and climb the northwest edge of the pinnacle.

34. Voie Ancien   6
The following is a direct quote from Walter Fricke's old guidebook:
"From the left (west) gully climb up along a string of old pitons (5.6), traverse right across the valley face, and belay from a terrace. From the top of the terrace, traverse up and left and continue up to the top (5.2)."

35. Penis Chimney   9 ★
Locate a deep chimney formed by a collapsed pillar on the west side of the pinnacle. Rack up to five inches (Is that all?). FA: Harry Kent and Scott Kimball, 1976.
1a. Climb the chimney, cream out through the top as it narrows to offwidth, come straight up (9), or take an easier option to the right, and belay on a broad ledge.

1b. (*French Tickler* 8+) Above the neck of the chimney, work left and climb an exposed hand crack.

2. Walk left on the ledge, jam a short steep crack on the west side of the summit fin (8), then continue up the south edge of the fin.

36. Plan A   11a
FA: George Hurley and Chris Reveley, 1976.
Begin at the left side of the south face.
1. Work up shallow cracks (10c) followed by a reddish, right-leaning, very difficult crack. Belay on a large ledge.
2. Jam the left of the two cracks that pass through a bulge (10a). Continue up the south edge of the summit fin.

37. Manhole Cover   8
The middle of the south face is split by a deep slot.
1. Climb the left-facing inside corner at the back of the slot, squeeze past a wedged block, and belay on a broad ledge or terrace below the bulging summit formation.
2. Climb the right of two cracks in e summit block (8+), then up the south edge of the fin to the top.

38. Fall Out   9
FA: Hurley and Reveley, 1976.
Work in from the left (9) or climb straight up (10d) and jam up the crack in the right wall of the chimney that splits the lower south face (8).

39. Crack of No Return   11b
FA: George Hurley and Dave Rearick, c. 1975.
Rack up to a #4 Friend.
Locate a fist crack with no apparent entry in the right side of the south face. Climb in from the right with considerable difficulty. Escape from the top of the crack by descending a chimney to the right.

40. Son of a Pitch   10c
FA: Hurley and Rearick, c. 1975.
Rack up to #4 Friend.
Climb a groove with a bolt halfway up. The climbing is fairly sustained with the crux above the bolt. Climb off to the east.

41. East Side   8+ ★
Climb a right-facing dihedral system along the southeast side of the pinnacle to the broad ledge beneath the summit block and belay (7). Climb through a bulge via the right of two cracks (8+), then up the south edge of the fin to the top (7).

BOOKMARK PINNACLE AND BOOK BINDING AREA
on opposite page)

42. Cave Route 7
FA: Bill Forrest and Don Briggs, 1966.
Scramble up along the right (east) side of the pinnacle for a couple of hundred feet to a sandy-bottomed cave.
1. Follow a clean crack to the upper terrace on the east side of the summit fin (7).
2. Ascend the exposed south rib of the fin to the summit (7).

Book Binding. Between the Left Book and Right Book are two long narrow buttresses: the Left Buttress and the Isis Buttress. These are defined by three deep chimneys: the Left Chimney, the Requiem Chimney, and The Book of the Dead Chimney. No routes are recorded on the Left Buttress.

43. Left Chimney 6
Old pitons in the left of the three large chimneys suggest a very early route, likely dating back to the 1950s. Scramble in from the Requiem Chimney to get started. Three easy leads.

44. Requiem 9
FA: Layton Kor and Bob Culp, 1967.
This route ascends the steep chimney at the left of the Isis Buttress.
1. Jam cracks in the back of the chimney (7).
2. Continue in the same mode and pass a roof near the top (9).

SIS BUTTRESS
The following routes ascend the Isis Buttress, the formidable rib that stands between the Requiem Chimney and The Book of the Dead Chimney. The first four routes are on the west-facing wall of the buttress, that is, the right wall of the Requiem Chimney. More routes are likely to be established on either side of the chimney in the future.

45. Renaissance Wall 12c ★
FA: Randy Ferris and Mike Caldwell, 1992. Rack: Eight QDs.
This is a long, sustained, bolt-protected face climb on the sheer right wall of the chasm. Begin about 400 feet up in the chimney beneath a crack that curves up to the left (*Trials of Copernicus*). Three pitches.

46. Trials of Copernicus 11a
FA: Randy Ferris and Mike Caldwell, 1992.
SR to a #4 Friend.
Begin as for *Renaissance Wall*. Climb up past two bolts to gain a crack that curves up to the left. Join *Renaissance Wall* or rappel.

47. Steppenwolf 9
FA: Carl Harrison and Dennis Laird, 1979.
Hike up along the west wall of the buttress for about 100 feet to a large chockstone and a tree.
1. Follow flakes up and right and gain a crack system to the left of two trees on the ridge crest (8).
2. Do a long easy pitch up and right to the base of an orange fin of rock.
3. Jam the offwidth crack that splits the fin (9).
4. Scramble to the summit of the Isis Buttress.

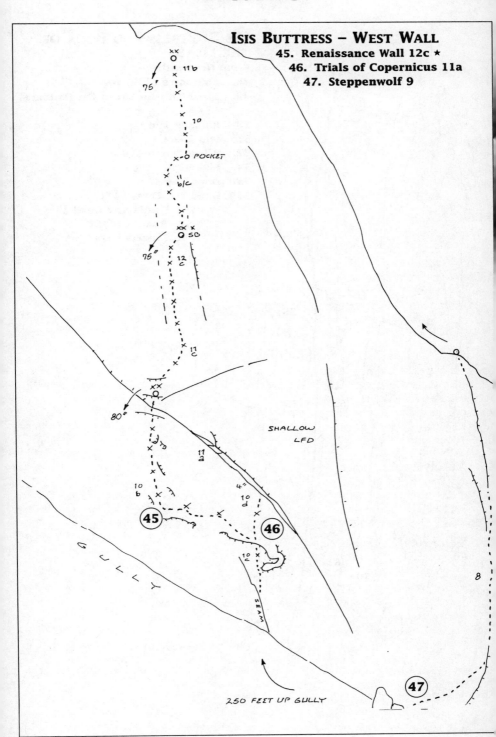

ISIS BUTTRESS – WEST WALL
45. Renaissance Wall 12c ★
46. Trials of Copernicus 11a
47. Steppenwolf 9

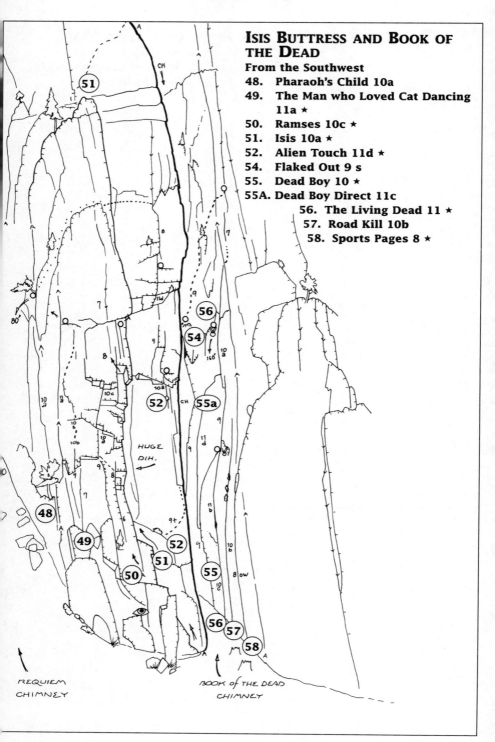

Isis Buttress and Book of the Dead

From the Southwest

48. Pharaoh's Child 10a
49. The Man who Loved Cat Dancing 11a ★
50. Ramses 10c ★
51. Isis 10a ★
52. Alien Touch 11d ★
54. Flaked Out 9 s
55. Dead Boy 10 ★
55A. Dead Boy Direct 11c
56. The Living Dead 11 ★
57. Road Kill 10b
58. Sports Pages 8 ★

REQUIEM CHIMNEY

BOOK OF THE DEAD CHIMNEY

HUGE DIH.

48. Pharaoh's Child   10a
FA: Scott Kimball and Chip Salaun, 1979.
Begin around on the west side of the buttress, on a ledge with a tree.
Climb the obvious, left-angling crack via a lieback (crux) to hand jams
(9), and rappel from a tree with slings.

49. The Man who Loved Cat Dancing   11a ★
FA: Kimball and Salaun, 1979.
Begin just right of the southwest corner of the buttress. Climb up
through a roof (9) and some small overlaps, lieback a left-facing corner
(crux), then go around to a crack on the west wall and rappel from the
tree on *Pharaoh's Child.*

50. Ramses   10c ★
FA: Doug Snively and Billy Westbay, 1978.
Begin as for **Isis.**
1. Work up and left into a smaller dihedral. Zigzag up through a series
of cleanly-cut, stepped roofs and belay at a small ledge above the last
roof.
2. Continue up over easier terrain, then go left and down to the top of
Pharaoh's Child to rappel.

51. Isis   10a ★
FA: Steve Hickman, Paul Anderson, and John Bryant, 1969. FFA:
unknown; hand crack finish, Carl Harrison and Scott Kimball, 1979.
The south face of the Isis Buttress is offset by a large, right-facing dihedral.
1. Angle up and left across the slab that forms the right wall of the
dihedral (7) and continue up for nearly 100 feet. Now, move out right,
jam over a roof (8), and belay.
2. Climb through the strenuous second roof to where the angle eases
and jam a short hand crack in the left wall (10a). Traverse left and rappel via *Pharaoh's Child.* The original route continues to the top of the
buttress via easier terrain.

51A. Brutus   11>
FA: Hidetaka and M. Suzuki, 1984.
This variation exits the main dihedral after 100 feet via a left-angling
overlap in the left wall.

52. Alien Touch   11d ★
FA: Dan McClure and Billy Westbay, 1981.
This fierce route ascends the far right side of the south face of the buttress.
1. Work right across a slab to reach the southeast arête (9+). Ascend the
airy arête, changing sides as needed, and power up an overhanging
flake (10a) to a good belay.
2. Work up to a large roof that is passed via an extremely difficult,
flared finger crack (crux). Belay at a good ledge above the roof.
3. Climb a bit higher in the same crack system until it is easy to traverse left to the top of *Pharaoh's Child.*

53. Book of the Dead 9
> FA: Mike Stults and Dick Erb, 1967.
>
> Ascend the very steep chimney in the back of the chasm at the right side of the Isis Buttress and finish as for *Isis*.

RIGHT BOOK

The Right Book is the large, clean buttress that forms the east side of The Book massif. Viewed from a distance, it has a vague pear shape for which one of its most popular routes seems to have been named. This is not to be confused with The Pear, an independent feature one-half mile to the west.

Approach. Hike the Black Canyon Trail for about a mile to a junction near the national park boundary. Take the right branch and follow the signs for The Book.

Descent. From the summit, scramble down ramps and grooves to the east and gain the terrace above the Cave Exit. From the terrace (where many routes finish), downclimb eastward to a ledge with a big pine tree. Do not cross the ledge, but continue down a steep gully to another ledge (class 4). The descent continues in this fashion, staying near the Right Book, for several hundred feet. If you need to rappel, you've gone the wrong way. Another option (if gear is not left at the base of the wall) is to scramble north over the grooved summit to a sandy saddle and follow the Skyline Trail eastward to the Twin Owls parking area, or westward to the gully between the Bookend and the Left Book.

Book of the Dead Chimney. The following routes ascend the right wall of the narrow chimney between the Isis Buttress and the Right Book.

54. Flaked Out 9 s
> FA: Tim Hansen, Joe Hladick, and Robin Bell, 1981.
>
> Go deep into the chasm to the base of a crack that begins with some right-facing flakes and has two bushes about 150 feet up.
>
> 1. Climb the crack to a point about six feet above the first bush, then hand traverse right and belay on a flake (9).
>
> 2. Climb dubious flakes up and right to a small tree (8+ s) and onward to the arête. Continue with *Sports Pages*.

RIGHT BOOK, SOUTH FACE (on opposite page)

55. Dead Boy   10 ★
FA: Bill Wylie, Tim Hansen, and Scott Kimball, 1982. SR to a #2 Friend with extra stoppers.
Down and right from *Flaked Out* is a stepped, left-facing corner with a good crack.
Ascend the crack/dihedral for about 90 feet (9), then make a difficult traverse right to join *The Living Dead* (10).

55A. Dead Boy Direct   11c
FA: Malcolm Daly and Keith Schoephlin, 1983.
One also may continue straight up the crack/seam and join *Living Dead* in the midst of the second pitch.

56. Living Dead   11 ★×
FA: Scott Kimball and Randy Joseph, 1981. SR to a #2 Friend with extra stoppers.
This beautiful line takes the continuous crack about ten feet right of *Dead Boy*.
1. Climb through a bulge (10d), followed by a sustained thin section (crux), and belay at a flake.
2. Follow the crack up and left to belay on another small flake (10a).
3. Work up and right to join *Sports Pages*.

57. Road Kill   10b
FA: Tim Hansen and Joe Hladick, 1981.
This is the obvious finger crack immediately left of *Sports Pages*.

The Pages. *The following four routes ascend the deep cracks and grooves in the west side of the south face (The Pages). About 130 feet from the top, is a long sloping shelf called Fang Ledge, named for a spike of rock near its left end.*

58. Sports Pages   8 ★
FA: (?) Chip Salaun and Bill Alexander, 1979. SR plus a five-inch piece.
This long sweeping climb begins with a wide crack (up to eight inches) in the right wall of the Book of the Dead Chimney about 20 feet up from the low point.
1. Ascend the wide crack to a good ledge on the right side of the arête (8).
2. Climb grooves and flakes along the right side of the arête (8) and belay at a narrow stance after 100 feet.
3. Continue up a groove (6) and belay at the left side of The Fang.
4. Finish with a steep groove just right of the arête (6).

59. Wallet Eater   9 ★
FA: Paul Mayrose, 1970.
Begin in the last chimney left of *Osiris* on the south face.
1. Ascend the chimney and a right-facing corner (8) to a ledge shared with *Sports Pages*.
2. Jam a steep crack (7) up to the tree belay on *Osiris*.
3. Climb the long crack between *Osiris* and *George's Tree* to Fang Ledge (9).
4. Finish with either of these routes.

60. Osiris   7 ★
FA: Dave Johnson and Pete Robinson, 1964.
A very popular, moderate route.
Begin about 30 feet left of *George's Tree.*
1. Ascend a chimney in a left-facing dihedral to a good ledge (6, 130 feet).
2. Climb easy cracks to a ledge with a small tree (5).
3. Ascend cracks and flakes just right of a long, right-facing dihedral, then follow parallel cracks through a bulge (7). Move left, and belay beside a spike of rock (The Fang) on Fang Ledge.
4. Jam the slot behind The Fang and gain the summit of The Book (7).

61. George's Tree   9 or 10c ★
FA: George Hurley and Steve Pomerance (III 5.7 A2), 1967. FFA: unknown. SR to a #4 Friend.
Classic. Begin at a flared crack with a small pine tree 50 feet left of *Tombstone.*
1. Jam the crack (without stepping on the tree!) and move left to belay as for *Osiris* (9, 130 feet) – or rappel from bolts after about 70 feet.
2a. A short, easy pitch leads to the belay tree on *Osiris.*
2b. Jam a right-leaning crack past a bulge (crux), then work up and left to a belay stance (10c, 60 feet).
3. Climb straight up the last continuous crack on the right (8) and belay on Fang Ledge (8, 140 feet).
4. Jam a crack just left of the recess called The Box to a horizontal break (optional belay), then climb a left-facing dihedral to the top of the buttress (9, 150 feet). One also may finish with The Box (see Exit Pitches).

62. Bob's Climb   8+ s
FA: Bernard and Robert Gillett, 1987.
Begin about 50 feet right of *George's Tree.* Follow a ramp/crack up and left to *George's Tree,* up ten feet, then up and left into a wide crack just right of *Osiris.*

Fat City Area. The following routes ascend the smooth wall and arching roof in the middle of the south face. The right side of the wall is bounded by a large left-facing dihedral.

63. Frisky Puppies   12b ★
FA: Topher Donahue and Kennen Harvey, 1989.
A slab classic.
Follow ten bolts along a dike up the super-clean face about 50 feet up and right from *George's Tree.* This is a continuously difficult route with the crux at the fourth bolt. After the sixth bolt, move right and clip slings on a horn, then go back left into the line. Four more bolts lead up the dike to a roof that is protected with stoppers. Belay from slings around another horn and rappel 50 meters to the ground.

64. The 44   10b ★
FA: Paul Mayrose and Hans Leitinger, 1965.
This was the original line up the face (III 5.7 A4), joined later by *Fat City Crack*. Begin about 60 feet up to the right from *George's Tree* at a flared slot.
1. Jam up the slot (7) and move up left to belay.
2. Climb a flared chimney (7) and right-facing corner (8) up to a bombay slot, move right and turn the roof (10b). Belay just above.
3. Continue as for *Fat City Crack*.

65. New Music   11d s ★
FA: Jeff Lowe and Malcolm Daly, 1987.
A bold and original slab route. Begin just left of *Fat City*.
1. Angle up and left along discontinuous cracks and a groove, past two bolts, and belay at a stance with two bolts (11b).
2. Move up and left to *The 44* (11a), then climb down and left and turn a roof. Work straight up past a bolt to a faint groove (crux) that is followed up and left to a belay in a flared crack.
3. Angle up and right past a bolt and gain a sloping ledge that is shared with *High Plains Drifter* (optional belay). Climb a left-facing corner from the right side of the ledge and continue up a blank slab (9 s) to Fang Ledge (10b s, 170 feet).
4. Finish with *Willie's Way* (11a). See *Exit Pitches* below.

66. Fat City Crack   10b ★
FA: Bill Forrest and Ray Jardine (III 5.7 A1), 1970. FFA: unknown.
Classic. Begin on the ledge behind The Tombstone near a large, left-facing dihedral.
1. Jam a left-leaning hand crack up the middle of the slab and belay at a fixed anchor (8, 120 feet).
2. Continue up the crack (9+ fingers), traverse left, and squeeze up to the top of a bomb bay slot (8+). Move right and jam through the roof to a stance on the slab above (10b, 60 feet).
3. Follow a right-leaning crack and corner up to The Cave (9, 150 feet).
4. Chose an *Exit Pitch* (see below).

Right Book, The Pages and Fat City Area

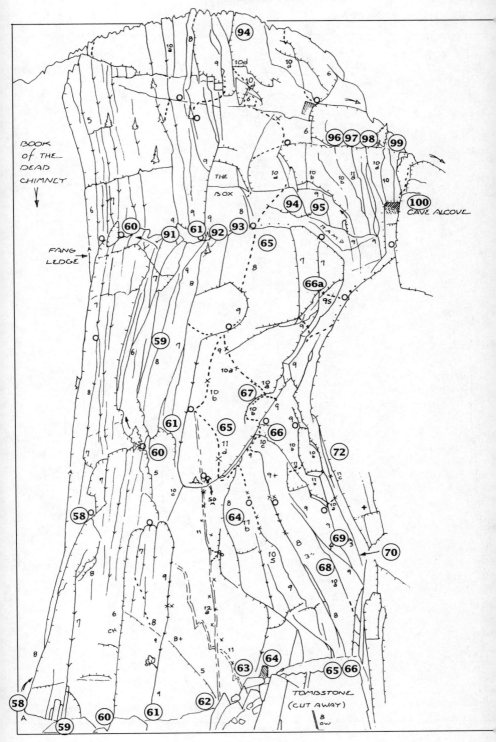

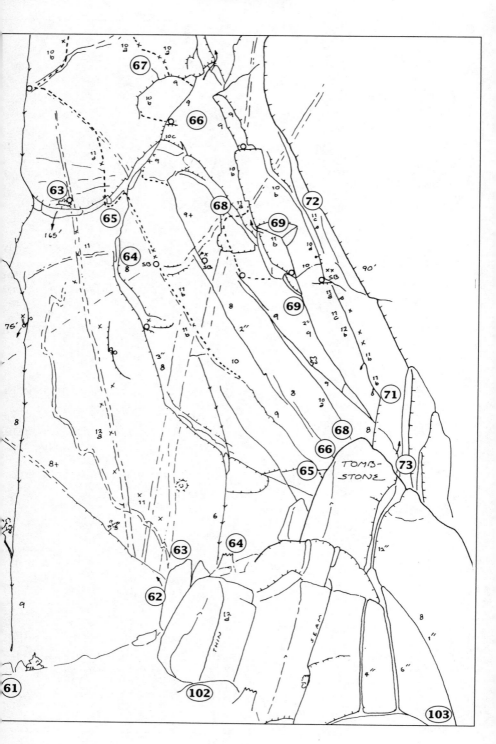

66ᴀ.Fat City Variation
FA: The Gilletts, 1987.
Before reaching The Cave area on the third pitch, ascend either of two right-facing dihedrals (9) on the left to reach Fang Ledge. The right dihedral is at first difficult to protect.

67. High Plains Drifter   10b ★
FA: Mike Caldwell and Randy Ferris, 1986.
This excellent slab route branches left from the third pitch of *Fat City Crack* (see topo). Unfortunately, one of the bolts pulled out while being unclipped and the remaining three are of the same quality. Note: It is possible to avoid the initial, dicey dihedral by continuing farther up *Fat City* and moving straight left through the roof.

68. Perelandra   11a ★
FFA: Larry Bruce and Dan McClure, 1975. SR to a #2.5 Friend.
No science fiction here – more of a reality check!
1. Climb the crack between the *Howling* dihedral and *Fat City* and belay at a stance as the crack fades (10a, 120 feet).
2. Work up around the left side of a flake and place pro overhead in the left-leaning dihedral. Crank right around the corner and make a harrowing traverse right into the upper dihedral of *Howling at the Wind,* then climb to a stance in the corner (11a, 75 feet).
3. Climb either of two small dihedrals above, then follow *Fat City* to The Cave area (9, 150 feet).
4. Choose an exit pitch such as *Cheap Date* or *Willie's Way.*

69. Howling at the Wind   11b ★
FA: Alec Sharp and John Cleaver, 1979. SR to a #4 Friend, or begin with *Perelandra* and skip the #3.5 and 4 Friends.
A route as wild as its name. Begin up behind The Tombstone pinnacle.
1. Lieback a massive left-facing dihedral to a stance on a wedged block (9).
2. Continue up the dihedral to a triangular roof. Crank left around the roof (crux) and continue up the corner (10b) to a belay stance.
3. Ascend the right of two small corners (9) and merge with the third pitch of *Fat City Crack.*

70. Fair Weather Friends   9 A3
FA: Bob Bradley and Aaron Walters, 1980.
This three-pitch route ascends the overhanging right wall of the huge dihedral behind The Tombstone. It begins and ends with *Howling at the*

Rɪɢʜᴛ Bᴏᴏᴋ, Fᴀᴛ Cɪᴛʏ Aʀᴇᴀ

Wind and was the last aid climb completed on The Book. The entire route has been climbed free, and with the addition of several bolts, the first pitch is no longer A3.

1. El Camino Real   12d ★
FFA: Bernard Gillett, 1992. Bring many stoppers up to a #2 Friend and nine or ten QDs.
This route free climbs the first pitch of *Fair Weather Friends.* Begin up behind The Tombstone at the base of a massive left-facing, left-leaning dihedral.
1. Begin with *Howling at the Wind,* but break right after about 20 feet. Ascend the thin crack in the right wall of the big dihedral past several bolts and belay on a small ledge with cold shuts about ten feet before reaching the traverse on *Corner Pump Station.* The crux is about halfway up the crack.
2. Continue with *Corner Pump Station* or rappel 90 feet to the ground.

2. Corner Pump Station   11c ★
FFA: Mike Caldwell and Charlie Gray, 1988. Bring stoppers to a #2.5 Friend (Friends up to a #4 for *Howling*).
This route climbs free the second pitch of *Fair Weather Friends.*
1. Climb *El Camino Real* or the first pitch of *Howling at the Wind.*
2. From *Howling,* hand traverse right (10a) to an alcove with fixed nuts and a pin (or reach the same point directly from *El Camino*). Lieback duel, overhanging cracks past a fixed knifeblade (11b) and continue up a lieback/finger crack that arches out to the left (10b). After about 25 feet, the lieback turns into an undercling (11a). A short corner (9) leads to a belay stance at the base of two left-facing corners.
3. Follow either corner to The Cave (9 in either case).

3. Toot   10d ★
FA: Dan McClure and Molly Higgins, 1976. SR to a #2 Friend.
Ascend a difficult finger crack in the right-hand wall of the long dihedral that splits the south face. It is customary to begin from stacked rocks.

Short Subjects. *The next four one-pitch routes ascend the wall above and left of the leaning flake of Pear Buttress and finish along a ramp some 60 feet up. Rappel from a horn at the west end of the ramp.*

4. Stepped On   11c
FA: Steve Levin and John Harlin, 1980. RPs and stoppers.
Climb a pair of cracks just left of the arête.

5. Thinstone   9
FA: Duncan Ferguson and Doug Snively, 1979. RPs to a #2 Friend.
Climb the dihedral just right of the arête behind The Tombstone.

6. Stretch Marks   11a ★
FA: Scott Kimball and Bill Wylie, 1981. RPs to a #2 Friend.
Climb the right side of a minor arête.

7. Thindependence   10c ★
FA: Randy Joseph and Tim Hansen, 1981. RPs to a #1.5 Friend.
Ascend parallel thin cracks from the top of the leaning flake.

Pear Buttress Area. *The following routes ascend the smooth and beautiful wall between the big left-facing dihedral that splits the south face and the buttress of Endless Crack at right.*

78. Pear Buttress   8+ ★
FA: Layton Kor and partner, 1962. SR with an extra #2.5 and #3 Friend.
An excellent primer in jamology. This very popular route follows cracks up the far west side of the face. The protection is all quite good except for the beginning of the first pitch, which has ground-fall potential.
Begin about six feet right of a 60-foot flake that leans up against the wall.
1. Face climb up and left about 25 feet (7, no pro) , then stretch left into a perfect hand crack along the right edge of the flake – or lieback the flake from the bottom (9 s). From the top of the flake, jam parallel finger cracks (8+) and belay on a ramp beneath a pod.
2. Angle up to the left on the ramp, then up and right to belay on a good ledge (4).
3. Jam a beautiful hand crack (8), go right at a roof, and up to another good belay ledge. Or climb the long dihedral on the right (8).
4. An easy pitch leads up to The Cave area.
5. Choose an exit (see *Exit Pitches* below).

79. Loose Ends   9 ★
SR to a #3.5 Friend.
Classic crack climbing on perfect rock.
This line begins with the shallow, left-facing flake a few feet to the right of Pear Buttress.
1. Climb the left edge of the flake (9), then angle up and left to the belay on Pear Buttress (8).
2. Ascend the left of two long finger cracks to a ledge atop a flake (9).
3. Climb a left-facing, left-leaning dihedral (9) to a big ledge at its top.
4. Scramble up to The Cave area and choose a final pitch.

80. Visual Aids   10a ★
SR to a #3.5 Friend. A classic crack.
1. Climb the first pitch of *Loose Ends* (9) or *Pear Buttress* (8+) and belay at the pod.
2. Step left and jam the right of two thin cracks to a belay on a flake (10a, 100 feet).
3. Climb up to a left-facing dihedral, then pull up and right around a bulge (8). Jam a wide crack to a ledge on the right (7), then work easily up and left to The Cave area and choose an exit pitch.

81. J Crack   9 or 11c ★
FA: Steve Hickman and John Bryant, 1964. FFA: of headwall, Dan McClure, Michael Covington, and Billy Westbay, c. 1975. SR to a #3 Friend with extra mid-range pieces.
This is *the* classic crack at Lumpy Ridge. Begin just right of the leaning flake of Pear Buttress or farther to the right as described.
1a. Climb easy cracks and corners up and right to a long, flat ledge (4).
1b. Climb up into a gigantic solution hole called The Cavity and reach the same ledge via a steep, left-facing dihedral (10a).

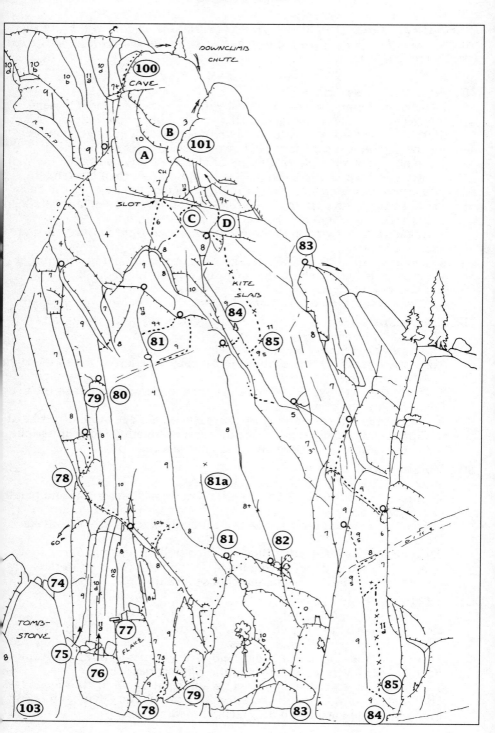

1c. Scramble up and left from the start to *Fender* (0).

2. Traverse left to reach the crack, then jam the peerless, flared finger-and-hand crack and belay in a pod (9, 150 feet).

3a. Climb the right-leaning finger crack through the headwall and belay on a ledge beneath an arched roof (11c, 50 feet).

3b. Traverse right at a horizontal break and climb up to the ledge (9+).

3c. Take a lower traverse right with better footholds and climb to the ledge (8+).

4a. Climb an easy groove up and left, then up and right to The Cave and choose a final pitch.

4b. Finish as for *Femp*.

81A. Loose J   10b ★

1. Climb *Loose Ends* to a point shy of *Pear Buttress* and belay at a narrow stance (9, 100 feet).

2. Climb up and right past a pin and a bolt (crux) and join the second pitch of *J Crack*.

82. Femp   9 ★

FA: Ren Fenton and Charlie Kemp, 1962.

SR plus a few extra mid-range pieces.

Classic. *Femp* takes the next continuous crack system right of *J Crack*.

1. Climb the first pitch of *J Crack* and belay on a flat ledge at the base of the main crack (4).

2. Jam the flared crack to its end, then step left into another crack (crux) and jam to a belay just left of Kite Slab (9, 155 feet).

3a. Move the belay up and left to the ledge on *J Crack*. Follow a crack through an arching roof (7), work up a slab, and finish with a steep, right-leaning chimney (7).

3b. Climb the dihedral that forms the right side of the arch (8) and exit right in a finger crack (8) – optional belay at a horn. Choose one of the *Roof Exits* (below).

82A. Hemp   10c

FA: Kimball and Hanson, 1980.

Legalize it! Climb the left-leaning, overhanging corner directly above the belay at the top of the second pitch, then work up and right and take one of the *Roof Exits*.

RIGHT BOOK, PEAR BUTTRESS AREA

74. Stepped On 11c	83. Fender 8
75. Thinstone 9	84. Endless Crack 9 ★
76. Stretch Marks 11a ★	85. Pizza Face 12a ★
77. Thindependence 10c ★	100. Cave Exits
78. Pear Buttress 8+ ★	101. Roof Exits
79. Loose Ends 9 ★	A. Manhood 10b
80. Visual Aids 10a ★	B. Chimney 7
81. J Crack 9 or 11c ★	C. Pod 11a
82. Femp 9 ★	D. Wind And A Prayer 9+ ★
82A. Hemp 10c	103. Tombstone 8

Endless Crack Buttress. *The following routes are located on a buttress at the eastern side of the south face. Kite Slab is a beautiful diamond-shaped slab up and left from the top of the buttress.*

83. Fender 8

FA: Tom Fender and Jack Turner, early 1960s.

This forgotten route ascends a deep groove along the left side of the Endless Crack Buttress and finishes with a beautiful crack pitch to the right of Kite Slab. Begin on a ledge about 60 feet up the gully.

1. Climb the groove past a steep section and belay near its top (7, 150 feet).

2. Jam a braided crack to a triangular roof, work up the left side of a hanging flake, and exit right at the top (8, 100 feet).

84. Endless Crack 9 ★

FA: George Hurley and Dave Rearick, c. 1975.

An ironic name. Identify a clean, flared finger crack that begins and ends in the midst of the slab along the left side of the buttress. Begin at the bottom of *Mission Impossible.*

1. Work up and left past a bolt to gain the crack, then jam to near its top. Work right past a bolt into a left-facing dihedral, then go up to belay at a block (9, 140 feet). One also may go straight up from the top of the crack (9 s) and hand traverse right along a horizontal crack to the same belay.

2. Traverse out left and jam a three-inch crack, then follow cracks up and left to a belay shared with *Femp* (7, 130 feet).

3. Crank right above a small evergreen and jam a thin crack up the left side of Kite Slab, then follow a crack up and right (8) and belay at a horn beneath a roof (9, 75 feet).

4. Climb up and right and pass the roof at a bombay slot with a wedged block, then move up and left to a chimney and follow it to the top of the wall (9+, 80 feet).

84A. F.I.N.E. Alternative 9 s ★

FA: Richard Rossiter and Greg "Cafe" Carelli, 1995

1. Climb the first pitch of *Endless Crack* to the top of the "endless crack," then continue straight up past a horizontal crack (good one-inch pro) and up the arête another 40 feet until it is possible to traverse left into a flared groove with a hand crack (9 s 130 feet).

2. Jam straight up the crack/groove (9) and continue with the second pitch of *Endless Crack* (9, 165 feet).

85. Pizza Face 12a ★

FA: Malcolm Daly and Jim Brink, c. 1985.

This is a face climb between *Mission Impossible* and *Endless Crack.*

1. Climb past five bolts just right of *Endless Crack* (12a, 140 feet).

2. Do the second pitch of *Endless Crack* to a stance at the left of Kite Slab (7, 130 feet).

3. Move out right to a bolt, then work up the steep slab past two more bolts and gain a stance at a horn beneath a roof (11a, 80 feet).

4a. Climb through the roof at an A-shaped slot with a wedged block, then work left and finish in a chimney (9+, 80 feet).

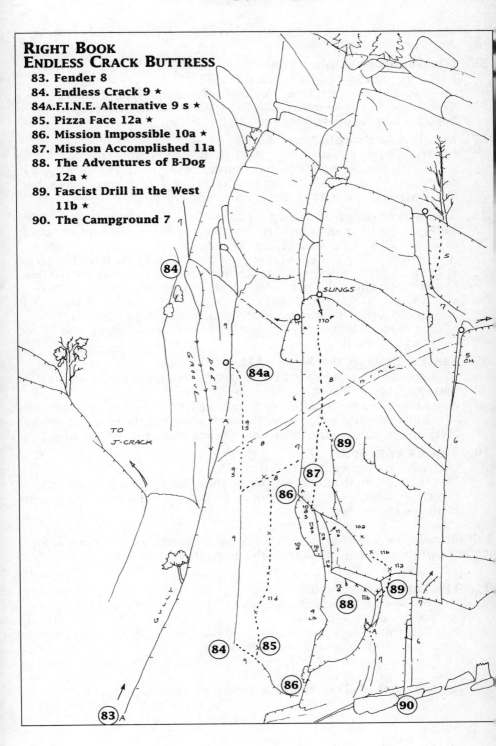

4b. Turn the roof at a pod, six feet left of the A-shaped roof (11a). See *Roof Exits* (below).

86. Mission Impossible   10a ★
FA: George Hurley and Dave Rearick, 1975.
This route ascends the long, clean dihedral to the right of *Endless Crack*. The crux is an undercling/lieback around a flake. Belay as for *Endless Crack*. Rappel or continue with that route.

87. Mission Accomplished   11a s
FA: Bernard and Robert Gillett, 1990. SR to a #2 Friend.
Begin with *Mission Impossible* but continue straight up the corner and over a small roof to join *Fascist Drill* at its last bolt. The pro sucks, but if you are into that sort of thing, it's a good climb.

88. The Adventures of B-Dog   12a ★
FA: Bernard Gillett and Chris Hill, 1990. Rack: RPs, double set of Rocks to a #6, #0.5 and 1.5 Friends, and lots of QDs.
A very demanding route. Begin as for *Fascist Drill in the West,* but go left at the roof. Make a desperate undercling past two pins and a fixed nut to a bomber jam in the left-facing corner at the end of the roof. Place a #5 Rock or a #0.5 Friend, lieback up the dihedral, then crank right to join *Fascist Drill.* One may avoid the crux undercling by climbing *Mission Impossible* and moving right into the dihedral where that route goes out to the left.

89. Fascist Drill in the West   11b ★
FA: Mike Caldwell and Randy Ferris, 1987. Rack up to a #2 Friend with four long runners for the initial clips.
Also known as *Fascist Bolts*, this is an excellent route. Climb up into the left-facing dihedral as for *B-Dog*, but crank right at the roof and follow bolts up the classic face. Belay on a sloping ledge with some slings.

90. The Campground   7
FA: (?) Robert and Bernard Gillett, 1987.
This is the farthest right route on the rock. Start with a pair of cracks just left of a large pine tree. Work up through a small roof and continue as shown in the topo.

Exit Pitches. *The following variations ascend the upper headwall and are listed from left to right, beginning from the west side of Fang Ledge.*

91. The Interceptor   10b
This follows a relatively clean crack system a few feet left of the last two pitches of *George's Tree.*
1. Follow the slightly left-leaning hand crack up the steep wall (10b) and belay at a break beneath the final headwall.
2a. Climb a finger and hand crack with an offwidth section near the top (10a).
2b. Ascend parallel cracks with a broken pillar between them.

92. The Box   9 ★

Climb a steep crack up the left side of the squarish inset called The Box (9) and belay beneath a buttress in the middle of the headwall. Move right and jam a crack through a stepped roof and follow it to the summit (9), or go straight up the corner as for *George's Tree* (8).

93. Midway   8 ★

Midway takes the right side of The Box, then goes up and right to the summit.
1. Climb cracks up and through a clean, left-facing dihedral (8), veer right across *Willie's Way* to a ledge at the far right side of the headwall and belay.
2. Climb up and left in a right-facing corner to the summit area, or once above The Box, move up and left and finish as for *George's Tree* (8).

94. Willie's Way   10d ★

FA: Bob Bradley and Paul Mayrose, c. 1962. FFA: unknown.
Begin beneath the more vertical left-facing dihedral just left of *Outlander.*
1. Ascend the strenuous, bulging dihedral to an easy slab (10d). The route seems to have gone originally right and up a right-facing corner to the top. A more challenging version goes left up the slab to belay at a bolt.
2. Work up and left to a small, cavernous overhang and make a difficult exit from either side of the roof (10d). Continue up and left through another cave/roof (10d) and follow a crack to the top.

95. Outlander   10d ★

Begin about 50 feet left of The Cave alcove.
1. Climb up into a left-arching dihedral (9), turn a roof at its high point, and ascend a finger crack to a sloping ledge (10b).
2. Climb an easy left-facing dihedral, hand traverse left to a hole, then jam a very strenuous crack to the top of The Book (10d).

96. Cheap Date   10b ★

SR plus extra #0.5 to 1.5 Friends.
Begin on the south-facing wall just left of The Cave alcove. Climb up to a stance at a bifurcation in the crack, then follow the left branch to join *Willie's Way* or the last pitch of *Outlander*...or scramble off to the east.

97. Final Chapter   11a ★

FA: (?) Randy Ferris and Mike Caldwell, 1986. SR to a #2 Friend.
Begin as for *Cheap Date,* but stay right. Face climb up the wall to the right of the seam (11a) or stem off *Cheap Date* (10d). Belay on a large, sloping ledge. Scramble off to the east or join *Outlander* or *Willie's Way.*

98. Mountaineers Indirect Cave   11a ★

FFA: Jeff Lowe and Paul Sibley, 1979; name via Mic Fairchild.
Climb up the wall just left of The Cave alcove and lieback over a flake, then move right to a crack with a bush and pin scars and continue up to a tree (crux).

99. Parable of The Cave 10b/c
FA: Kimball and Sapp, 1984.
Lieback up the thin, right-facing dihedral at the left margin of The Cave alcove. Above the roof, move right into a good hand crack.

100. Cave Exits.
These are the standard finishes for routes from *Fat City Crack* to *Femp.* Above the last pitch of *Pear Buttress,* ascend an easy groove up and right to a deep alcove and choose from the following options:

A. The Cave Exit 7+
Climb into The Cave and jam out through the right side of the roof.

B. The Hurley Traverse 7+
Climb up toward The Cave, then hand traverse out right and pull around to an easy arête.

C. Direct 9 ★
Climb a crack in the right wall of the alcove to the end of the hand traverse.

101. Roof Exits.
Down and right from The Cave, a roof cuts across the top of the wall and offers final pitches to such routes and *J Crack, Femp,* and *Endless Crack.* There are at least four ways to pass the roof:

A. Manhood 10b
Gain the chimney that cuts through the left end of the roof, but after about eight feet, break left and follow a left-facing corner to the top of *The Hurley Traverse.*

B. Chimney 7
Gain the chimney that cuts through the left side of the roof and follow it to the top of the wall.

C. Pod 11a
FA: Bernard and Robert Gillett, 1989.
About eight feet right of the chimney, climb through the roof at a pod, then move left into the chimney.

D. Wing and a Prayer 9+ ★
Directly above Kite Slab and six feet right of the pod, climb up into a bombay slot and crank past a wedged block, then work up and left into the chimney. This is the regular fourth pitch of *Endless Crack.*

The Tombstone. The following two routes are associated with a small pinnacle below the middle of the south face of the Right Book.

102. Wolfie and the Scientists 12d
FA: Hidetaka Suzuki, TR, 1986; led by Leonard Coyne. SR to a #2 Friend.
This is a 25-foot finger crack in a boulder just left of *Tombstone.*

103. Tombstone 8
This mini-route ascends an obvious left-arching wide crack up the south face of The Tombstone. The approach trail leads nearly to the start of the route.

Weekend Warrior   12d

FA: Randy Ferris, 1992.

Also known as the *Ten Meter Mile*. This is a single route located on a south-facing, 40-foot boulder about 200 yards east from the base of the Right Book. Climb an overhanging, flared, diagonal crack with four bolts and a chain anchor at the top.

Pee Wee's Big Adventure   11c/d

FA: Mike Caldwell and Dan Ludlam, 1986.

This short climb is located about 300 feet above the Black Canyon Trail a few hundred yards east of the old, more easterly cutoff to The Book. Climb a hand crack with a wide section through an oval-shaped roof.

The first pitch of Orange Julius, The Bookend.

The author on a solo ascent of Clowntime Is Over, Batman Rock.
Photo: Greg Carelli

BATMAN ROCK

Batman Rock is the striking skyline dome west-northwest of the Twin Owls parking area. It features many high-quality routes on solid granite with an abundance of handy knobs and rugosities.

Approach. Approach via the Batman Rock Trail.

Descent. To escape from the summit, scramble north into the forest slope, then back around to the east and south. Stay close to the edge of the face.

1. **Randy-O   9**
   FA: Randy Joseph, Bill Wylie and Scott Kimball, 1981.
   Begin a good way to the left of *Summer Breeze* and ascend a diagonal flake that leads to a right-facing dihedral with a bush.

2. **Summer Breeze   7**
   FA: Carl Harrison, 1979.
   Jam a crack directly above the notch between Batman Rock and Batman Pinnacle. Belay at a pine tree and continue in an easy crack.

3. **No Known Cure   8**
   FA: Kimball and Rusty George, 1984.
   Climb the dihedral immediately left of *Hand Jive*. After about 100 feet, angle left beneath an obvious break.

4. **Hand Jive   9 ★**
   FA: Mike Neri and friends, 1976.
   This is a sort of Bat classic.
   1. Jam up the large, right-facing dihedral at the left side of the south face (9). Belay above an overlap.
   2. Climb a steep, thin crack through the left wall of the dihedral, then go on to the summit (8).

5. **Old Route   9 s**
   FA: George Hurley and Charlie Fowler, 1971.
   This route climbs the face between *Station to Station* and *Hand Jive*. Begin about ten feet right of *Hand Jive* and aim for a crack.

6. **Station to Station   9 s ★**
   FA: Neri and Kimball, 1975.
   A Bat Classic.
   Begin about 40 feet left of the southeast corner of the rock and just right of a 20-foot Douglas fir tree.
   1a. Step off a pointed boulder and make a difficult mantle onto a right-angling dike (9 s). Work straight up into a shallow right-facing corner and climb to its top (8). Climb another 15 feet straight up (8+ s) and belay from cams under a flake (good stopper at left).
   1b. One also may begin the route from a flake to the left of the tree and make a nice hand traverse right into the shallow corner (5).
   2. Climb a short right-facing corner, then work left into the top of the *Hand Jive* dihedral. Climb a short, steep step (8), go right on a ramp, then straight up (5) to easy terrain.

BATMAN GROUP From the Southwest

LIGHTNING ROCK
1. Short Circuit 9 ★
2. Meltdown 11d s ★

BATMAN PINNACLE
3. Bat Flake 11a ★
4. Robin's Secret 10a
5. Batman and Robin 6 ★

BATMAN ROCK
3. No Known Cure 8
4. Hand Jive 9 ★

6. Station to Station 9 s ★
8. Backbone Arête 11c ★
9. Rockheads 9
10. Clowntime is Over 9+ ★

CHECKERBOARD ROCK
1. Ziggie's Day Out 10d ★
3. Checkerboard Crack 10a ★
4. Rainy Day Woman 9+ s
7. Fallen Shark 9
12. Icarus 10d ★

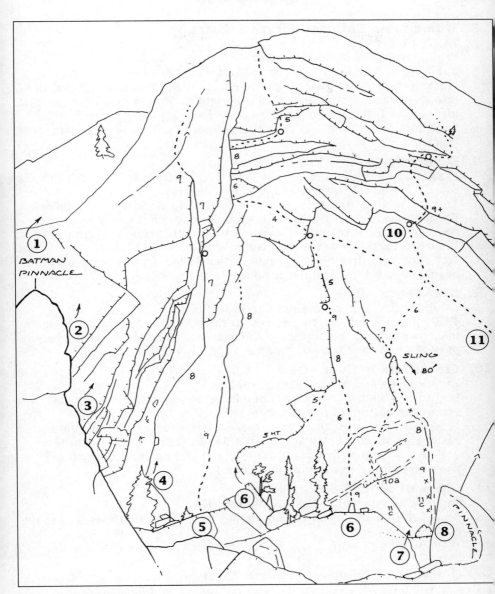

Batman Rock From the South

1. **Randy-O 9**
2. **Summer Breeze 7**
3. **No Known Cure 8**
4. **Hand Jive 9 ★**
5. **Old Route 9 s**
6. **Station to Station 9 s ★**
7. **Women and Children First 11b/c s**
8. **Backbone Arête 11c ★**
10. **Clowntime is Over 9+ ★**
11. **Globs of Blobs 8 ★**

7. Women and Children First   11b/c s
FA: Tim Hansen and Scott Kimball, 1983.
Begin just left of *Backbone Arête*.
1. Place pro from a shoulder stand and work up a steep, left-angling crack system (crux). Pass a knobby bulge (10a), then move up and right into a left-facing flake system (to the right of *Station to Station*). Belay after about 140 feet at a sloping stance from a good stopper.
2. Climb up and right and pass a large roof at a fixed wire (missing) (10a).

8. Backbone Arête   11c ★
FA: Richard Rossiter and Beverly Bien, 1992. QDs only for first pitch; SR to a #2 Friend to continue to the top of the crag.
This stimulating line ascends a white dike (The Backbone) just left of the southeast corner of the wall. A sandy ledge contours around the southeast side of the crag above an initial cliffy section. Begin where the ledge passes between the main face and a large pinnacle. Smear and face climb past five bolts and belay after 80 feet from a sling around a horn. Lower off or continue as shown in the topo.

9. Rockheads   9
FA: Richard Rossiter and Greg Carelli, 1990.
This route ascends flared grooves up the south-facing wall of the huge detached flake at the bottom of the east face and finishes at the beginning of *Clowntime is Over*. Stay just right of center.

10. Clowntime is Over   9+ ★
FA: Bill Wylie and Randy Joseph, 1981.
Begin from the top (south end) of a large detached flake/ledge that runs across the bottom of the east face.
1. Stem across to the main face, make a few steep moves, and follow easier rock up to a belay at the left side of the *Marlin Alley* roof (6).
2. Find a good jug (that you can't see) and crank over the airy roof (9+). Work straight up to the top via two roofs.

11. Globs of Blobs   8 ★
FA: Billy Westbay and Mike Covington, 1974.
Begin left of a shrub juniper on the big flake/ledge that runs across the bottom of the east face.
1. Climb a steep wall, then work up and left via knobs and jugs to a belay at a flake (5).
2. Work left to finish with *Station to Station* (8 at the roof).

12. Marlin Alley   11b/c s ★
FA: Mark Wilford and Bill Wylie, 1981.
Begin as for *Globs of Blobs*.
1. Climb into the dihedral just left of *Hand Over Hand* and belay a short way up (7).
2. Climb the face left of the dihedral and step right (10b) or jam up the dihedral (10c). Undercling out past your pro, turn the roof (crux), then go up and right to the top.

13. Hand Over Hand   7 or 8 ★
Classic. Begin left of a juniper bush on the big flake/ledge that runs out across the east face.
1. Climb knobby rock to a conspicuous flake and jam a good crack to a roof (6). Hand traverse left, turn the roof (7), and pull up to a good belay ledge.
 2. Go left around a corner (6); or (better) go up and right through an overlap, then up along the edge of the roof and back right to the top of the face (8).

14. Bat Crack   9 ★
FA: Bill Forrest and Don Briggs, 1970.
This route ascends the middle of the east face and turns a dramatic roof.
1. Move up and right to an incipient crack just left of *Spaziergang*. Climb the crack and the face above to a belay beneath a roof (8). Pro is a bit sparse.
2. Crank through the roof (9), then up a slab (8) to the summit.

15. Spaziergang   8 ★
FA: George Hurley and Charlie Fowler, 1971.
This is a good tour up the right side of the east face.
Begin with a short, overhanging, right-facing corner a bit right of *Bat Crack*.
1. Work up and left to a good crack, up past a small tree, and right to belay.
2. Go up and right past a small roof (7) and finish as for *Carpenter's Corner* (8).

16. Carpenter's Corner   8
FA: (?) Scott Kimball and Joe Hladick, 1977.
1. Climb the large right-facing dihedral at the right side of the east face (8) and belay beneath the big roof.
2. Crank around the left side of the roof, then go up and right over a bulge (8).

17. Stepping Stones   9 s
Climb the crack and dihedral system that leads up to the big roof at the far right side of the face. Exit to the right or go left and join *Carpenter's Corner.*

18. Coors Roof   8 A4
FA: Kevin Donald, c. 1980.
Begin with *Carpenter's Corner* or with an easier system to the right (6). Aid a shallow, flared crack through the middle of the big roof, then climb the face above (7).

Insignificant Crag is a formation to the northeast of Batman Rock.

Significant Route   9+
FA: Keith Hayse and Jim Detterline, 1987.
This route takes the 300-foot face to the left of a major crack system.
1. Climb the face using incipient cracks for protection and belay beneath an overhanging slot (9+).
2. Climb the slot.

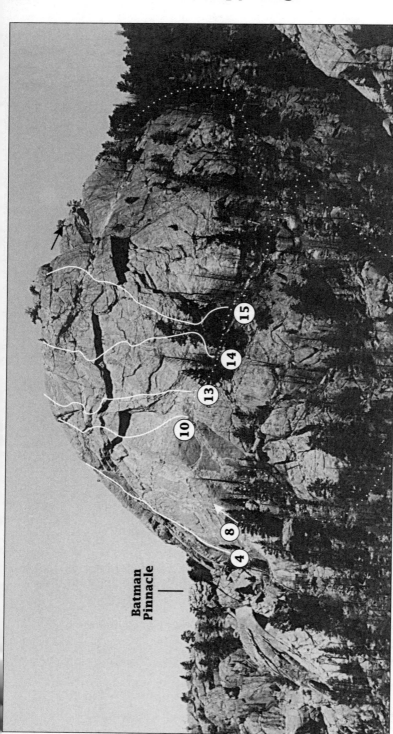

BATMAN ROCK From the East

4. Hand Jive 9 ★
8. Backbone Arête 11c ★
10. Clowntime is Over 9+ ★
13. Hand Over Hand 7 or 8 ★

14. Bat Crack 9 ★
15. Spaziergang 8 ★

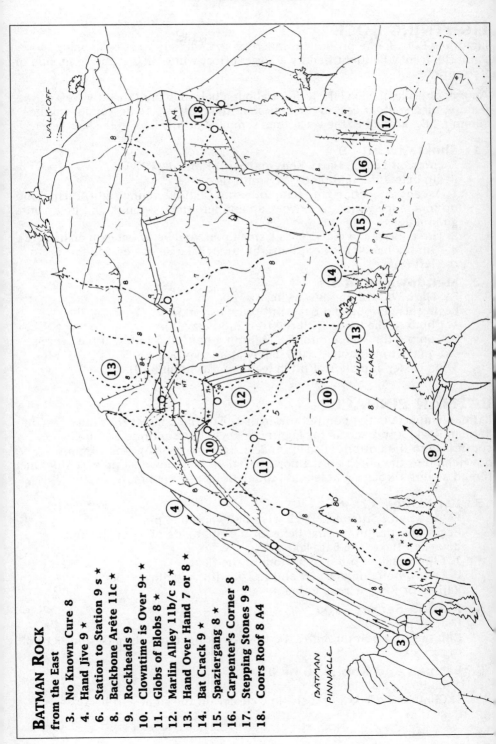

BATMAN ROCK
from the East

3. No Known Cure 8
4. Hand Jive 9 ★
6. Station to Station 9 s ★
8. Backbone Arête 11c ★
9. Rockheads 9
10. Clowntime is Over 9+ ★
11. Globs of Blobs 8 ★
12. Marlin Alley 11b/c s ★
13. Hand Over Hand 7 or 8 ★
14. Bat Crack 9 ★
15. Spaziergang 8 ★
16. Carpenter's Corner 8
17. Stepping Stones 9 s
18. Coors Roof 8 A4

LIGHTNING ROCK

Lightning Rock is the prominent buttress immediately west of Batman Pinnacle. It may be identified by a large, offset white dike at the right side of its south face.

Approach. Hike the Skyline Trail for about a half mile until directly west of the feature, then contour east to the bottom of the buttress. To descend from the summit, hike around to the west, then scramble down slabs to the southeast.

1. Short Circuit   9 ★
FA: Warren Young, Harry Kent and Scott Kimball, 1976.
Begin below the middle of the south face.
1. Ascend a small, right-facing dihedral (9), undercling right, then climb up to a ledge with a tree. Work up and left along a ramp, and belay on a good ledge.
2. Jam a nice hand crack, pass a small roof, and belay beneath an apex (8).
3. Climb a hand crack on the right (9), or take an easier option just to the left (8).

2. Meltdown   11d s ★
FA: Mark Wilford and Bill Wylie, 1981.
Begin this serious and beautiful route as for *Short Circuit.*
1. Climb to the ledge with the tree and belay (9).
2. Climb a thin crack into the "lightning bolt" and follow it past three old quarter-inch bolts (crux). Belay at an overlap.
3. An easier and shorter pitch leads to the summit (9).

BATMAN PINNACLE

Batman Pinnacle is the pointed tower that leans up against the south face of Batman Rock. Approach as for Lightning Rock, but continue east below its south face to the bottom of the pinnacle. To descend from the summit, downclimb to the notch on the north (4), then hike down along east side, or thread a sling through a hole and rappel 45 feet to the notch.

3. Bat Flake   11a ★
FA: Lawrence Stuemke, 1992. Five bolts and one pin.
Begin in a shallow corner beneath the right side of a conspicuous detached flake (the Bat Flake).
1. Climb easily up to the bottom of the flake.
2. Follow bolts up and left and finish with a shallow groove.
Rappel or jump across to main wall.

4. Robin's Secret   10a
FA: Stuemke, 1992.
Clip the first bolt on *Bat Flake,* then work up and right past another bolt to a crack.

5. Batman and Robin   6 or 8 ★
A moderate classic.
1. Climb easy flakes or a shallow corner on the right and belay atop a flake (5).

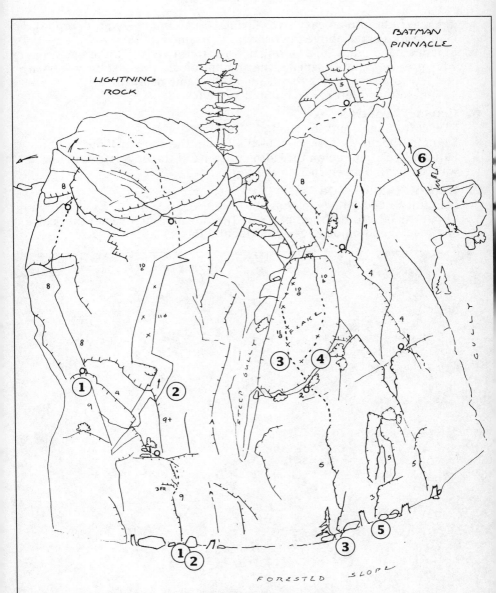

LIGHTNING ROCK AND BATMAN PINNACLE From the South

LIGHTNING ROCK
1. **Short Circuit 9 ★**
2. **Meltdown 11d s ★**

BATMAN PINNACLE
3. **Bat Flake 11a ★**
4. **Robin's Secret 10b**
5. **Batman and Robin 6 ★**
6. **Cross Threaded 9**

2. Move right into an easy right-facing corner and belay at its top (4), or climb a thin crack above the belay to the same fate (8).

3. Jam a hand crack (6) or a finger crack to the right (7), then go up a wide groove to belay beneath the summit block. One also may work up and left to a steep crack that leads to the same belay (8).

4. Spiral up and left to the pointed summit.

6. Cross Threaded   9
FA: Scott Kimball and Joe Hladick, 1984.
Begin in a niche a short way downhill from the start to *Hand Jive* on Batman Rock. Jam up an offwidth crack, hand traverse left at the headwall, and climb steep rock to the top.

7. Within Reach   10a
FA: Kimball and Bill Wylie, 1981.
Climb the face to the right of *Cross Threaded*, stretch past a thin crack, and reach good holds above a horizontal flake.

The author "slipping a disk" on Backbone Arête, Batman Rock. Photo: Joyce Rossiter

CHECKERBOARD ROCK

Checkerboard Rock is the smaller, squarish buttress below and to the south of Batman Rock. Approach via the Batman Rock Trail and take a signed left branch (go straight) after about a half mile.

1. Ziggie's Day Out   10d ★
FA: Mark Wilford and Bill Wylie, 1979.
This is an excellent crack climb requiring finesse and skill at placing pro. SR with emphasis on thin gear.
Begin at the far left side of the face atop a gigantic boulder.
1. Undercling up and right across the face (9) and follow a seam through a difficult bulge (crux). Continue up a thin crack to a stance on a ledge (10d).
2a. Move left on the ledge until it is possible to angle up and right along a crack (9).
2b. Climb straight up a hand crack (8) and a short wall (9).

2. Ziggie's Brother Hank   10b ★
FA: Matt Smedley, Dave Larsen and Bill Anderson, 1989. Stoppers, a #1.5 Friend and QDs.
Begin down to the right from the start to *Ziggie's*, behind a massive boulder. Work up through a slit and up the slab above past a bolt (10a). Cross *Ziggie's Day Out,* step left, and work up the face past two more bolts (10b) to a bolt belay. Lower off or continue with the second pitch of *Ziggie's Day Out.*

3. Checkerboard Crack   10a ★
FA: Scott Kimball and Mike Neri, 1976.
1. Lieback up a left-facing corner for about 70 feet (8+), move up and right, then back left (10a), and jam up to a ledge (9).
2. Jam straight up a crack and jog right below the headwall (8) or go straight up (9).

4. Rainy Day Woman   9+ s ★
FA: Kimball and Nancy Heron, 1979.
Climb the dihedral to the right of *Checkerboard Crack* to a tiny stance (8), go up to a flake (9), left to *Checkerboard,* then friction over to the crack on the right which is thin (9+) at the top. Finish as for *Checkerboard.*

5. Crystal Catch   9 ★
FA: Kimball and Harry Kent, 1976.
Begin near a large pine, about 15 feet left of a large chimney.
1. Ascend a flake/crack past a bulge, balance to the right on crystals (9), then work up to belay on a small flake.
2. Climb the crystal-studded face (7) and the groove above (7).

6. Non-Alignment   10c
FA: Joe Hladick and Kimball, 1982.
Begin in the chimney up and right from *Crystal Catch.* Undercling and lieback up and left along flakes to join *Crystal Catch.*

7. Fallen Shark   9
FA: Kimball and Chip Salaun, 1979.
1. Climb up behind the huge block wedged in the chimney and move out to the belay on *Crystal Catch.*

2. Lieback up a crack on the right side of the chimney (9) and continue up a higher crack (9). Move down and left across a wedged block and out onto the left wall.

3. Finish as for *Crystal Catch.*

8. Southeast Pillar   8
SR to a #4 Friend.

This route ascends the east side of the massive pillar at the southeast corner of the rock.

Begin in the chimney at the right side of the pillar.

1. Step off from a pedestal and face climb up to an S-shaped hand crack.

2. Climb the crack and the wide groove above to the top of the pillar.

3. Climb the chimney behind the pillar to the top of the rock.

9. Number 8 Beartrap   8
FA: Kimball and Salaun, 1979.

This route grunts up the chimney between the pillar and the main wall.

10. Tim's Troubles   10 s
FA: Hansen and Hladick, 1982.

1. Climb a wide crack to the right of the *Beartrap* to the long ledge that runs across the rock.

2. Jam and lieback up the crystalline crack and right-facing dihedral at the upper southeast corner of the crag.

11. White Line   9 s
FA: Gary Sapp and partner, 1982

Begin pitch two of *Tim's Troubles,* but before the corner arches to the right, move left and ascend white crystalline rock to a left-facing corner that runs to the top of the crag.

12. Icarus   10d ★
FA: Jim Detterline, Rick Guerrieri, Paul McLaughlin and Bill Webster, 1988. SR with ten QDs.

This is a two-pitch line up the east-facing buttress just around to the left from *Broken Wing.* It should probably be renamed so as to avoid confusion with a route done earlier on Sundance Buttress. Due to poor rock on the first pitch, most parties climb only the second pitch. Begin on the ground below the buttress.

1. Lieback up a curving crack/flake, continue up the face via short cracks, and belay on a long ledge (9, 120 feet).

2. Work up the buttress following bolts, flakes, and cracks (10d, five bolts, four pitons, 165 feet).

13. Broken Wing   9
FA: Kimball and Hladick, 1977.

Hike up around to the northeast corner of the crag to the base of a steep and narrow north-facing wall.

1. Ascend a short right-facing dihedral (7).

2. Climb steep rock up to a right-arching crack. Jam up the crack, lieback up a wide section (9), and jam on the top.

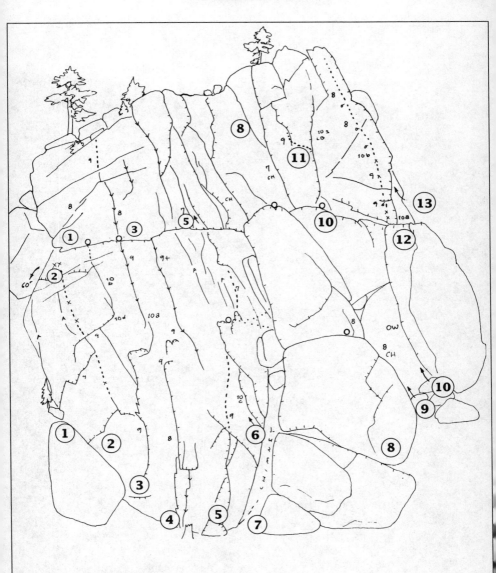

CHECKERBOARD ROCK From the South

1. Ziggie's Day Out 10d ★
2. Ziggie's Brother Hank 10b ★
3. Checkerboard Crack 10a ★
4. Rainy Day Woman 9+ s
5. Crystal Catch 9
6. Non-Alignment 10c
7. Fallen Shark 9
8. Southeast Pillar 8
9. Number 8 Beartrap 8
10. Tim's Troubles 10 s
11. White Line 9 s
12. Icarus 10d ★
13. Broken Wing 9

Randy Joseph on Gollum's Arch. Photo: R.J. Collection

SKYLINE ROCKS

Running between Batman Rock and the Twin Owls is a row of smaller crags that forms a jagged skyline above the Twin Owls parking area.

Approach. Fallen Down Crag, Christmas Crag, and Flounder Rock are reached most easily by starting out on the Batman Rock Trail, then cutting upslope to the north at an appropriate point. All the crags from Fan Rock through Rock One are reached via the Rock One Trail which begins at the drinking fountain on the north side of the Twin Owls parking area. This trail leads into the gully between Rock One and Rock Two and is marked with cairns and red tape. Rock One also may be reached from the trail to *Conan's Gonads* described under the Twin Owls.

LITTLE TWIN OWLS

This is a popular top-roping rock about 75 yards west of the Twin Owls parking area. All routes but *Arête* can be led safely. Approach via the Batman Rock Trail, then branch right after about 50 yards.

1. **Little Twin Owls Crack   11a ★**
   Climb the obvious, overhanging finger crack on the south side. Rack: many stoppers, TCUs, #2 and 3 Friends.

2. **Arête   11c ★**
   Climb the right side of the southeast arête around to the right from *Little Twin Owls Crack.* The right side of this narrow face also may be climbed (11d).

3. **Knee Catcher   6**
   Climb the crystal-toothed offwidth crack that splits the east face.

4. **Flake   8+**
   Begin at the chimney in the middle of the east face, then undercling right along a flake and head for the top. One also may begin with a thin seam that leads up to the flake.

FALLEN DOWN CRAG

This small buttress sits just south of Christmas Crag. It may be recognized by a long pointed flake resting against its southeast side. Rappel from a tree or downclimb at the southwest corner of the crag.

1. **Loop-Ty-Loop   9**
   FA: Kimball and Hansen, 1980.
   Work up a slot left of the flake at the southeast corner of the rock, hand traverse out left above a drop-off, then jam a crack to the top.

2. **Ruffian   9**
   FA: Kimball and Johnson, 1980.
   Climb the crack in the middle of the east face.

SKYLINE ROCKS OVERVIEW

A. **Batman Rock**

B. **Fallen Down Crag**

C. **Christmas Crag**

D. **Flounder Rock**

E. **Little Twin Owls**

F. **Fan Rock**

G. **Rock Six**

SKYLINE ROCKS OVERVIEW

H. The Dike Dome
I. Rock Four
J. Rock Three
K. Rock Two
L. Twin Owls Glacier Rock
M. Rock One
N. Twin Owls

CHRISTMAS CRAG

Christmas Crag is located about 150 yards northeast of the Little Twin Owls. It may be recognized by its clean east buttress which has a vertical crack with a small tree in it. All routes by Kimball and Harrison, 1980.

1. Neanderthal Slide   9

Ascend a water trough at the southwest corner of the crag, pass a small overhang, go left to the crest, and tackle a bulge.

2. Men in Granite   9

Climb a chimney that narrows to a squeeze, up and right from Neanderthal Slide.

3. Botany Crack   9

Climb a wide crack to the right of *Men in Granite*.

4. Tree Crack   5 ★

Climb a crack with a small tree in the middle of the east buttress, then hand traverse right under a roof.

5. Precambrian   9

Climb the face just right of *Tree Crack* (9), then step left and climb through the roof at a left-facing flake (9).

FLOUNDER ROCK

This formation sits about 50 yards east of Christmas crag and may be distinguished by cracks that intersect to form an X on its southeast face and a large flounder-shaped block at left. Rappel from the summit.

1. Piranha Crack   10a

FA: Kimball and Harlin, 1981.

Jam a short, overhanging finger crack on the west side of the block.

2. Flounder   9+ s

FA: Charlie Fowler and John Harlin, 1981.

Face climb up the middle of the east side of the Flounder Block and belay at its top (8). Follow discontinuous cracks up the main wall.

FAN ROCK

Fan Rock is the seventh large formation counting west from the Twin Owls. It consists of five narrow towers in a vague radial arrangement that might be likened to a folding fan. The only known route is on the second tower from the right, (and that is if I have identified this route in its actual location – I could not find the bolt).

1. Jack-Booted Thugs   10

FA: (?) Jeff Rickerell and Scott Miller, 1992.

Climb the face left of a dihedral in a sustained 120-foot pitch. A new one-quarter inch bolt sans hanger was found part way up the climb. Rappel 80 feet from the summit.

Rock Six *is located just north of Fan Rock. It is an attractive buttress with obvious cracks in its east face, but has no known routes.*

THE DIKE DOME

Rock Five or The Dike Dome is located a short way east of Rock Six. It is the highest of the group and has a single known route up the middle of its south face.

1. Uphill Gardeners   9
FA: Richard Rossiter and Greg Carelli, 1995.
Scramble up a ramp from the southeast corner of the buttress and belay beneath a flake/crack. Lieback up the flake/crack, then cut back left and gain a crack system that angles up and right through the middle of the south face. Leave this system and climb a steep ramp that leads to the summit.

Rock Four *or* *The Stupa* *is located a short distance east of The Dike Dome. The only known route is a short scramble up its north side (cl3).*

ROCK THREE

Rock Three is the third major buttress west of the Twin Owls. It features a long south-facing slab of excellent rock that is evident from the Twin Owls parking area. Escape from the summit by scrambling off to the north.

1. Amazing Grace   10a vs ★
FA: Richard Rossiter, solo, 1995.
I climbed this route site unseen wearing only rock shoes and a tonga. High up, the holds got smaller and smaller. I passed the point of no return. An amazing grace led me through.
From the bottom of the south face, scramble up and right to a belay niche right of three dwarfed trees at the right edge of the face. Note: I'm guessing the pitch lengths since I had no rope.
1. Crank up and left into the crack above the trees and jam to its end. Continue on good holds and jam a short crack through a bulge (7, last pro). Work up the beautiful, rounded arête for 30 feet (8), then angle up and left on diminishing holds until the angle eases off (10a, 140 feet with a 50-60 foot run-out).
2. Move left and climb a flared crack to a sloping shelf (8, 75 feet). Scramble to the top (4, 75 feet).

ROCK TWO

Rock Two is the next large buttress east of Rock Three or the second large buttress west of the Twin Owls.

1. Somewhere   6
FA: Bob Bradley and George Hankin, sometime.
Ascend cracks and slabs to the right of the large central dihedral.

TWIN OWLS GLACIER ROCK

This small, triangular buttress is located just west from the bottom of Rock One. It is named for a spring that runs down a slab at the east side of the feature. The spring freezes in winter and sometimes may be climbed.

1. **Basic   2**

   Around to the left from the spring and to the left of a fin, climb a low-angle slab. Rappel.

2. **Skipping School   8**

   Climb a vertical crack on the east side of a fin and traverse left below a roof to belay. Jam up a short fist crack.

3. **The Dead Kennedy   11b** ★

   FA: Terry Kennedy, 1989. Rack: four QDs. Climb the black water streak about 20 feet right of the spring. Four bolts with the crux near the third. Go right and up from the last bolt.

ROCK ONE

Rock One is the 300-foot buttress across the gully to the west from the Twin Owls. Its notable features include a large, left-facing dihedral that is capped by a roof. To escape from the summit, walk off to the north.

1. **Rock One Route   4** ★

   Begin to the left of the large left-facing dihedral at the bottom of the rock.
   1. Climb a short wall by a small tree, then angle right to a good ledge.
   2. Climb a chimney to another ledge.
   3. Jam a crack system to a third ledge (crux) but continue up past a short left-facing dihedral and easy slab to the summit.

2. **Lucky Seven   10a**

   FA: Dan Hare and Olaf Mitchell, 1970s. Climb the large left-facing dihedral and roof at the bottom of Rock One.

3. **No Exit   9**

   FA: Snively and partner, 1977. Climb the hand crack in the right wall of the large dihedral. Finish with some interesting face work.

4. **Hole in the Wall   10a**

   FA: Kimball and Wilford, 1979. Locate a large detached flake on the right side of the crag.
   1. Climb up through offwidth terrain and belay above where the flake tapers to a point.
   2. Work left and finish over easy ground.

TWIN OWLS From the Southwest

ROCK ONE
1. Rock One Route 4 ★
2. Lucky Seven 10a
3. No Exit 9
4. Hole in the Wall 10a

LITTLE TWIN OWLS
1. Little Twin Owls Crack 11a ★
2. Arête 11c ★

TWIN OWLS
5. Conan's Gonads 9 ★
6. The Organ Pipes 6 to 9 ★
7. Tilted Mitten 8 or 9 ★
8. Senseless Meaning 10a s ★
13. Prow 10b
15. Pin Route 4
16. Sky Top 8
18. West Chimney 5 or 7
22. Wolf's Tooth 8 ★

TWIN OWLS

As one drives up the road through McGregor Ranch, the Twin Owls rise majestically and unmistakably to the north. This commanding buttress is the nearest to the parking area of the large crags at Lumpy ridge, and as a consequence, is rather popular. The rock, however, is characterized by coarse, steep granite and an abundance of wide cracks and chimneys, which has the contrary effect of diminishing its popularity.

The East and West Owls rise steeply above a long ledge system called the Roosting Ramp that slices all the way across the south face of the crag. The Owls are divided by a deep cleft called the Central Chimney. The most prominent feature on the West Owl is a narrow detached column called the Wolf's Tooth Pinnacle. The big south face of the East Owl features the obvious Crack of Fear. Below the Roosting Ramp is a broad buttress called the Lower Owls.

Approach A. From the Twin Owls parking area, set out on the Gem Lake Trail. Just beyond an initial aspen grove, a path cuts back to the left and leads up the slope to the *Conan's Gonads* and *Organ Pipes,* which lie on the west side of the Lower Owls. The path continues up the gully and reaches the west end of the Roosting Ramp.

Approach B. A short way farther up the Gem Lake Trail from the aspen grove, a massive boulder appears on the left. Not far beyond it, another path breaks off to the left and climbs to the East Owl and the east end of the Roosting Ramp.

Descent. To descend from either summit, scramble to the notch between the summits and downclimb the *Bowels of the Owls.*

Hangover Overhang   A4
FA: Keith Loeber, solo, 1970s.
The massive boulder on the north side of the Gem Lake Trail (five minutes from the parking area) has a 50-foot route up the big overhang on its southwest side.

1. Bowels of the Owls Class   4
From the highest point of land on the north side of the Owls, a path leads up into a deep, dank fissure. Climb back behind a couple of chockstones and squeeze up to the notch between the two summits. To descend from summit area, scramble to the farthest west of the grooves between the East and West Owls (cairn) and downclimb north to the top of the deep chimney of the *Bowels.* Begin all the way in the back and bridge down behind the chockstones to easier ground.

2. Cheechako Class   4
About 50 feet right of the *Bowels* is a larger gully system that leans left. Climb the back of the gully, then follow cracks up and left to the area above the *Bowels.*

3. Sneaky Pete's North Rib   9
FA: Chip Salaun and Bruce Stoebner, 1979.
Begin as for *Cheechako,* but climb a scaly right-leaning chimney to a wall with many cracks and jam to easy ground near the top.

Lower Owls. *The following routes ascend the broad buttress below the Roosting Ramp. The southeast face of the buttress has two tiers offset by a big ledge.*

4. **Bloop** **8**
   Climb a conspicuous dihedral up and left from *Conan's Gonads.*

5. **Conan's Gonads** **9** ★
   FA: Larry Bruce and Mark Hesse, 1970s. SR plus an extra #3.5 or 4 Friend.
   Classic. Also known as *Conads.* Begin on the west-facing wall around to the left from *The Organ Pipes.* Ascend the obvious crack that varies from hand to fist width and leads to the Roosting Ramp.

6. **The Organ Pipes** **6 to 9** ★
   FA: John Chapman and Steve Hickman, 1963.
   This popular route ascends flared, bottoming cracks up the wall, just around to the right from *Conads.* More difficult variations lie to the left of the line described. The last crack on the left is rated 9.
   Begin from a large pedestal at the bottom of the dihedral.
   1. Climb the first continuous crack to the left of the corner and belay on a marginal ledge (6, 120 feet).
   2. Continue via similar terrain to a good ledge near the top of the dihedral (6).
   3a. From the left side of the ledge, jam up a curving crack with a wide section (8, 35 feet).
   3b. Jam a hand crack a short way to the left (7).
   3c. Jam and stem up the corner on the right and gain the Roosting Ramp (6).

7. **Tilted Mitten** **8 or 9** ★
   FA: Michael Covington.
   This route is named for a peculiar, leaning block about halfway up the lower buttress. It is a good climb for those who enjoy chimneys, especially if the climb is begun with pitch 1c.
   Begin near the low point of the buttress, just where the terrain begins to climb uphill to the right.
   1a. Climb a wet brushy chimney past a small roof, then continue up and right to a belay beneath a long, curving crack (4).
   1b. Hike about 50 feet up and right from the chimney mentioned above to a smaller flared chimney with a clean hand crack at its left. Jam the crack for 30 feet, then hand traverse left to the previous option (7).
   1c. Just up and right from the previous pitch is a black inset that leads to another chimney. Stem up the inset (pro in a finger crack at left) and continue in a 14-inch chimney (9 ★).
   2. Climb the crack and continue past the right side of the Mitten (8), then pass through a hole and belay on a ledge.
   3. Move the belay right to the base of a right-angling chimney. Ascend cracks in the back of the chimney to the big ledge beneath the upper Owls. The left side of the Mitten feature also may be climbed (8 s).

LOWER OWLS

From the Southeast
7. **Tilted Mitten 8 or 9 ★**
8. **Senseless Meaning 10a s ★**
9. **Sunset Arête 6 ★**
11. **One of Life's Little Problems 7+**
12. **Second Thoughts 10a**
13. **Prow 10b**
14. **Fist Fight 10c**

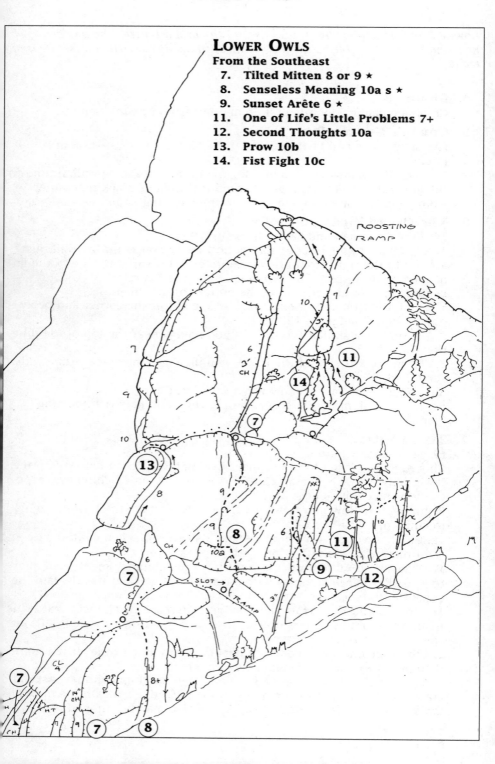

8. Senseless Meaning   10a s ★
FA: Doug Snively and Bill Wylie, 1980.
Begin about 150 feet up and right from *Tilted Mitten*.
1. Ascend a vertical groove (8+), then scramble right until beneath another wall with a flake/roof. This point may also be reached by scrambling in from the right.
2. Crank over the flake/roof and gain good holds above, then swing left (crux) to a stance beneath a left-facing flake. Jam along the flake, then work up and right to a big ledge (9). Walk off or continue with a route on the upper tier.

9. Sunset Arête   6 ★
FA: Scott Kimball and Tim Hansen, 1984.
Begin up to the right from *Senseless Meaning* in a large alcove that is bound on the left by a big right-leaning, right-facing dihedral.
Work left across the bottom of the dihedral, then crank up and left on good holds and follow the rounded arête to a bolt anchor at its top. Rappel 75 feet.

10. Chip's Tantrum   10a
FA: Chip Salaun and Tim Hansen, 1982.
Climb the inside of the big dihedral that forms the left side of the alcove. Note that there are two possibilities: a steep thin crack at left, or a six-inch slot a few feet to the right. These features merge after about 40 feet and it is not known in which Chip had his tantrum.

11. One of Life's Little Problems   7+
FA: Bob Bradley, 1960s.
Begin about 50 feet right of the big dihedral mentioned above.
1. Ascend either of two right-facing flakes that lead to a large right-leaning flake with a crack that opens to ten inches. Lieback up the wide crack and belay on the big ledge that runs across the buttress.
2. Climb a right-facing flake and dihedral just right of *Fist Fight*.

12. Second Thoughts   10a
FA: Kimball, Heron, Salaun, 1979.
Begin toward the right side of the alcove mentioned above behind a large boulder. Climb a finger/hand crack through a bulge with a horn, then go up and right along a dike and finish with a shallow left-facing flake. Rappel 80 feet from a pine tree.

12A. Alignment of the Misaligned   10c/d
FA: Lawrence Stuemke and Dusty Hardman, 1991.
Climb through the bulge of *Second Thoughts,* then work straight up the face past a bolt. Rappel 80 feet from a pine tree.

Thin Crack. Ten feet to the right of Second Thoughts is a beautiful fingertip crack. This has to have been climbed, but no record exists (10b?). Could easily be toproped from a 30-foot pine, but looks leadable.

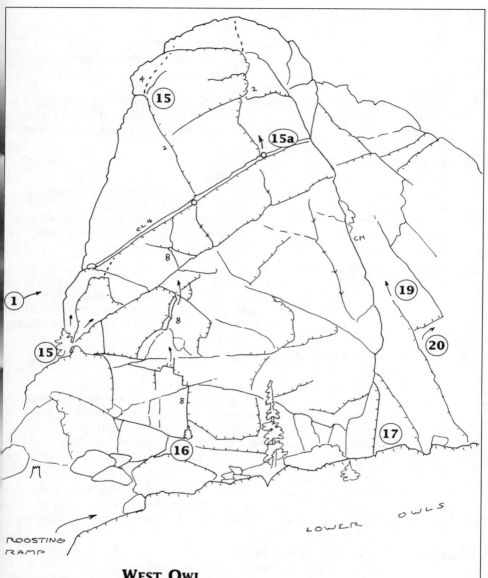

WEST OWL
West Buttress
1. **Bowels of the Owls Class 4**
15. **Pin Route 4**
15A. **Sky Route 2**
16. **Sky Top 8 ★**
17. **Arm and Hammer 5 A3**
19. **Jacob's Ladder 9 A2**
20. **Eclipse 9 A2**

13. Prow   10b
FA: John Long and Lynn Hill, 1980.
This route ascends the arête that divides the southwest and southeast faces of the lower buttress.
1. Climb the first two pitches of *Tilted Mitten* (or any route on the lower tier) and gain the left end of a long ledge that runs across the buttress.
2. Hand traverse left to the arête, then jam a steep crack (crux), pass a roof, and belay on the Roosting Ramp.

14. Fist Fight   10c
FA: McClure, Kimball, Hansen, 1980.
Locate a right-leaning crack on the upper tier of the lower wall well to the right of the *Tilted Mitten* route and just left of *One of Life's Little Problems.*

West Owl, West Buttress.

15. Pin Route   4
An ancient tour of the west buttress and a good beginner route. Begin above and north of the west end of the Roosting Ramp, about 100 feet right of the Bowels.
1. Climb either of two short chimneys to gain a ramp system, then traverse up and right to a belay at the bottom of a long crack/groove that angles up to the left.
2. Follow the long crack to the summit area. The final moves are the most difficult.

15A. Sky Route   2
1. Proceed as for *Pin Route,* but set the belay farther to the right along the ramp at the base of a right-facing flake.
2. Climb straight up along flakes and scoops to the summit.
To reach the descent route, scramble east through a deep groove and look for a cairn that marks the downclimb.

The following routes begin from the west side of the Roosting Ramp.

16. Sky Top   8 ★
FA: Pettigrew and Craig, 1976.
Begin about 30 feet from the northwest end of the Roosting Ramp beneath a small limber pine up on the wall. Climb a left-facing corner system through a roof, work up and right along a slot, and jam a finger crack up to join *Pin Route.*

17. Arm and Hammer   5 A3
FA: Mike Neri and Jim Johnson, c. 1977.
Begin this aid line just around the corner to the right from the wall of *Sky Top.*
1. Aid up a somewhat rotten crack in reddish rock to the ridge crest.
2. Climb free up the rib to the right of *Pin Route.*

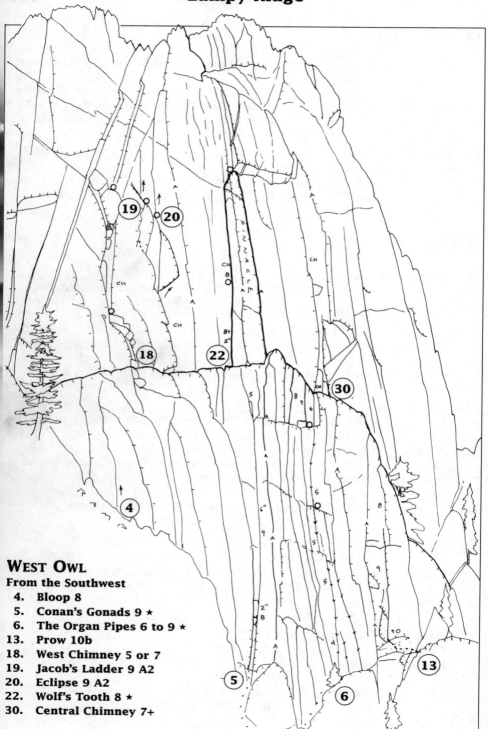

WEST OWL

From the Southwest

4. **Bloop 8**
5. **Conan's Gonads 9 ★**
6. **The Organ Pipes 6 to 9 ★**
13. **Prow 10b**
18. **West Chimney 5 or 7**
19. **Jacob's Ladder 9 A2**
20. **Eclipse 9 A2**
22. **Wolf's Tooth 8 ★**
30. **Central Chimney 7+**

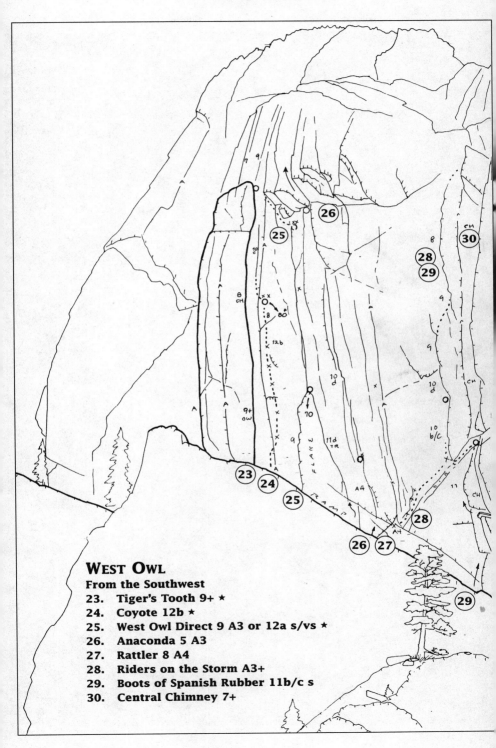

West Owl

From the Southwest

23. **Tiger's Tooth 9+ ★**
24. **Coyote 12b ★**
25. **West Owl Direct 9 A3 or 12a s/vs ★**
26. **Anaconda 5 A3**
27. **Rattler 8 A4**
28. **Riders on the Storm A3+**
29. **Boots of Spanish Rubber 11b/c s**
30. **Central Chimney 7+**

18. West Chimney 5 or 7

The southwest side of the West Owl forms a dihedral of monumental proportions with a reddish groove running up the center. Begin about 35 feet to the right of the corner at a five-foot fin of rock.

1. Climb a low-angled chimney up and left into the main groove (4) or take harder lines to either side (7).
2. Climb up to a chockstone, into a cave, and out onto a ledge (5).
3. Finish with a right-facing dihedral (3) or take an early exit (easier).

19. Jacob's Ladder 9 A2

FA: Hickman, Chapman, and Lord, 1963.
An early aid climb, seldom done.

1. Begin as for *Eclipse,* but continue farther up the ramp. After about 90 feet, make some difficult free moves up a short, overhanging wall, then aid a thin crack which widens to three inches. Belay on top of a ramp.
2. Aid a vertical thin crack to the right of the belay and free climb to the top of the West Owl when the angle eases off.

20. Eclipse 9 A2

FA: Billy Westbay and Michael Covington, 1974.
A short way to the right of the rock fin, a chimney/ramp runs steeply up the shaded north face.

1. Ascend the chimney for about 25 feet, then aid out to the right along a thin flake. Continue free to a small, inset ledge.
2. Work up and right along a left-facing flake, hand traverse right, then continue upward (9).

West Owl, South Face. *The following routes are located between the Wolf's Tooth Pinnacle and the Central Chimney.*

21. Idiot's Delight 6 A4

FA: Bradley and Mayrose, 1960s.
This obscure route begins with the *Wolf's Tooth* crack, then branches left into a system of rotting grooves and flared cracks.

TWIN OWLS From the Southeast

LOWER OWLS

7. Tilted Mitten 8 or 9 ★
13. Prow 10b
14. Fist Fight 10c

West Owl

23. Tiger's Tooth 9+ ★
25. West Owl Direct 9 A3 ★

EAST OWL

30. Central Chimney 7+ ★
34. Crack of Fear 10d ★

36. Peaches and Cream 11 ★
37. Twister 10c ★
38. Last Dance 11d ★
39. Tighter Squeeze 8
47. Yosemite Crack 9 ★

THE HEN AND CHICKEN

48. Rooster Tail 9+ ★
51. Rhode Island Red 10a ★

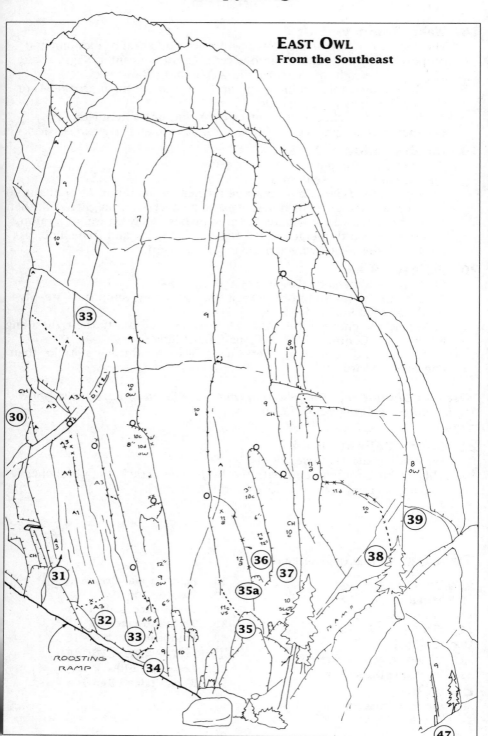

EAST OWL
From the Southeast

22. Wolf's Tooth   8 ★

FA: Tink Wilson and George Lamb, 1958. SR with a #3.5 and 4 Friend. Climb the fist crack and chimney at the left side of the pinnacle and belay on a flat, triangular ledge after 130 feet. Choose an exit from the *Tiger's Tooth*. Two pitches, lots of old, fixed pins.

23. Tiger's Tooth   9+ ★

FA: Layton Kor and Pat Ament, c. 1965. Rack up to five inches. A classic wide crack.
1. Climb the crack and chimney at the right side of the pinnacle and belay short of the top.
2a. Climb a deceptive crack on the right (9).
2b. Climb the flared crack above the belay (7).
2c. Bridge up between the pinnacle and the main wall, then left and up (6).

24. Coyote   12b ★

FA: Mike Caldwell, 1989. SR to a #1.5 Friend.
Cast Off Your Old Tired Ethics is an acronym borrowed from the American Prostitute's Union. This striking route ascends the arête between the *Wolf's Tooth* Pinnacle and *West Owl Direct*.
1. Begin just left of the arête and pull up around to the right side. Five bolts mark the line. The crux is at the last bolt and consists of desperate palming and liebacking. The final 20 feet may be protected by a sling on a horn (7).
2. Rappel 80 feet from a bolt anchor or climb a crack on the left side of the arête (10b). When the crack fades, continue straight up. One also may join the *Tiger's Tooth*.

25. West Owl Direct   9 A3 or 12a s/vs ★

FA: Bill Eubank and Brad Van Diver, 1956. FFA: John Bachar and Doug Snively, 1978.
This route ascends the huge dihedral about 70 feet left of the *Central Chimney*. The first pitch is fairly popular.
1. Climb the left side of a flake that sits in the bottom of the dihedral (9). The crack on the right may be toproped (11d).
2. Work up the crack in the dihedral and belay at the base of the roof (11d, some fixed gear).
3. Go left around the roof and continue to the top.

EAST OWL From the Southeast

30.	Central Chimney 7+ ★	35A.	Rip Curl 12a ★
31.	Autumn Mist 8 A3	36.	Peaches and Cream 11 ★
32.	Copperhead A4	37.	Twister 10c ★
33.	Viper 8 A4	38.	Last Dance 11d ★
34.	Crack of Fear 10d ★	39.	Tighter Squeeze 8
35.	Epitaph 11c vs	47.	Yosemite Crack 9 ★

26. Anaconda   5 A+
FA: Layton Kor and Larry Dalke, 1965. SR plus an assortment of pins, hooks, copperheads, et cetera.
A classic aid line.
1. Nail a crack up the bulging right wall of the *West Owl Direct* dihedral (A4).
2. Continue on aid until near the roof (optional belay), then angle up to the right and over the roof. This pitch has been free-climbed (11a).

27. Rattler   8 A4
FA: Keith Lober, 1979. Rack as for *Anaconda*.
This ascends the arête and crack system to the right of *Anaconda*.
Begin with *Anaconda* and move right into the system or take a very difficult direct start up through a rotten roof (crux).

28. Riders on the Storm   A3+
This aid route begins with the first 20 feet of *Rattler*, then breaks right at the initial roof via fixed gear. Continue up and right along a large dike to a bolt near the *Central Chimney*. Climb straight up along flakes and cracks for two more pitches to the saddle between the Owls.

29. Boots of Spanish Rubber   11b/c s
FFA: Hidetaka Suzuki and Scott Kimball, 1984.
This three-pitch route ascends the face and outside corner just left of the *Central Chimney*. The second and third pitches are the same as an aid climb called *Riders on the Storm*, which works up and right from the start to *Rattler* (see above).
1. Gain a pedestal in the bottom of the *Central Chimney*, then jam out left and climb to the top of a small rib. Continue on better holds and belay in the Central Chimney at the level of a large diagonal dike (11b/c).
2. Climb down and left to a bolt (see *Riders on the Storm*), then jam 30 feet to a stance and belay (10b/c).
3. Climb an overhanging flake (10d), then follow a thin flake (hard to see on the left) to better holds (9). Continue along flakes and cracks to the left of the Central Chimney.

30. Central Chimney   7+ ★
FA: Dick Sherman, Harbert Higgins, and Tom Hornbein, c. 1950.
This is one of the oldest routes on Lumpy Ridge. It is sure to please those with a flare for spelunking.
1. Climb up onto a 30-foot pedestal in the bottom of the chimney and belay (2, 60 feet).
2. Ooze up through a squeeze (7+), pass a chockstone on the left, and belay.
3a. Climb a good crack out on the left wall (8) and continue to the saddle between summits (150 feet).
3b. Pass the chockstone on the right or left wall (7).
3a. Tunnel behind the giant chockstone (6).

East Owl, South Face. The following routes lie right of the Central Chimney.

31. Autumn Mist 8 A3
FA: Bill Todd, 1980.
Begin at the right side of the *Central Chimney.* Work up discontinuous cracks to a bolt belay. Nail over a roof (A3), up nearly to *Viper* (7), then back left to the arête.

32. Copperhead A4
FA: Aaron Walters and Bob Bradley, 1994. Bring two sets of Friends #1-4, various wired stoppers, copperheads 1 through 4, one-inch angle piton, two hooks.
Set the first belay just right of a small triangular slab, just below and right of the *Central Chimney.*
Climb the right side of the slab for about 12 feet until a copperhead can be reached. Aid right for 20 feet past a bolt and another copperhead and gain the bottom of an overhanging crack (A3). Follow the scaly crack until it fades (A1, 60 feet). Two A3 placements lead to four fixed copperheads that are used to reach a bolt (A4). Another bolt and two hook moves bring one to a bolt that was placed on the first ascent of *Autumn Mist.* Move up and right to a three-bolt belay. Rappel or continue with *Viper* in the next crack system to the right.

33. Viper 8 A5
FA: Layton Kor and Larry Dalke (II 5.6 A5), 1965. SR plus pins, hooks, copperheads, et cetera.
Begin a short way left of *Crack of Fear,* beneath a bolt.
1. Nail up to the bolt, then follow seams until it is possible to move left to more of a crack (A5, possible zipper).
2. Nail up the vertical crack, then reach left to a deeper V-shaped crack. Continue on aid and belay in a light-colored area (A3).
3. Climb mixed aid and free straight up, nail left around a flake (A4), then free climb up and left, and finish in a steep crack just right of the Central Chimney.

34. Crack of Fear 10d ★
FA: Layton Kor and Paul Mayrose, 1963. FFA: Chris Fredricks and Jim Logan, c. 1966. SR to 4 inches; larger gear may be used.
No waiting in line here. This area classic ascends a horrific 300-foot, offwidth/chimney in the south face of the East Owl.
Begin about 40 feet down and right from the *Central Chimney.*
1. Jam the left (9) or right (10) side of the Rat's Tooth, a small pillar at the beginning of the crack, then battle up the unrelenting slot to a bolt belay atop a flake (9).
2. Work up and left through a jog in the crack (crux) and belay at a stance just above. One also may proceed to a better belay after about 50 feet.
3. The challenge continues above with an offwidth slot (10) followed by a six- to ten-inch crack. Belay beneath a roof after a long pitch.
4. Jog left beneath the roof and scramble to the top.

Twister Area. *The following routes begin from the low point of the East Owl and along a ramp that climbs right to the notch above the Hen and Chicken (described below).*

35. Epitaph 11c vs
FA: Layton Kor and Steve Komito, 1963. FFA: Earl Wiggins and Dan McClure.
This route takes the crack system between *Peaches and Cream* and *Crack of Fear.* The first free ascent began left of the original start; the first pro is a piton 30 feet off the deck.

35A. Rip Curl 12a ★
FFA: Bernard Gillett, 1990.
This is a free version the original aid start to *Epitaph.* The crux is by a fixed nut. Belay in the main crack after moving left past the arête.

36. Peaches and Cream 11 ★
FA: Jimmy Dunn, c. 1978.
Just left of *Twister* is a formidable route. Climb the crack formed by an 80-foot flake. An off-width section is the crux. Rappel or continue with *Twister.*

37. Twister 10c ★
FA: Layton Kor and T.J. Boggs, 1963. FFA: Jim Logan and Mike Stultz, c. 1973.
This is the distinct chimney at the right side of the south face.
1. Struggle up through two cruxes to a good belay.
2. Work up and around a chockstone and complete the upper chimney (9).
3. Ascend flakes and cracks to a horizontal break, then tackle a wide, hanging, crystal-studded crack (the Barracuda) to reach easier terrain (9).

East Owl, East Buttress. *The following routes begin above and around to the right from the Hen and Chicken and finish with a broad A-shaped roof near the top of the east buttress.*

38. Last Dance 11d ★
FA: Mike Covington and Ketchum, 1973. FFA: Topher Donahue and Mike Caldwell, 1990.
This is the free version of the aid climb *East Wing* (7 A2). Begin just left of *Tighter Squeeze.* Work up the face past a bolt and gain a horizontal crack that runs out left to an arête – the "East Wing." Hand traverse or foot traverse through the crux and belay at the base of a crack on the arête. Proceed as shown in the topo.

39. Tighter Squeeze 8
FA: Mayrose and O'Connor, 1963.
Begin from a ramp that descends to the south from the notch behind the Hen and Chicken.
1. Climb the conspicuous chimney about 35 feet south of the notch and belay beneath an A-shaped roof.
2. Choose a finish from the *East Ridge.*

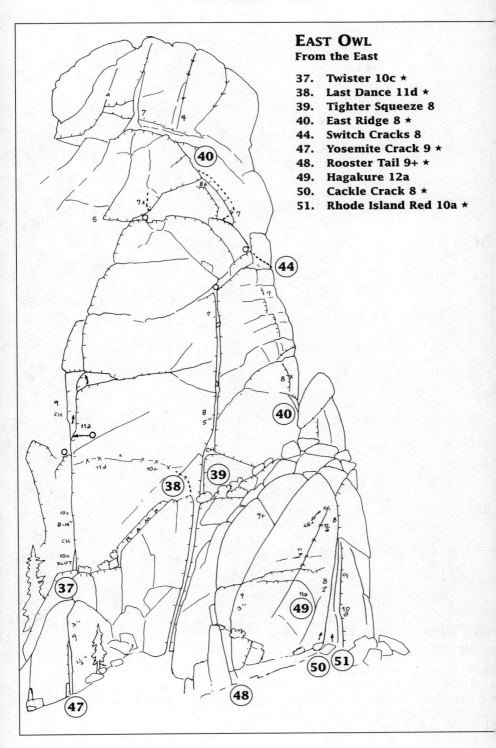

East Owl
From the East

37. Twister 10c ★
38. Last Dance 11d ★
39. Tighter Squeeze 8
40. East Ridge 8 ★
44. Switch Cracks 8
47. Yosemite Crack 9 ★
48. Rooster Tail 9+ ★
49. Hagakure 12a
50. Cackle Crack 8 ★
51. Rhode Island Red 10a ★

EAST OWL (from the northeast)

40. East Ridge 8 ★
41. Thimbleberry Jam 8
42. Jamesia Jam 10c ★
43. Turn, Turn, Turn 6

44. Switch Cracks 8
44A. Rather Fight than Switch 10a ★
45. Lady and the Tramp 9

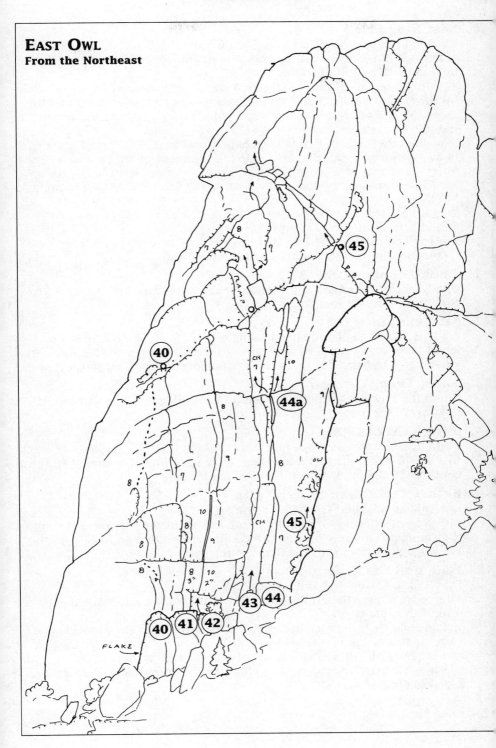

EAST OWL
From the Northeast

40. East Ridge 8 ★

FA: Bob Bradley, Steve Hickman, John Chapman, 1962.
Classic. Begin from a flake a short way up and right from the notch behind the Hen and Chicken.
1. Clip a fixed angel piton and pull around onto the east buttress. Work up the right side of a flake with a fixed piton and continue up to a big ledge (8). It also is possible to begin with the fist crack to the right of the initial crack (9+).
2a. Climb up through a broad, A-shaped roof that is managed most easily by swinging around its right side (7), then face climb up and left just outside the roof to a ledge. Finish via a cleft on the left (7).
2b. Climb through the top of the roof in a wide crack that slants up and left (8).
2c. Climb a short crack just left of the A-shaped roof (7 s) and work straight up through the headwall.
2d. Traverse left beneath a small roof, ascend an exposed left-facing flake, and join the other options at the headwall.

41. Thimbleberry Jam 8

Climb the fist-sized crack just right of the *East Ridge* and merge with that route after 70 feet.

42. Jamesia Jam 10c ★

FA: (?) Scott Kimball and Mike Covington, 1976. SR to a #3.5 Friend.
Begin three or four feet to the right of the *East Ridge* and jam this very sustained hand-and-fist crack to the big ledge on the *East Ridge* route.

43. Turn, Turn, Turn 6

Climb the obvious chimney that splits the wall about 30 feet right of the *East Ridge* route.

44. Switch Cracks 8

Begin at a clean hand crack just right of *Turn, Turn, Turn.* Jam the crack to a small stance after 60 feet, then move left into the chimney and continue to the big ledge on the *East Ridge* route.

44A. Rather Fight than Switch 10a ★

FA: (?) Mike Neri and Casey Swanson, 1977.
Climb *Switch Cracks* for about 60 feet, but instead of escaping left into the chimney, continue up the flared slot above (crux) and belay on the big ledge system of the *East Ridge* route.

45. Lady and the Tramp 9

FA: (?) Chip Salaun and Lynn Albers, 1979.
This route climbs the 80-foot pinnacle that stands against the north wall of the East Owl.
1. Jam the offwidth crack between the main wall and the pinnacle and gain the top of the pinnacle (9). Traverse ten feet right and go up to a roof, then work left past some old pins to a belay stance.
2. Work left up a black ramp to a rib, turn the corner and face climb on big holds to the summit.

46. Tail Feathers 6

Walk uphill from the pinnacle of *Lady and the Tramp* and climb the deep cleft about 20 feet east of the *Bowels of the Owls*.

The following routes ascend the lowest tier of rock below the east buttress of the East Owl.

47. Yosemite Crack 9 ★

Begin on the ground about 60 feet left of the Hen and Chicken, below the ramp of *Twister* and *Last Dance*. Jam the steep hand-and-fist crack to the ramp.

The Hen and Chicken. *When is a hen not a chicken? This is the 100-foot buttress at the eastern extreme of the East Owl, below the east buttress.*

48. Rooster Tail 9+ ★

Begin near the left edge of the flat south face. Jam a hand-and-fist crack up to the right, then take a thinner crack up and left.

49. Hagakure 12a

FA: H. and M. Suzuki, 1984.
Begin a few feet left of *Cackle Crack*. Follow a seam up and left, then angle up to the right along an incipient crack.

50. Cackle Crack 8 ★

Jam the crack in the left-facing dihedral at the right side of the face.

51. Rhode Island Red 10a

FA: Kimball and Harlin, 1980.
Jam a steep crack a few feet right from *Cackle Crack*.

Gollum's Arch From the South

1. Smeagol's Riddle 8+ s
2. Frigidaire 7
3. Seam-Stress 11c s
4. Gollum's Arch 10a ★

5. Facial Hair 10c ★
6. Close Encounters 11a
7. Latch-Hand 11c

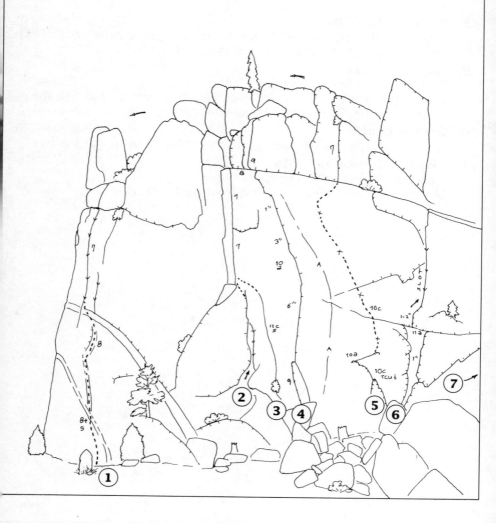

GOLLUM'S ARCH ROCK

This crag lies roughly midway on a contour between Triangle Rock and the East Owl. The namesake feature is a large left-facing, left-arching dihedral with a wide crack in the middle of the south face.

Approach as for the East Owl but angle up and right once at the level of the Hen and Chicken. Descend via the gully at the west side of the wall or rappel.

1. **Smeagol's Riddle   8+ s**
   FA: Bernard and Robert Gillett, 1987.
   Begin about 50 feet left of *Gollum's Arch* near the left edge of the south face. Climb an unprotected water streak for 30 feet, set pro in a crack on the left, then go up a wide groove (7).

2. **Frigidaire   7**
   FA: Chip Salaun and Nancy Heron, 1978.
   Begin at a flake a short way left of *Gollum's Arch.* Climb a black groove up the right side of the flake and continue up the right of two parallel cracks.

3. **Seam-Stress   11c s**
   FA: Mark Wilford and Skip Guerin, 1980. Rack: RPs to one inch.
   Climb the seam just left of *Gollum's Arch.*

4. **Gollum's Arch   10a ★**
   FA: Duncan Ferguson and Dudley Chelton, c. 1972. Rack: SR plus extra #3.5 and 4 Friends (could include #4 Camalot).
   Classic. Climb the long, curving, variable-width crack/dihedral in the middle of the south face.

5. **Facial Hair   10c ★**
   FA: Mike Caldwell and Dan Ludlam, 1985. Rack: Three runners, stoppers, TCUs, a #2.5 Friend, six QDs.
   Begin around to the right from *Gollum's Arch.* Mount a flake and continue up and left along a short crack (10c, TCUs). Mantle up, then work up the face past three bolts.

6. **Close Encounters   11a**
   FA: Billy Westbay and Doug Snively, 1978.
   Fifty feet right of *Gollum's Arch* climb a fist crack in a corner (8) or the flake to its right, then take a rounded crack out left through a roof. The trough above is easy.

7. **Latch-Hand   11c**
   FA: Hansen and Kimball, 1983.
   Begin several hundred feet up to the right from *Gollum's Arch* at a short, bulging wall. Climb a hanging flake (10a) and a difficult seam. A variation called *Hannibal Crosses the Alps* (11c) goes right beneath the roof (FA: Billy Westbay and Scott Kimball, 1981).

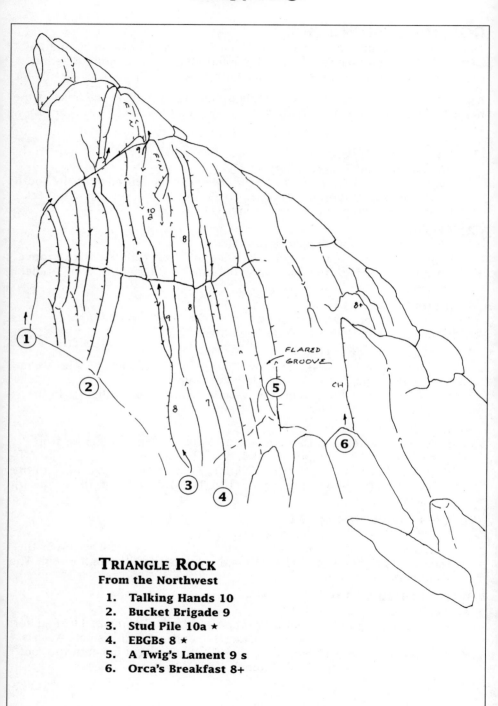

TRIANGLE ROCK
From the Northwest

1. Talking Hands 10
2. Bucket Brigade 9
3. Stud Pile 10a ★
4. EBGBs 8 ★
5. A Twig's Lament 9 s
6. Orca's Breakfast 8+

TRIANGLE ROCK

This small crag has a couple of routes that make it worth the walk, but the walk is fairly short! Hike the Gem Lake Trail about half a mile to an obvious inside bend and find a footpath on the left. Proceed as though heading for the East Owl. After several hundred feet, if you are paying attention, find another path that breaks off to the right and follow it north up the slope to Triangle Rock. To get off the summit, scramble southeast, then counterclockwise around the rock.

1. **Talking Hands   10**
   FA: Kimball, Wylie, Wilford, 1980.
   Climb a finger crack at the left edge of the north face.

2. **Bucket Brigade   9**
   FA: Westbay and Kimball, 1981.
   Begin to the right of *Talking Hands*. Climb right-facing flakes to a horizontal break and reach right to a jug.

3. **Stud Pile   10a ★**
   FA: Kimball and Wylie, 1980. Rack: SR to a #2 Friend.
   Odd name, good route. Ascend the groove and dihedral left of *EBGBs*.

4. **EBGBs   8 ★**
   FA: Chip Salaun and Jim Johnson, 1979.
   Ascend the groove and dihedral just left of the northwest arête.

5. **A Twig's Lament   9 s**
   FA: Salaun and Albers, 1979.
   Climb a deep water groove at the left side of the west face.

6. **Orca's Breakfast   8+**
   FA: Salaun and Johnson, 1979.
   Bridge up a chimney to the top of the pinnacle on the west side, then climb an offwidth crack to the top.

PACMAN CRAG

This is a small buttress just right (south) of the usual cut-off to Crescent Wall.

1. **Limp Wristed   8**
   FA: Caldwell and Hedlund, 1985.
   On the southwest side of the buttress, climb a hand crack in the left wall of a west-facing gully.

2. **Mad Monk   10b**
   FA: Caldwell, 1986.
   This is an offwidth crack left of *Rambozo*.

3. **Rambozo   10c**
   FA: Caldwell, 1986.
   Climb the overhanging offwidth left of the second pitch of *Ferris Peels*.

4. Ferris Peels 10b
FA: Randy Ferris and Mike Caldwell, 1985.
Climb an open book dihedral on the north side of the buttress and belay above a roof (10b). Climb a concave face with a bolt (10b).

CRESCENT WALL
Crescent Wall is the broad dome near the east end of Lumpy Ridge. Its steep south face has several excellent routes that justify the rugged approach. Hike the Gem Lake Trail about one mile to where the wall comes into view. Leave the trail and work southeast along a wooded and rocky ridge until south of the wall, then drop into the ravine and scramble up the other side through large boulders to the bottom of the south face. It is easier walking to leave the trail before the wall can be seen and work around the outside of a rock formation, but it is difficult to tell when to leave the trail if you have not done it before. To descend from the summit, walk off to the west.

1. Milk Run 7 vs
FA: Doug Snively and Scott Kimball, 1981.
Begin at the left edge of the south face. Climb a right-facing dihedral and the face above.

2. Root Canal 9 ★
FA: Caldwell, Solem, Lazar and Quigley, 1986.
Climb the first 100 feet of *Cleft Palate* and belay. Move out left and work up the slab past two bolts, then back toward the right.

3. Cleft Palate 11a s ★
FA: Scott Woodruff, Mike Gilbert and Dan Hare, 1975.
Begin near the left side of the south face.
1. Climb up to a hook-shaped crack and climb to its top, then traverse right beneath a long roof and belay (10b/c s). Another option is to climb up to the right of the crack past a bolt (9).
2. Climb the "cleft" beneath the long roof (11a).
3. Work up easier rock to the top.

4. Hair Lip 11c ★
FA: Mike Caldwell and Randy Ferris, 1986.
Climb the first 40 feet of *Wintergreen,* take a short crack that veers off to the left, then climb past three bolts to the middle of the *Cleft Palate* roof (10a) and move left to a belay. Go back to the right and tie off

CRESCENT WALL, SOUTH FACE

1. Milk Run 7 vs
2. Root Canal 9 ★
3. Cleft Palate 11a s ★
4. Hair Lip 11c ★
5. Wintergreen 8 vs
6. Heaven Can Wait 9 or 10b ★
7. Flight for Life 12a ★
8. Lycra Bikers from Hell 12a ★
9. Cool Aid 10d A3
10. Pressure Drop 11a ★
11. Politics of Scarcity 12b s
12. Finger Licking Good 11a ★
13. Strategic Arms 11d s
14. Crescent Arch 11c ★
15. Poultry in Motion 11d ★

horns at the lip of the roof. Crank over the roof and climb the slab past two bolts (11c).

5. Wintergreen   8 vs
FA: Snively and Kimball, 1981.
Begin about 70 feet left of *Heaven Can Wait* and climb a wall of knobs and crystals to the high point of that route.

6. Heaven Can Wait   9 or 10b ★
FA: unknown; of third pitch, Caldwell and Barlow, 1984.
Begin near the middle of the south face beneath a left-leaning, left-facing dihedral.
1. Climb the dihedral to a ledge (9).
2. Walk off or climb an easy right-facing dihedral to the big roof.
3. Turn the roof and climb the steep face past two bolts (10b). Finish as for *Cleft Palate.*

7. Flight for Life   12a ★
FA: Randy Ferris, 1991. Seven QDs.
Begin near the left end of a long ramp that runs up and left from the start to *Pressure Drop* (see topo).
1. Follow four bolts up the wall (12a), traverse up and right over scaly rock and join *Lycra Bikers* at the roof (see below).
2. Climb the wall above past two more bolts (10a/b) or rappel 80 feet.

8. Lycra Bikers from Hell   12a ★
FA: Mike Caldwell and Randy Ferris, 1987.
Begin on a ramp about 60 feet up and left from *Pressure Drop.*
1. Follow a crack out to the right past two pins, then work straight up past a bolt, climb a crack and the face above (two more bolts) to a belay at a two-bolt anchor (11d, 70 feet).
2. Traverse straight left, turn the roof (two bolts), and belay at a two-bolt anchor (11b, 45 feet).
3. Climb the wall above past two more bolts (10a/b, 100 feet) or rappel 80 feet.

9. Cool Aid   10d A3
FA: Layton Kor and partner, 1964.
Begin at the bottom of the ramp that angles up and left across the wall. Climb a vertical finger crack (10d) and continue straight up to the roof on aid. Turn the roof (A3) and belay from bolts. The short second pitch requires a pendulum.

10. Pressure Drop   11a ★
FA: Dan Hare and Pete Steres, 1974. Rack up to a #2.5 Friend.
This fine route can be completed in two 70-foot pitches with an uncomfortable belay or one long pitch. Climb the finger crack of *Cool Aid,* then break right and follow an arching thin crack to a bolt belay.

11. Politics of Scarcity   12b s
FA: Steve Muehlhauser and Sarah Spalding, 1988. Rack up to one inch.
Begin as for *Finger Licking* but continue straight up a thin crack/seam with an unidentifiable piece of metal glued into the crack and a bolt a little higher. When the seam fades, continue upward to join the last few moves of *Pressure Drop.*

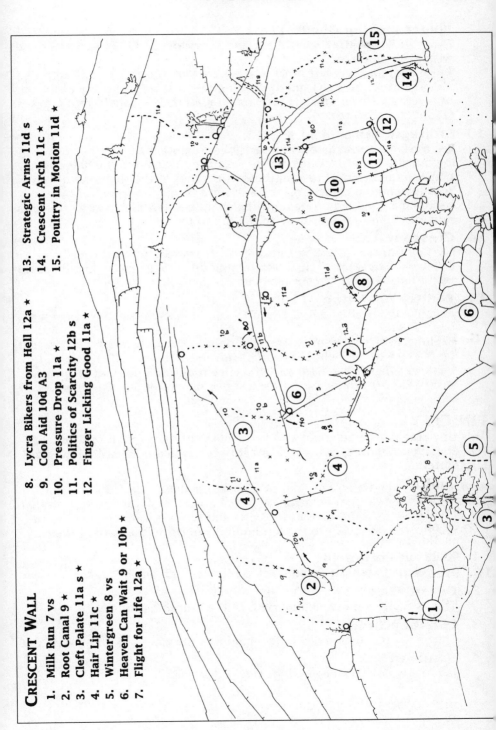

CRESCENT WALL

1. Milk Run 7 vs
2. Root Canal 9 ★
3. Cleft Palate 11a s ★
4. Hair Lip 11c ★
5. Wintergreen 8 vs
6. Heaven Can Wait 9 or 10b ★
7. Flight for Life 12a ★
8. Lycra Bikers from Hell 12a ★
9. Cool Aid 10d A3
10. Pressure Drop 11a ★
11. Politics of Scarcity 12b s
12. Finger Licking Good 11a ★
13. Strategic Arms 11d s
14. Crescent Arch 11c ★
15. Poultry in Motion 11d ★

12. Finger Licking Good   11a ★

FA: Scott Woodruff, Mike Gilbert, and Dan Hare, 1974. SR to a #2 Friend with extra stoppers.

Begin about 40 feet left of *Crescent Arch*. Work up to a crack/ramp that shoots out to the right and undercling this feature to a belay at the base of a vertical finger crack (11a). Jam straight up the superb thin crack (11a). Rappel 80 feet.

13. Strategic Arms   11d s

FA: Mark Rolofson, Eric Doub, and John Allen, 1981.

Begin with *Finger Licking Good* or *Pressure Drop*. From the bolt anchor, climb up and right (11d s) and belay in slings at the right end of the roof (two-bolt anchor). Work up and right through a trough (11a) and belay on a good ledge. Move the belay up and left past a large tree (now fallen). Climb the face above to the top of the wall (11a).

14. Crescent Arch   11c ★

FA: Ken Duncan. FFA: Ken Duncan, 1977. Rack up to six inches.

Climb the large, left-facing, left-arching dihedral at the right side of the south face. Rappel or continue with *Strategic Arms*.

15. Poultry in Motion   11d ★

FA: Mike Caldwell and Brian Bornholdt, 1987. Rack: small wires and #2.5 or #3 Friend.

Begin as for *Crescent Arch*. Traverse right to the arête and follow six bolts up the face to the right of the arch. Traverse left to a bolt anchor and belay in slings at the right end of a huge roof (third belay of *Strategic Arms*). Rappel 120 feet or do the last two pitches of *Strategic Arms*.

FIN CITY

This tiny crag is located about 150 yards north of the summit of Crescent Wall and about 200 feet east of Out West Crag – which is to say, a long walk for some short cracks.

Approach via the Gem Lake Trail. Walk past the usual cutoff to Crescent Wall. Where the trail first comes near to the ravine, look for a faint trail that drops down to the right. Cross the ravine and hike up slabs to near the top of Crescent Wall, then exit to the left and hike north to the base of the crag.

1. Kids on Coffee   8+

This is the first clean hand crack on the left side of the crag.

2. Out of Time   8+

This is the second crack line right of the preceding route.

3. Chimney Sweep   7

This is the flared chimney in the middle of the west face. Bring wide gear.

4. Hands Off   9

Jam the wide crack at the right side of the wall.

OUT WEST CRAG

This small crag is located about 1.3 miles up the Gem Lake Trail. Look for a square-ish, grey and yellow rock up along the ridge to the right of the trail, a short way before reaching the lake. Routes on this crag were established by Scott Kimball, Tim Hansen, and Doug Snively during 1981.

1. Rawhide   11a
Jam a deceptive finger and hand crack up the northeast rib (the main wall faces northwest).

2. Small Caliber   10c
Climb the finger crack near the left side of the northwest face.

3. Hanging Tree   10d
Begin near the middle of the northwest face. Make a delicate traverse out right and climb a thin, left-leaning crack with a small tree partway up.

4. Rough and Ready   9+
Ascend the right-leaning, right-facing dihedral at the right side of the northwest face.

Cosmic Commode   11a
FA: Caldwell and Ferris, 1985.
Hike the Gem Lake Trail to a solar outhouse a short way south of Gem Lake. This route climbs the giant dihedral to the west of the outhouse.

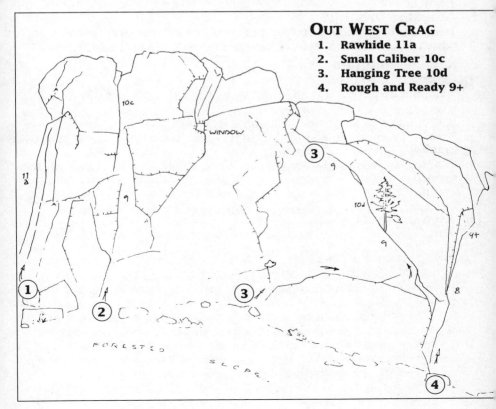

OUT WEST CRAG
1. **Rawhide 11a**
2. **Small Caliber 10c**
3. **Hanging Tree 10d**
4. **Rough and Ready 9+**

SALAMANDER ROCK

Salamander Rock is a small buttress about 500 feet to the left (southwest) of Alligator Rock (see below). It has a single known route.

Salamander Crack 10b/c
FA: Tim Hansen and Inguan Raastad, 1983.
Climb the crack near the middle of the feature.

ALLIGATOR ROCK

Alligator Rock is located at the eastern extreme of Lumpy Ridge just within the boundary of Rocky Mountain National Park. It does resemble an alligator, with the head at left. The "head" has a large scooped-out area with a pronounced buttress at right. The "body" has another buttress with the route *Pine Tree Arête*. A long "tail" tapers off to the right. Note the uncanny "eye" above the scoop.

Approach. From Estes Park, take Devil's Gulch Road (McGregor Avenue) north and continue about 1.5 miles past the turn-off to McGregor Ranch (Lumpy Ridge). The rock comes into view above a ranch and appears as a long arched wall with two distinct buttresses left of center. The approach involves going up a private driveway onto the ranch. Stop at the house and ask permission before proceeding.

1. **Alligator Drool 8**
   The left side of the scoop features a wide crack that overhangs at the bottom. Scramble up slabs to get started. Walk off to the west.

2. **K Mart Mountaineer 7**
   FA: Scott Kimball and Liz Lehmann, 1977.
   Scramble up a trough at the right side of the scoop and belay at the base of a left-leaning chimney.
   1. Climb the chimney and belay on a ledge (7).
   2. Move to the north end of the ledge. Climb unpleasant cracks and continue to a notch.
   3. Angle up around the summit block and climb to its top. Walk off to the west.

The following routes ascend a compact buttress that forms the posterior mandible of the alligator.

3. **No Purchase Necessary 10a ★**
   FA: Hansen, Kimball, Raastad, 1983
   Begin down to the right from *K Mart Mountaineer* and left of the rounded ridge crest.
   1. Face climb up the steep wall past a horizontal break and continue left of the crest until it is possible to move right and clip a bolt, then friction up to another break in the face (crux). Work up to a flake that straddles the ridge and go right to a common belay with *Possum Hang*.
   2. Finish with the second pitch of *Possum Hang*.

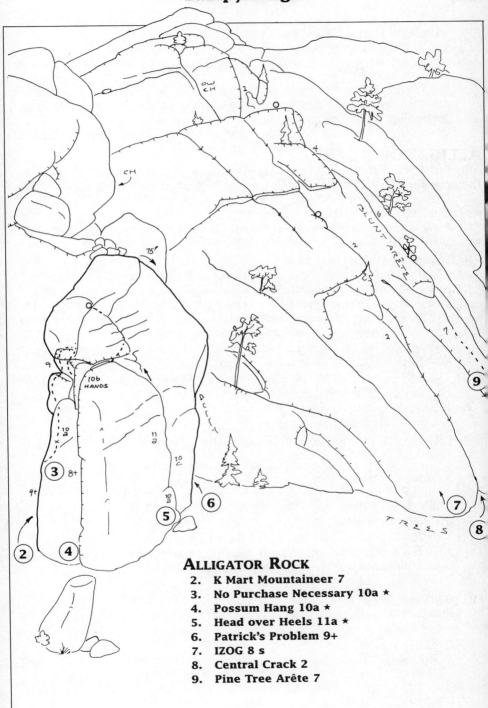

ALLIGATOR ROCK

2. **K Mart Mountaineer 7**
3. **No Purchase Necessary 10a** ★
4. **Possum Hang 10a** ★
5. **Head over Heels 11a** ★
6. **Patrick's Problem 9+**
7. **IZOG 8 s**
8. **Central Crack 2**
9. **Pine Tree Arête 7**

4. Possum Hang   10a ★
FA: Kimball and Wylie, 1980.
This route ascends the obvious crack and corner just left from the prow of the buttress.
1. Climb a finger crack in a clean, left-facing dihedral (8+), step left into a small alcove, then jam a fist crack along a pointed flake to a bucket, and belay above the roof.
2. Climb an easy slab to the rock-littered ledge on top. Walk north and rappel 80 feet from a chockstone into a gully.

4A. Hawk's Nest   9 ★
Hand traverse right from the alcove onto the face, then make a scary step left to belay.

4B. Orangutan   10b ★
This is the best option of the three. Climb the overhanging hand crack where the main crack jogs left and continue to the top of the buttress.

5. Head over Heels   11a ★
FA: Westbay and Snively, 1978. SR with extra #1.5 to 2.5 Friends.
The right side of the buttress mentioned above forms a slightly over-hanging wall that is pierced by a dramatic crack. This is the route. The crack arches up and left in three distinct phases, each harder than the preceding. Tape up. Rappel as for *Possum Hang.*

6. Patrick's Problem   9+
FA: Mark Wilford and Pat Morris, 1980.
Locate a fist crack followed by a chimney to the right of *Head over Heels* and left of the rappel chimney.

7. IZOG   8 s
FA: Jim Detterline and Lisa Reilly, 1986.
Climb the center of the slab between the rappel gully and *Central Crack.*

8. Central Crack   2
This route takes the obvious crack/chimney in the broad wall to the right of the rappel chimney.

9. Pine Tree Arête   7
This route ascends the foreleg of the alligator.
1. Climb a thin crack on the left side of the arête to a stance with a pine tree, continue up the arête, and work left to belay.
2. Follow the obvious line above.

10. Archie   6
Climb slabs with right-leaning arches in the tail of the alligator.

COW CREEK CANYON

The next drainage to the north of Lumpy Ridge is Cow Creek Canyon, which is geographically separate from the Estes Valley and drains into the North Fork of the Big Thompson River. At least three crags in this beautiful mountain valley offer interesting climbing. The largest of these is Sheep Mountain Rock, which presides on the north slope above Cow Creek about two miles from the trailhead.

Approach. From Estes Park, take Devil's Gulch Road as though going to Glen Haven. After 4.5 miles, turn left (actually, go straight) on McGraw Ranch Road (unpaved) and drive about two miles to its end at McGraw Ranch inside Rocky Mountain National Park. Follow signs for parking. The trail starts at the ranch and heads west along a dirt road that narrows to a good trail after about one-half mile. Cow Creek Canyon also may be reached from the Twin Owls Parking area via the Gem Lake Trail (4.5 miles). While this will be of little interest to those going rock climbing, it provides an excellent three-trail loop with the Cow Creek Trail and the Black Canyon Trail. This is a wonderful hike or, for the more athletic, a great trail run of about ten miles.

Climbing on Combat Rock.

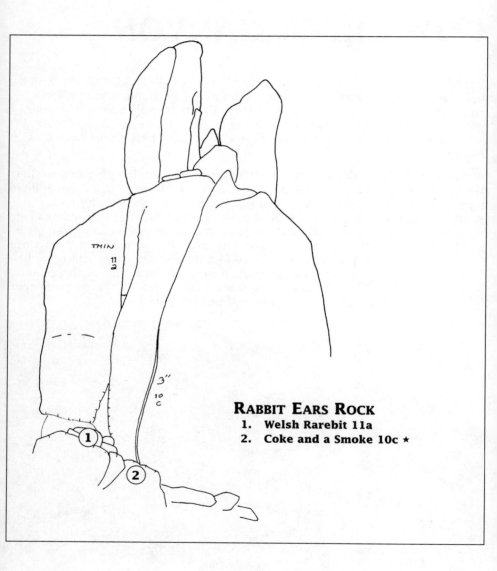

THIN
11
a

3"
10
c

RABBIT EARS ROCK
1. **Welsh Rarebit 11a**
2. **Coke and a Smoke 10c ★**

RABBIT EARS ROCK

Rabbit Ears Rock sits above a backcountry campsite on the south side of Cow Creek, about 1.5 miles from the trailhead. The rock is easily identified by two granite prongs (the ears) above a square-cut, 50-foot block. The following routes ascend the vertical faces of the block.

1. **Welsh Rarebit   11a**
   FA: Scott Kimball and Joe Hladick, 1984.
   This is the left-hand crack on the west face.

2. **Coke and a Smoke   10c ★**
   FA: Tim Hansen, 1984. Rack as for *Small Paradise*.
   This is the right-hand crack.

3. **Small Paradise   10b**
   FA: Hansen, 1984. Medium stoppers to a #3.5 Friend with extra #2.5 to #3.5 Friends.
   This is a fist crack in the east side.

KELLOG'S CRAG

This is a south-facing crag about 0.75 mile west of Rabbit Ears Rock in a south fork of Cow Creek Canyon. Hike to Rabbit Ears Rock campsite, then follow a faint streambed southwest until the rock can be seen on the north (right) side of the drainage. There is a large overhang at the right side of the main face. This crag is largely hidden from view during the approach.

1. **Steak and Eggs   10a**
   FA: Bernard and Robert Gillett, 1988.
   Climb an easy chimney at the left side of the south face and arrive at a ledge. Step left and jam an offwidth crack.

2. **Corn Flakes   6**
   FA: The Gilletts, 1988.
   Begin at some jumbled flakes to the right of *Steak and Eggs.* From the top of the flakes, climb an easy crack.

3. **Fruity Pebbles   8 vs**
   FA: The Gilletts, 1988.
   Begin at a right-facing flake about 40 feet right of *Corn Flakes.* Climb the flake (8) and the crystal-studded face above (8 near the top).

4. **Fruit Loops   9+ ★**
   FA: Bernard Gillett and Doug Snively, 1988.
   Climb a clean, vertical, right-facing dihedral in the middle of the crag (9+), turn a roof on the left (8), and follow a crack to a belay.

SHEEP MOUNTAIN ROCK From the South

1. **Double Fantasy 10a** ★
2. **Wuthering Heights 9 s**
5. **Gimmerton Corner 10b/c** ★
6. **Stone Pillar 10b/c**
7. **Himmelfahrt 10b/c**

8. **Thrushcross Grange 7**
9. **High Road 1**

SHEEP MOUNTAIN ROCK

Sheep Mountain Rock is the large buttress on the north slope of Cow Creek Canyon that is visible to the west from McGraw Ranch. The crag is about 350 feet high, 1,500 feet wide, and consists of a fine-grained granite.

Approach via the Cow Creek Trail. From the cutoff to Rabbit Ears Rock Camp (1.5 miles), hike northwest up the grassy slope and through open forest directly to the buttress. The off-trail hiking can be shortened, however, by continuing on the trail until below the southwest face, whence a direct line up the brushy slope leads to the right side of the crag.

Descent. Escape the top of the buttress by walking west until the rock changes from granitic to metamorphic and descend a gully. Feature of note: Near the middle of the southwest face is a distinct, left-facing dihedral with the route *Gimmerton Corner*. All routes begin from a ledge system along the bottom of the face.

1. Double Fantasy   10a ⋆
FA: Scott Kimball, Carl Harrison, and Sandy East, 1980.
Some 180 feet left of *Gimmerton Corner,* locate a pair of flake/dihedrals that face toward each other about 50 feet up. Belay from a 35-foot pine.
1. Climb a short crack through a bulge (8), move up and right along a ramp, step left, and climb the channel between the two flakes (10a).
2. Work up and right, hand traverse along an arching, black roof, turn the roof, and belay above (9+).
3. Climb straight up, turn another roof (8), and follow easier terrain to the top of the wall.

2. Wuthering Heights   9 s
FA: George Hurley and Walter Fricke, 1970.
About 90 feet left of *Gimmerton Corner,* identify two 20-foot flakes behind a small Douglas fir tree.
1. Climb the right flake, move delicately up and left, then back right (9 s) into a flared crack system. Above the crack, climb steep rock with rounded holds (8 s) to a groove that leads to a belay left of a prominent pillar (135 feet).
2. Work up and left via easier terrain to a final headwall. Mantel onto a sloping ledge (8), climb a small rib to the left, and friction up a slab to the top (150 feet).

3. Pennystone Crag   9+
FA: George Hurley and Bob Beal, 1971.
A coin is hammered into a groove at the start of this climb.
Begin 60 feet left of *Gimmerton Corner* behind a three-foot Douglas fir.
1. Climb a small, left-facing dihedral and flared crack for 25 feet, move right at a fixed pin (9+), and follow a flared crack and corner system to a ledge on the right.
2. Climb a long pitch that begins with left-facing corners and ends in vague terrain (9).
3. A short pitch leads to the top (7).

4. Lamb's Skin   8
FA: Scott Kimball and Warren Young, 1977.
Begin about 30 feet left of *Gimmerton Corner* in large dihedral system between two slight buttresses.
1a. Start back in the left-facing dihedral, climb about ten feet, then hand traverse left along a one-inch crack to its end. Work up into a flared crack and corner system and follow it to a belay stance (8).
1b. Climb a clean fist crack straight up to the end of the hand traverse and continue (8).
2. Work up and left along similar terrain (7).
3. An easier pitch leads to the top.

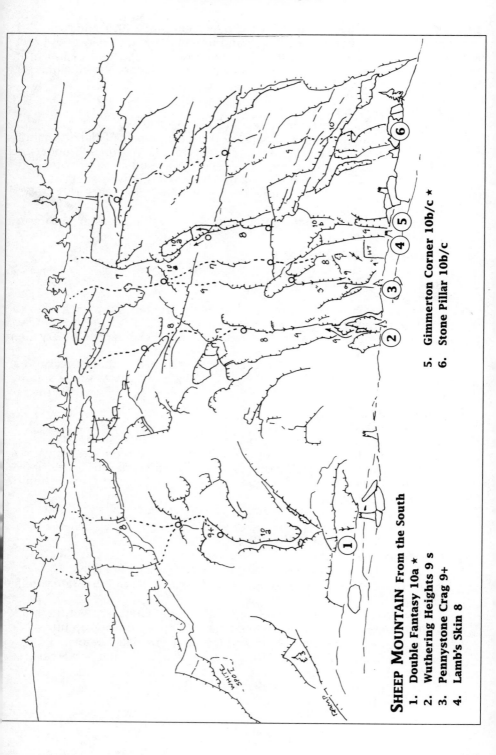

SHEEP MOUNTAIN From the South

1. Double Fantasy 10a ★
2. Wuthering Heights 9 s
3. Pennystone Crag 9+
4. Lamb's Skin 8
5. Gimmerton Corner 10b/c ★
6. Stone Pillar 10b/c

5. Gimmerton Corner   10b/c ★

FA: George Hurley and Phil Fowler, c. 1971. FFA: Jim Erickson, c. 1972.

This is perhaps the best route on the wall.

Begin below a conspicuous left-facing dihedral in the middle of the southwest face, just right of *Lamb's Skin*.

1. Step off a two-foot spike and climb the left side of a pillar (9). Work up and right along a flake (10b) to the main corner, then squeeze up and left to belay.
2. Climb the dihedral for about 100 feet (8).
3. Continue in the corner as it bends left along a smooth slab (sustained 9 to 10) and finish with 50 feet of easier terrain (7).

6. Stone Pillar   10b/c

FA: George Hurley, Richard Smith, and Tim Grove, 1971.

Begin 20 feet right of *Gimmerton Corner.*

1. Climb the right side of pillar or flake, then continue over flakes and knobs to a good belay (10b/c). There may be a fixed nut at the crux — then again...
2. Continue upward for a long pitch (9).
3. Climb a double crack to the top.

7. Himmelfahrt   10b/c

FA: George Hurley and Dave Rearick, 1973.

No doubt the name of some Norwegian ski race or the like – A very steep, impressive route in any case.

Begin about 200 feet right from *Gimmerton Corner* on a pedestal with a flat rock above an abrupt step in the ledge system.

1. Climb up into a slot formed by a protruding block, lieback up the dihedral for about 75 feet and belay in a bombay slot (9).
2. Above the slot, tackle a very sustained crack and corner system (10b) and belay at right after the difficulties ease.
3. Climb a moderate slab to another roof.
4. Climb a right-leaning slash in the overhang (10b/c) and finish with a moderate slab.

8. Thrushcross Grange   7

FA: Hurley and Beal, 1971.

Locate a massive, left-facing dihedral system with orange lichen at the right side of the main wall.

1. Begin in the dihedral system, but veer slightly left into a black, left-facing corner, continue up a steep ramp, and belay on a ledge 20 feet below and 20 feet out left from the initial overhang in the dihedral (150 feet).
2. Follow the line of least resistance to the left of the overhangs until it is possible to pass the upper roof on the right (155 feet).

9. High Road   1

This is a pleasant line up clean rock at the southeast end of the crag. Approach via a perfect ledge that runs east from the bottom of *Thrushcross Grange.*

EAGLE ROCK, West Face
1. **Left Dihedral 6**
2. **The Great Escape 7**
3. **Golden Eagle 7 ★**
4. **Spread Eagle 7 s ★**
5. **Center Dihedral 7 ★**
6. **Kay's Caravan 6**
7. **Guides' Route 5 s**

DRY GULCH

Dry Gulch is the broad, grassy draw north of Lake Estes and east of Lumpy Ridge. To reach Dry Gulch Road from the junction of Highway 34 and Highway 36 in Estes Park, drive east about 1.5 miles on 34 and turn north (left) on Dry Gulch Road. Dry Gulch Road climbs north along Dry Gulch Creek for about three miles, and ends at an intersection with County Road 61 (unpaved). Devil's Gulch Road may be reached by traveling west on the dirt road for a quarter mile. Two excellent rock formations, Eagle Rock and Crosier Dome, are located on the east side of Dry Gulch, about two miles north of Lake Estes.

EAGLE ROCK

Eagle Rock, a stately exfoliation dome, hosts several fine moderate routes, and has become popular over the years. To reach Eagle Rock, follow the directions above to Dry Gulch Road. The dome appears on the east side of the road after about two miles. Turn east on the new road to Eagle Rock School and park just after crossing a cattle grate. The road passes directly beneath the west face of Eagle Rock, but apparently parking is not allowed along this stretch. The road and Eagle Rock lie within the boundaries of the McGregor Public Trust lands, and the trust's position on climbing is not known.

1. **Left Dihedral   6**
   This line follows the large, right-facing dihedral at the left side of the west face. Begin about 30 feet right of a seven-foot "tombstone" flake and belay from an aspen tree. Three pitches. Exit left (8) or right (6) from the top of the dihedral.

2. **The Great Escape   7**
   This is an early route described in Walter Fricke's guide; its exact location is not known. Begin near the middle of the slab; look for a seam with a fixed pin about 50 feet up. Climb two pitches up to a roof, climb around the roof, and finish with a chimney/dihedral.

3. **Golden Eagle   7 ★**
   FA: Jon Estabrook, 1988.
   At the right side of the central slab, locate a compelling crack that shoots up and slightly left.
   1. Climb an awkward, left-facing dihedral, then follow the crack past the left end of a roof and belay after 120 feet.
   2. Follow the crack through a bulge and belay beneath a roof (140 feet).
   3. Climb straight up and finish as for *Left Dihedral* (100 feet).

4. **Spread Eagle   7 s ★**
   FA: John Spezia and Fred Sphax, 1974.
   This route begins at a large, triangular flake/slab just right from the start to *Golden Eagle.*

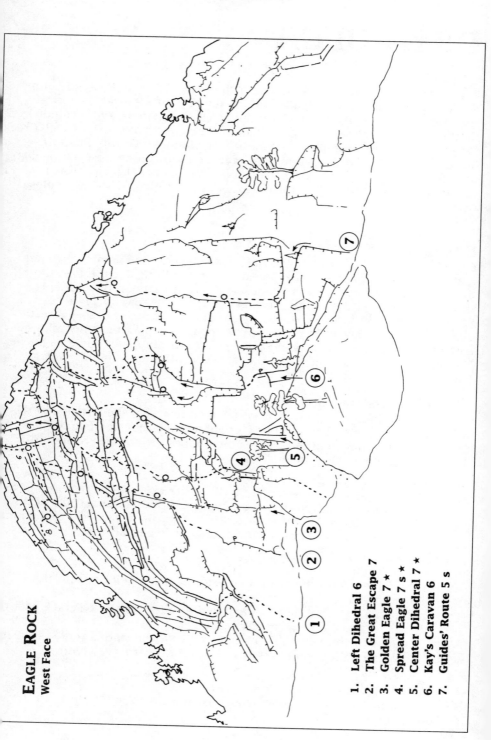

EAGLE ROCK
West Face

1. Left Dihedral 6
2. The Great Escape 7
3. Golden Eagle 7 ★
4. Spread Eagle 7 s ★
5. Center Dihedral 7 ★
6. Kay's Caravan 6
7. Guides' Route 5 s

1. Climb the slab to a pine tree at its top, continue up the face, turn a roof at a break (7), and belay on the slab above (7 s, 135 feet).
2. Climb straight up the face past some overlaps and an old bolt (no hanger), pass a roof on the left, continue along some right-facing dihedrals, and belay (7, 165 feet).
3. Work up and left and finish as for the previous route or go straight up through a fist crack (The Raven, 9).

5. Center Dihedral   7 ★

This route begins just to the right from the slab/flake of *Spread Eagle*. Identify a right-facing dihedral above and right of the horizontal roof at mid-face.
1. Climb a slab via short cracks and seams and continue up the right-facing corner to a good belay (7, 165 feet).
2. Work more or less straight up to finish just right of the summit overhangs (4, 140 feet).

6. Kay's Caravan   6

FA: Kay Westbay and Lynn Albers.
Begin about 150 to the right from *Spread Eagle* in the left of three left-leaning grooves.
1. Work up past a fixed pin, then up and left to belay beneath the left side of a roof.
2. Turn the roof and finish with a right-leaning, right-facing dihedral. It is also possible to belay beneath the right side of the roof on the first pitch, then merge left into the right-facing dihedral.

7. Guides' Route   5 s

FA: Bradley and Hankin.
Begin about 200 feet down and right from *Kay's Caravan* and to the left of a large pine up on the wall.
1. Climb up onto a ledge, walk to its north end, then work straight up to an obvious belay (5, 130 feet).
2. Climb straight up into a right-facing dihedral and belay (4, 160 feet).
3. Continue up the dihedral and finish on easy ground.

CROSIER DOME

Crosier Dome is an impressive, south-facing buttress about 0.5 mile south-east of Eagle Rock. The rock is steep and solid with an abundance of flared grooves and a few chimneys. Access availability is not known.

Approach as for Eagle Rock but continue along the road toward Eagle Rock School for about 1.5 miles. The dome is visible from a saddle, beyond which the road goes downhill. About 0.25 mile beyond the saddle, take a left branch in the road and follow it to the bottom of a draw. Park here at a 90° bend in the road. Cross the draw to the northeast and follow a good trail until the full south face of Crosier Dome may be seen at left (north), then hike straight up the hillside to the base of the wall. Look for cairns. To descend from the summit, carefully downclimb grooves on the west edge.

1. **Fledgling 7** ★
   FA: Estabrook and Norlin, 1989.
   From the bottom of the south face, hike left (west) up a gully/ramp to the far left side of the face and scramble up onto a big ledge.
   Begin just right of a juniper tree. Climb flakes to the right of an obvious crack, then up a thin crack that leans to the right, and head for a chockstone in a notch (80 feet).

2. **Expecting to Fly 9**
   FA: Estabrook and Norlin, 1989.
   This line takes the blank face to the right of *Fledgling* and finishes in a short, vertical crack. The first ascent party protected the face by climbing halfway up *Fledgling* and placing a #2 Camalot, then downclimbing back to the ledge to begin.

3. **Edge of a Feather 7**
   FA: Estabrook, 1989
   Begin down on the ramp/groove at a wedged boulder below the right end of the ledge where the preceding routes begin.
   1. Start up the face behind the boulder and reach a crack. Continue with the crack and belay on the big ledge of *Fledgling* (5).
   2. Follow a crack straight up the face to a ledge beneath an overhang (7). Walk off or continue with a third pitch.
   3. Lieback up into a water groove (being wary of a loose flake) and climb to the top (5).

4. **Crosier Cave 5 or 7**
   FA: Estabrook, 1989.
   Belay from a large juniper just down to the right from *Edge of a Feather*.
   1. Climb a crack to the right of a hanging flake, then work up and right to belay on a large ledge (130 feet) or continue up and left to walk off (165 feet).
   2. Climb up and right to a ledge at the bottom of a chimney (optional belay). Climb the chimney (easy) or the face on the right via short cracks.

5. **Dirty Hula 8**
   FA: Estabrook, 1989.
   This route takes the prominent groove on the left side of the wall.

Photo: Jon Estabrook

CROSIER DOME, South Face

1. **Fledgling 7 ★**
2. **Expecting to Fly 9**
3. **Edge of a Feather 7**
4. **Crosier Cave 5 or 7**
5. **Dirty Hula 8**
6. **Crosier Direct 8 s ★**
7. **Komito Route 7 ★**
8. **Danger Bird (Flies Alone) 8 or 9 s (unfinished)**
9. **Another Komito Route 7**
10. **Flown Home 7**

Begin a short way down and right from the *Crosier Cave* route below a bulge with a black crack through it.
1. Climb the crack through the bulge (6), then follow the groove to a lichenous recess (150 feet).
2. Climb the nasty recess and the nice crack above to a ledge (8, 80 feet).
3. Climb the face and crack above the belay (7, 80 feet) or do the right-hand finish to *Crosier Cave* (7).

6. Crosier Direct   8 s ★

FA: Estabrook, 1989. SR plus lots of runners.

This is a good, solid route up the middle of the face. It has a runout section with good holds (5) on the first pitch; the crux is well-protected. Begin from the right end of a ledge down and right from *Dirty Hula*.

1. Climb straight up via discontinuous cracks, continue in a groove, and belay in a small alcove (6, 165 feet).
2. Move right and up the face to a ledge beneath a crack (4, 50 feet).
3. Climb the crack up to a ledge (8) and continue in the same system (6) to the top (140 feet).

7. Komito Route   7 ★

FA: (?) Steve Komito and Michael Covington.

Begin a short way left of three deeply cut grooves at mid-face, just right of two five-foot junipers.

1. Climb the face left of the deep grooves and belay in an alcove at the bottom of a right-facing dihedral/slot with a chockstone (5, 155 feet).
2. Climb straight up, passing the chockstone on the right, and belay in another alcove (7, 130 feet).
3. Wander up and right to a crack system and follow it to the top (6, 150 feet).

8. Danger Bird (Flies Alone)   8 or 9 s (unfinished)

Begin in the right of the three deep grooves at mid-face. The rock above the groove has not been climbed.

9. Another Komito Route   7

FA: (?) Steve Komito and Michael Covington.

Begin about 100 feet to the right from the three deep grooves at mid-face. Scramble 30 feet up onto a ledge with a small pine tree.

1. Follow a prominent groove to where it bends right, continue up into another groove and belay in a recess (6, 165 feet).
2. Continue in the same system as it tapers to a crack and reach a ledge beneath a headwall (optional belay). Angle up and left into a groove in a large open book dihedral and belay on a ledge at its top (7, 150 feet).
3. Work up and left into a groove and continue to the top (5, 120 feet).

10. Flown Home   7

FA: Estabrook and Norlin, 1990.

This route follows a system of deep chimneys and grooves along the right side of the south face.

Scramble up into the initial chimney to belay.

1. Follow the chimney/groove to a horizontal break, continue straight up in a steep corner/crack to a good ledge (7, 165 feet). One also could step right at the break and climb either of two steep cracks to the belay.
2. Continue up the groove for about 20 feet, then work up and left to a crack with a chockstone. Pass the chockstone (crux) and belay in an alcove with a bush (7, 120 feet).
3. Wander up the east ridge (6, 90 feet).

BIG THOMPSON CANYON

The rugged Big Thompson Canyon, which descends eastward from Estes Park, is a vast climbing area unto itself. Touring the canyon on Highway 34, many towers and buttresses catch the eye and distract one from the duty of driving. An occasional glint of sunlight reflected off a bolt hanger suggests the activity of modern climbers. While it is true that many routes have been established here, little has been published. The only crag to have gained wide recognition is Combat Rock, which is located off a forest service road about one mile north of the little town of Drake. A magnificent slab known as Seam Rock is located three miles north of Combat Rock.

COMBAT ROCK

Combat Rock is located about 12 miles east of Estes Park, near the town of Drake in the Big Thompson Canyon. It is host to many good bolt-protected face climbs as well as a few notable cracks. The main wall faces south and is a short hike from the road. All routes, including those fixed with bolts, require transient protection; thin to medium width, flexible pieces are especially useful due to a prevalence of horizontal cracks.

Approach. To reach the crag from Boulder or Denver, take Highway 36 to Lyons, turn east (right) at the light and, after 3.8 miles, turn north (left) on County Line Road. Go about 3 miles and turn left on North 83rd. Drive 5.5 miles and go left at a stop sign. Go past the road to Carter Lake and, after 2 miles, go left on Road 12 (gravel). After 7.1 miles, go left on Highway 34 and drive 9 miles up the Big Thompson Canyon to Drake. At 9.3 miles, turn right on the road to Glen Haven and right again after 0.3 mile on a dirt "forest access" road from which the crag is visible. Follow the road up past four steep switchbacks and park at a pullout on the left where the road straightens.

One also may reach Drake by taking Highway 34 east from Estes Park or west from Loveland. If approaching from the east via Highway 36, turn north on Mall Road just before Lake Estes, then turn right on Highway 34 and proceed to Drake.

From the pullout, follow a footpath down into the draw on the north. Note *Elmer Fudd's Wok* on the north bank, a toprope slab. Walk west along the draw, then make an ascending traverse to the northwest along a path that leads to the low point of the face.

Descent. For routes that finish along the west side of the south face, traverse off to the left to where it is easy to scramble down into the wooded gully along the west side of the rock. For routes that finish nearer the top of the rock, scramble east to a grassy gully that descends to the south. One also may rappel from various bolt anchors on the face.

COMBAT ROCK From the South
1. Arkansas Patriot 9+ ★
6. Eight Clicks to Saigon 10d s ★
8. Across Enemy Lines 11b ★
11. Blood for Oil 12b ★
15. Lizzard Warrior 11b ★
17. G.I. Joe does Barbie 9+ s A1
18. Nuclear Polka 10a ★

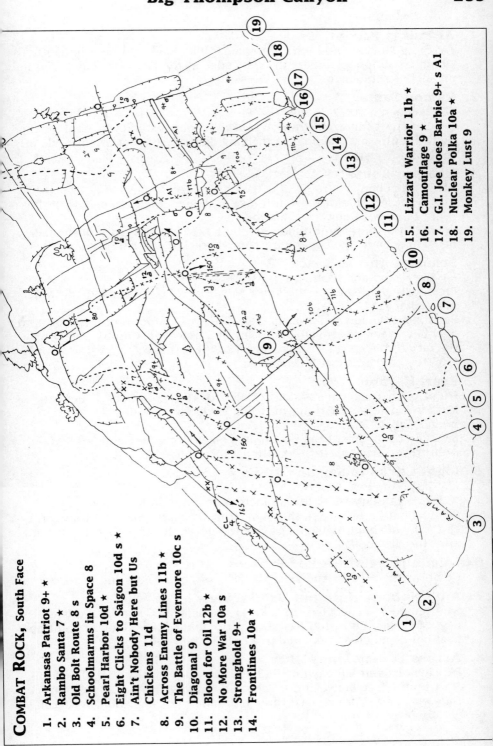

COMBAT ROCK, South Face

1. Arkansas Patriot 9+ ★
2. Rambo Santa 7 ★
3. Old Bolt Route 8 s
4. Schoolmarms in Space 8
5. Pearl Harbor 10d ★
6. Eight Clicks to Saigon 10d s ★
7. Ain't Nobody Here but Us
8. Chickens 11d
9. Across Enemy Lines 11b ★
10. The Battle of Evermore 10c s
11. Diagonal 9
12. Blood for Oil 12b ★
13. No More War 10a s
14. Stronghold 9+
15. Frontlines 10a ★

15. Lizzard Warrior 11b ★
16. Camouflage 9 ★
17. G.I. Joe does Barbie 9+ s A1
18. Nuclear Polka 10a ★
19. Monkey Lust 9

1. Arkansas Patriot 9+ ★
FA: Craig Luebben and John Shireman, 1990. Rack: stoppers and QDs.
Climb an 80-foot slab near the west edge of the face. Three bolts up to an anchor with chains.

2. Rambo Santa 7 ★
FA: Luebben and Ginny Sawyer, 1992. Rack: stoppers to a #3 Friend.
Begin a short way right from *Arkansas Patriot.* Six bolts to a bolt anchor on the southwest shoulder of the crag. Rappel 165 feet or scramble off to the left (west).

3. Old Bolt Route 8 s
FA: Keith Lober.
The lower left side of the south face is shaped like a triangle with the route *Diagonal* along its right side.
Begin left of center and follow six old bolts up to the apex of the face. A belay may be necessary at a horizontal crack about halfway up.

4. Schoolmarms in Space 8
FA: Gary Sapp and partner, c. 1987.
Previously published as the *Kinko Memorial Roof,* this is a good primer in overhangs.
Begin near the low point of the face. Turn a five-foot roof (one bolt that may have been destroyed) and belay at a pine tree. Climb straight up the face to the apex (7). Traverse off to the left and rappel from *Rambo* (165 feet), or finish with *Diagonal.*

5. Pearl Harbor 10d ★
FA: of pitch 1, Luebben and Lizz Grenard, 1991; of pitch 2, Luebben, Mark Beardsley, Jeff Brisslawn, 1992. Rack: #3 Lowe Ball, #0 to #3 Friends, six QDs.
Banzai! This is one of the best routes on the crag. Begin about 30 feet right from *Schoolmarms.* Two pitches.

6. Eight Clicks to Saigon 10d s ★
FA: Gary Sapp and Tom Henry, 1989.
"Click" is military slang for kilometer and a pun in this case.
Begin about 50 feet up to the right from *Schoolmarms.* This route crosses *Diagonal* about halfway up. The second pitch has a notable runout after the first bolt.

6A. Saigon to Pearl Harbor Express 10d ★
Combine the hardest and safest pitches of *Eight Clicks* and *Pearl Harbor.*

7. Ain't Nobody Here but Us Chickens 11d
FA: Grenard and Luebben, 1991. Rack: stoppers, #3.5 Friend, and five QDs.
Begin in a small dihedral to the right of *Eight Clicks.* Climb straight up past bolts and cross *Diagonal* to a bolt anchor.

8. Across Enemy Lines 11b ★
FA: Luebben and Bill Taylor, 1992. Rack: a #2 Friend and six QDs.
Start up the face between *Chickens* and *Diagonal* (three bolts), cross *Diagonal,* and continue past three more bolts to an anchor on Peacenik

Ledge. Rappel 80 feet or continue up smooth rock past three bolts (12a) to an arching roof that is followed up and right to the belay at the top of *Blood for Oil*.

9. The Battle of Evermore 10c s
FA: Sapp and Luebben, 1987.
From the bolt belay on Peacenik Ledge, climb a dihedral at left, then work right beneath a long roof to the bolt anchor on *Blood for Oil*. Rappel 150 feet or choose an upper pitch.

10. Diagonal 9
FA: Gary Sapp and Scott Kimball, 1984.
Follow the crack and corner system that forms the right edge of the apex, then climb up and right beneath a large, diagonal roof.

11. Blood for Oil 12b ★
FA: Luebben and Grenard, 1991.
Follow bolts up the steep wall to the right of *Diagonal* (thin edging). Rappel 150 feet or climb the very steep and difficult second pitch (12a).

12. No More War 10a s
This route apparently begins in the same crack system as an obscure line called *Beetle Bailey* (8+), to the right of *Blood for Oil*. Rappel or climb the second pitch of *Stronghold*.
Ascend a deceptive, flared crack to where it fades, continue straight up past a bolt and a small tree, up the slab past another bolt (10a), and belay at the bolt anchor on Blood for Oil.

13. Stronghold 9+
FA: Kimball and Sapp, 1984.
Begin in a shallow right-facing corner. Crank over a roof (9) and work up the steep wall to a belay on a tiny ledge. Work up and left and pass some roofs on the left (8).

14. Frontlines 10a ★
FA: Scott Kimball and Randy Joseph, 1984.
Begin about 15 right of *Stronghold*.
1. Ascend two thin offset cracks up to a roof (9) that is passed near a bush. Move up and right, overlapping *Stronghold* a short way, and continue right to a streaked bulge. Jam a left-facing flake to a belay.
2. Go right up a hand crack and pass a roof via a finger crack (10a). Finish on the right. The second pitch has four fixed pins.

15. Lizzard Warrior 11b ★
FA: Luebben and Grenard, 1991. Rack: a #1.5 Friend and six QDs. The first pitch is excellent.
Begin below the large roof at the right side of the wall. Climb straight up past the first bolt (11b) or climb in from the side (10b). Continue up the face past five more bolts to an anchor beneath the left side of the roof (10d). Lower off (75 feet) or turn the roof and climb past three bolts (12?). Join *Camouflage*.

16. Camouflage   9 ★
Follow cracks up past the left edge of a large roof at the right side of the face. This is a very good two-pitch climb.

17. G.I. Joe does Barbie   9+ s A1
FA: Luebben and Taylor, 1991. SR to include Lowe Balls, #0 and #0.5 Friends for first pitch.
Climb the face just right of *Camouflage* past three bolts to a bolt anchor. Lower off or aid the roof via a single bolt and continue to another bolt anchor. A third pitch continues to the top of the crag (9).

18. Nuclear Polka   10a ★
FA: Kimball and Sapp, 1984. Rack should include RPs and TCUs.
Ascend a left-facing dihedral past the big roof at the right side of the face (crux), and continue up a crack with two pins to a belay on a sloping stance. Traverse left and jam a two-inch crack. Finish on the right.

19. Monkey Lust   9
FA: Sapp and Matt Renbaum.
Begin to the right of *Nuclear Polka* and just left of a tree that grows against the wall. Follow cracks and flakes for two pitches to a ledge with a tree. Step left and join the last pitch of *Nuclear Polka*.

S&M WALL
Continuing up the road from Combat Rock, note S&M Wall on the left (north) after about 0.5 mile. Three routes are listed from left to right.

1. Pop Rock   11
Follow six bolts up the left side of the face. Six QDs only.

2. I Love Little Girls   10d s
Five one-quarter-inch bolts.

3. My Name is not Elvis   9 s
Look for two or three bolts.

SEAM ROCK

This large slab was described in a climbing magazine as Cedar Park Slab, however, it is known by people who live in Cedar Park as Seam Rock. The 600-foot, south-facing crag is located in Roosevelt National Forest about three miles north of Combat Rock. The face is angled at 55 to 70 degrees and consists of a very hard, fine-grained granite. Though one excellent route has been established, the crag yet sees little traffic. The approach is brushy and unpleasant and takes about 45 minutes from the car.

Approach. From Combat Rock, continue up the road to a T intersection and turn left (2.2 miles from the Glen Haven road). Go 0.2 mile to a Y intersection and veer right. Follow the road downhill, avoiding a right turn at 0.4 mile, to a second T intersection at 0.6 mile. Park here or turn left and park along the road on the near side of a gate marked "private property." Do not drive through the gate or hike up the road. Hike up the hillside to the north and drop into the bottom of a draw on the other side, which is at the foot of Seam Rock. Scramble up brushy slabs to the base of the main wall. It is probably easier to reach the stream bottom from the right branch in the second T intersection but the "no trespassing" signs are thicker than the trees.

Descent. From the top of the wall, hike east until it is possible to follow a ramp down along the base of the wall to its bottom.

1. **Slab Ants   7 s**
   Begin on a ledge with trees up and left from the low point of the face or do the first pitch of *Dags*. Climb four pitches with occasional runouts well to the left of *Dags in Beanland* and join that route at the tree atop its fourth pitch. Six pitches.

2. **Dags in Beanland   8 ★**
   This route could win the prize for having the weirdest name in the book, however, *Thrushcross Grange* and *Himmelfahrt* are strong contenders. It is otherwise a very good route. Begin at the low point near the center of the face.
   1. Angle up and right past a bolt and belay on a ledge (7, 150 feet). Walk-off possible here.
   2. Climb the short crack just right of the belay, then continue up the beautiful slab past four bolts (8), turn a roof (7, #1 Friend), work up the slab past another bolt, and belay at a stance with two bolts (160 feet).
   3. Climb straight up to a bolt, follow a curving pink dike, and belay on a small ledge (6, 155 feet).
   4. A short pitch leads up to a big ledge with a juniper tree and some bad-ass ants (5, 60 feet).
   5. Start with a short crack just left of the juniper and climb the beautiful slab past two bolts. Continue up a trough, go past a ledge with no cracks, and belay at a stance about 40 feet from the top of the wall (7, 155 feet).
   Scramble to the top.

Seam Rock, South Face
2. Dags in Beanland 8 ⋆

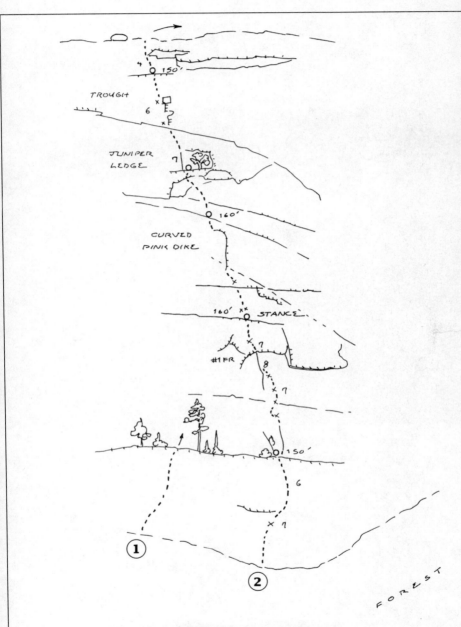

Seam Rock, South Face
1. Slab Ants 7 s
2. Dags in Beanland 8 ★

INDEX

Climbing is Dangerous: Stack the Odds in your favor.

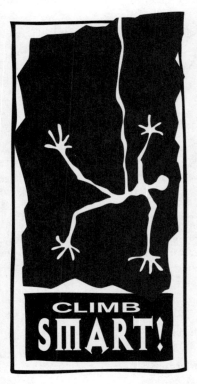

CLIMB SMART!

- Check your knots and harness buckle
- Inspect your gear and replace as necessary
- Know your partners and their habits
- Check your belay—are you sure you're on?
- Read all warnings—they can save your life
- Fixed gear is unreliable—back it up when possible
- Keep an eye on the weather
- Rock breaks—check your holds
- Always double check your rappel system

--Remember--
your safety is your responsibility

Climb Smart! is a public information program of the Climbing Sports Group, the trade association of the climbing industry.

Access: It's everybody's concern

the ACCESS FUND

THE ACCESS FUND, a national, non-profit climbers' organization, is working to keep you climbing. The Access Fund helps preserve access and protect the environment by providing funds for land acquisitions and climber support facilities, financing scientific studies, publishing educational materials promoting low-impact climbing, and providing start-up money, legal counsel and other resources to local climbers' coalitions.

Climbers can help preserve access by being responsible users of climbing areas. Here are some practical ways to support climbing:

- **COMMIT YOURSELF TO "LEAVING NO TRACE."** Pick up litter around campgrounds and the crags. Let your actions inspire others.

- **DISPOSE OF HUMAN WASTE PROPERLY.** Use toilets whenever possible. If none are available, choose a spot at least 50 meters from any water source. Dig a hole 6 inches (15 cm) deep, and bury your waste in it. *Always pack out toilet paper* in a "Zip-Lock"-type bag.

- **UTILIZE EXISTING TRAILS.** Avoid cutting switchbacks and trampling vegetation.

- **USE DISCRETION WHEN PLACING BOLTS AND OTHER "FIXED" PROTECTION.** Camouflage all anchors with rock-colored paint. Use chains for rappel stations, or leave rock-colored webbing.

- **RESPECT RESTRICTIONS THAT PROTECT NATURAL RESOURCES AND CULTURAL ARTIFACTS .** Appropriate restrictions can include prohibition of climbing around Indian rock art, pioneer inscriptions, and on certain formations during raptor nesting season. Power drills are illegal in wilderness areas. *Never chisel or sculpt holds in rock on public lands, unless it is expressly allowed* – no other practice so seriously threatens our sport.

- **PARK IN DESIGNATED AREAS,** not in undeveloped, vegetated areas. Carpool to the crags!

- **MAINTAIN A LOW PROFILE.** Other people have the same right to undisturbed enjoyment of natural areas as do you.

- **RESPECT PRIVATE PROPERTY.** Don't trespass in order to climb.

- **JOIN OR FORM A GROUP TO DEAL WITH ACCESS ISSUES IN YOUR AREA.** Consider clean-ups, trail building or maintenance, or other "goodwill" projects.

- **JOIN THE ACCESS FUND.** To become a member, *simply make a donation (tax-deductible) of any amount.* Only by working together can we preserve the diverse American climbing experience.

The Access Fund. Preserving America's diverse climbing resources.
The Access Fund • P.O. Box 17010 • Boulder, CO 80308